Dedication

To Emily, David's loving wife; a gracious, committed
follower of Jesus, and a faithful wise friend.

"There is no such thing as the age of miracles. There is a God of miracles who fills every age."

DAVID GREENOW

His Life & Legacy

Marcus Thomas

Published by
Maurice Wylie Media
Your Inspirational Christian Publisher

Publishers' statement: *Throughout this book the love for our God is such that whenever we refer to Him we honour with Capitals. On the other hand, when referring to the devil, we refuse to acknowledge him with any honour to the point of violating grammatical rule and withholding capitalisation.*

For more information visit
www.MauriceWylieMedia.com

David John Evans Greenow
26th May 1927 – 3rd May 2012

Contents

Acknowledgements

I would like to say 'thank you' to the many people who have helped me write this book on David Greenow. Thank you for your contributions, your stories and the memories that you shared with me about David.

For Pastor David and Sally Bell, for their inputs and the time they have spent reading and rereading the manuscript, making valuable comments and suggestions.

For Maurice Wylie and his team at Maurice Wylie Media, for their patience, humour and hard work in bringing this book to completion. My dear friend Emily who was the inspiration for this book.

My Lord and Saviour for blessing my life and the lives of many others through the life and ministry of David Greenow.

Introduction

My tribute to a legend...

I am writing this book to celebrate the life and ministry of David Greenow.

Before moving to Lurgan, Northern Ireland as a family in September 1999, I knew of David Greenow only by name. When we came to live in County Armagh it was David who made contact with me. After that initial meeting, we would then often meet over coffee and talk about ministry and, in particular, the churches that I was caring for in County Armagh. David knew these churches well. He had ministered regularly, over the years, at one of the churches and knew people from the other churches through various interdenominational events that David and they attended. David would have often been the guest speaker at these events.

David and I did have a spiritual link. In his early life David had, himself, been part of the denomination that I was ministering with during my time in Northern Ireland. We would remember different men of his generation from the denomination. Some of them he had spent time with in the Bible School. Although these men were much older than me, I knew some of them through my family. In fact, one of the men had pushed me in a pram when I was a baby!

David and his wife Emily were a real blessing to us as a family, introducing us to a wider group of Pentecostal believers and leaders in Northern Ireland. We enjoyed going to the International Gospel Conferences (IGO) held in Armagh and Belfast each year. In the latter years David and Emily attended the church that I led in Lurgan. He was always encouraging and supportive of my ministry and was always seeking to introduce me to other Christian leaders and ministries. I remember David bringing Andy Paget to meet me in a church coffee morning. Further, David helped me in one particular church that I was overseeing in County Armagh. We held a series of healing meetings where David led us in expecting the power of the Holy Spirit to fall in healing and saving power and we did witness God healing the sick.

The idea for this book came as a result of a visit to the home to see Emily. Over the years of knowing David, I became increasingly aware of all the different pamphlets and tracts that David had written during his life. They were rich in Biblical truth but also carried a challenge to live an abundant life for Jesus and to minister in His name and expect miracles. David's writings challenged us to have a life that is Christ-centred and Spirit-empowered. He ached for revival to come again and personally had been involved in a number of revivals during his life: he was asking God and encouraging others to stand with him to pray and expect God's power again. David believed he had a "big" God and he encouraged people to believe the same; a God that can do more than we can think or imagine (Ephesians 3:20).

During the visit I asked Emily if she would like David's writings to be put into a book. Emily agreed and, in 2017, work started on the book that you have started to read. But, no doubt, as you have already noticed, the idea grew to include not only the writings of David, but also, details about his life and the legacy he has left.

What do I want you to experience and receive from reading this book?

In 2016, a book that I had written was published and it carried this strap-line: '*We don't honour our fathers by following their ways but we honour our fathers by knowing their God.*' [1]

---

1 Thomas Marcus, 'The God of Our Fathers.' 2016

I trust the story of David Greenow, that is told in this book, will challenge and inspire you to *forget what is past* and with a renewed determination to reach out to God for the abundant, miraculous life that is yours in Christ Jesus. What does your village or town or city need at this time? People in your street need a real encounter with the God and Father of our Lord Jesus Christ in the power of the Holy Spirit. This is what David wanted for all Christians. Let's honour him by seeking God for ourselves and believing for demonstrations of His power.

James Packer in his book, "Knowing God"[2], wrote, "Christian minds have been conformed to the modern spirit; the spirit…. that spawns great thoughts of man and leaves room for only small thoughts of God." That is a sad indictment of the general apathy and lethargy that is around in Christian circles today. There are exceptions and David Greenow, I believe, was one such exception. I do hope this book lifts your vision of who God is and raises your expectations of what the Holy Spirit can do in and through your life. Be blessed as you read.

Marcus Thomas

2 Packer, James. "Knowing God". (1973). London: Hodder and Stoughton.

PART 1

The Legacy of David Greenow

'The steps of a good man are ordered by the LORD:
and he delighteth in his way.'
Psalm 37:23

TRIBUTES FROM DEAR FRIEND'S

Pastor Jim and Cynthia Wilkinson
Hollybush Christian Fellowship
North Yorkshire, England.

We had the privilege and joy of having David Greenow in our home, to stay, and also the privilege of his presence in the pulpit for almost forty years! He was always the same in private and also as a gifted expositor of the Scriptures, whether talking for five minutes or for an hour! He was highly esteemed wherever he spoke and a joy and pleasure to know as a dear friend and brother in the Lord: a great Bible teacher and personal confidant. 'Until we meet.'

Pastor Jim Wilkinson, who wrote this note of appreciation for David Greenow, leads a church in North Yorkshire called *Hollybush Christian Fellowship*. The story of this church has been captured in a book titled, '*Miracle Valley*.' There is a story about David in the book.

Each year, *Hollybush Christian Fellowship* holds a Holiday Bible Camp on their farm in North Yorkshire. David was a regular visitor. Pastor Jim tells how God gave him the vision for this camp and the arrangements that were put in place for the first meetings. He believed God had given him a Word of Knowledge about the first Bible week, that '*an American evangelist was going to be taking meetings at the camp.*' Other speakers were booked, including Selwyn Hughes.

Pastor Jim writes, "But the weeks were fast approaching and there was still no sign of such a man. Come the last few days and I was beginning to wonder whether that word had been from the Lord at all... By the Friday evening, the night before the camp was due to begin, I was ready to admit I'd been wrong. It was around 7pm and I was getting ready to go across to the granary for the fellowship meeting. Just before I left, the telephone rang; it was David Greenow, a friend who had ministered at *Hollybush* many times over the years and who was up in Fraserburgh helping with a tent crusade." David told Pastor Jim that the crusade tent had been burned down by a man who took exception to his partner being saved and she was not willing to live with him anymore. The tent campaign was over. David asked Pastor Jim, "Could you use a speaker? Our man up here is redundant."

Pastor Jim commiserated with him for a moment and asked David, "Well, what's the name of your speaker?" "Wilbur Jackson," David replied, "He's an American evangelist." Pastor Jim writes, "I almost leapt for joy! "He's the man we're waiting for. Send him down!"

Wilbur Jackson travelled down from Fraserburgh to North Yorkshire and spoke at the first Hollybush Bible Week.

Eric and Catherine Weaver
(retired leaders)
Glory Fellowship
Hereford, England.

I first met David Greenow while attending a College in Carmarthen. I originate from Bridgend and attended Beulah Mission Hall, Aberkenfig. The College course lasted three years and, while there, I attended a Glory fellowship in Llwynhendy. It was run by Mr Gwylfa Richards. David Greenow was one of his close friends and David had regular weekend engagements there, together with his brother, Glyn. David was ever an encourager, especially of the young.

David gave me his mother and father's address in Hereford. He told me if ever I was in Hereford, that I was to look them up. This was in 1962 and by 1964 I needed their address as I began my first job in

Hereford and was put in touch with a Christian lady who would be my landlady for a number of years.

Hereford had a *Glory Fellowship*. David's father, Lloyd Greenow, was a member. Whenever David visited his parents he came to minister there, and my husband and I were greatly blessed by his teaching. In the 1980s and 1990s David ministered at the farm camp at Lower Chilstone Farm, just outside Hereford and, of course, we as a family attended. David showed great interest in my husband's family. They had a child with special needs, and he sent many a parcel containing a video which would bless the family. He also ministered at a house prayer meeting which was held at their home near Hereford.

We miss David's ministry and encouragement very much. I have again read David's funeral eulogy. What a man! A very humble servant of God.

Pastor Keith Malcolmson
Limerick City Church
Limerick, Ireland.

David Greenow was one of several outstanding godly and gifted men who was always there during my childhood. He was a good friend to my grandparents, parents, and later a good friend to me. He visited our home outside Dromore many times.

In the late 50s and beginning of the 60s he led small teams south of the border into Dublin in Southern Ireland to minister and testify and my mother eagerly joined the team. Many in her generation highly respected him and looked to him as a father in the Lord and a godly example.

While growing up I always remember him either attending or speaking at meetings or conferences we attended such as IGO (International Gospel Outreach) and evening meetings at Mountain Lodge and many other places. Etched on my mind is seeing him play the accordion as he danced unto the Lord, hearing him pray with anointing, and sharing the Word with simplicity.

It was at the Railway Mission in Belfast, led by his brother-in-law Robin Honeyford, that I was baptised in the Holy Ghost at the age of 13 as evangelist Sandy Thompson ministered. Not far away at Ava Street, David ministered alongside Frank Brae at New Year's Day services for a few years. These were the meetings, environment, and ministers who impacted me as a teenager. I watched and listened very carefully. Each imparted something very unique.

Watching David's consistent character, conduct, and conversation over many years deeply marked my young life. As a kid I always thought of him as a holy man and this was only confirmed in later years. He was a Christ-centred man, a man of the Word. He always emphasised the work of the Cross; a humble man who always preferred others, and a man of prayer deeply burdened for a mighty visitation of God's Spirit. He breathed out humble authority. His example in character deeply impacted me.

His life of living by faith, not making his needs known to man nor begging for money, his faith in God's provision, and his integrity with money, impressed me.

As a shy kid I can remember Emily making efforts to speak to me. That always touched my heart. They were a special couple who complimented each other remarkably.

When I stepped out into full-time ministry at the age of 21, he was there guiding, encouraging, advising and praying. Over the next

20 years when we met up and talked, the time was never wasted. His words were always spiritual, weighty, and focused. He always encouraged me to walk holy, to spend quality time in prayer, and to pursue genuine *heaven-sent revival.* At times I would quiz him about the three revivals which he had witnessed and experienced during the 50s and I eagerly took down notes especially about the 1954 Belfast Revival when Evangelist James White was used by God in Pentecostal power. We talked about why God used men, things that hindered or quenched revival, and the consequence and fruit of genuine revivals that continued in the lives of those impacted by them.

He told me several times about a Word the Lord spoke to him in 1969. The troubles had just broken out in Northern Ireland and he was flying back into Belfast. As he looked out the window across the land, he spoke to the Lord asking where all this would lead to, not expecting an answer. But the Lord did answer saying, *'There will be a time of unparalleled bloodshed, then a false peace, then a time of unparalleled visitation across Ireland.'* He wrote this Word down in his Bible and he later lived to see much of it fulfilled apart from the unparalleled revival.

He first told me about this when I was in my late teens. In my thirties when I shared about encouraging things happening in Southern Ireland, he said; *'No this is not it. It will be an unparalleled visitation of God when it comes.'*

I loved his written tracts and leaflets; *Never Give Up! A Study on Going Through with God, Abundance in Christ, Be Filled with the Spirit, Christian Service, Ten Commandments of Ministry*, to name but a few. His bookmarks filled with teachings from the Word of God and his Christmas newsletters were always a blessing.

Once when we met up, he came armed with a set of all his leaflets as well as a number of old typed-up ones dating back many years with the hope that I could use them. When I published a book on Pentecostal history, he was most eager to get it out to preachers and to distribute it.

When I embarked on a new season of ministry in Northern Ireland and Europe, he was keen to open doors and to introduce me to friends who would benefit from it. There was no cynicism, scepticism, suspicion, jealousy, or competition with him. He was kind, willing to help all who were in ministry, never promoting himself. He was rare in his godly attitude. His motives were pure and he was without guile. When I found the girl I intended to marry, he was both wise and good-humouredly encouraging when I asked his counsel.

One last thing (although much more could be said) was how the Lord used him in prophecy. He believed in the real supernatural gift of the Spirit by which the Holy Spirit speaks through men to exhort, comfort, and edify. There was a period of time when I would pick him up on Boxing Day or on another day to spend time in fellowship. The testimonies were always wonderful but so were the times of prayer before departing. Several times as we prayed, he would give a precise, timely, edifying word from the Lord.

On one specific and unique occasion at a church convention where I knew everyone intimately and personally but where he only knew the leaders, the Spirit of God came down mightily and he began to prophesy personally to a great many individual persons, one after another. I listened carefully and closely as he ministered differently to each person, giving a word that was exact and very obviously precise to those who knew these individuals very well and were listening. They were very revealing, predictive words. The word he prophesied to me that day was simple but remarkable. It summed up my entire life; past, present, and future, depicting it as chapters of a book with God as the author. It also opened up and revealed the very intent of my heart. I will never forget it. While I had previously witnessed him operate in the edifying gift of prophecy, this was more than just prophecy: this was the gifted ministry of a prophet.

Some men have gifting but no character. Others have character but no gifting. But David Greenow was greatly blessed with both godly character and spiritual gifting. He was a true gift to the body of Christ but also a genuine Christian who loved Jesus Christ, loved people and always had time for them. His presence and friendship are missed, but his testimony, example, and warmth will always be carried in my heart and gladly remembered.

Pastor Mervyn and Lucy France
Kay's Farm Fellowship
Lancaster, England.

It is with a great feeling of thankfulness and gratitude we write a few words about times spent with David Greenow. As leaders of *Kay's Farm Fellowship* (Mervyn and Lucy France) we have good memories of great times of blessing.

Mervyn's sister, Mary, first heard him preach in the autumn of 1970; at the time she was staying with Jim and Cynthia Wilkinson at *Hollybush* and they took her to hear him preach at George Breckon's church in Northallerton. That night he preached on Hebrews 13:15; '*Therefore by Him let us continually offer the sacrifice of praise to God, that is the fruit of our lips giving thanks to His name.*' Mary, having recently been baptised in the Holy Spirit, had come into a new and dynamic experience of praise and worship. The message David spoke that night just added fuel to the fire that was already burning in her heart.

Shortly after that he began making his way across to *Kay's Farm Fellowship*, where he was a great source of blessing and encouragement to us all, as we had just been baptised in the Holy Ghost. David loved to stay on the farm with Mum and Dad France and one thing we remember when he was on the farm, he always enjoyed locally produced honey in his tea every morning. It was on one of his visits while staying at *Kay's Farm* he was walking round one of the cow pastures sharing Jesus with one of Mervyn's younger brothers and they both knelt down in the field and David led him to the Lord.

As a newly-married couple, David and Emily were amongst the first who stayed with us. We were only young at the time, but to us it was like having one of God's prophets in our home. He always brought a great blessing. One of Lucy's fond memories of him was in the summer of 1977; we were setting out in our car for the tent mission we were holding and David leaned forward, put his arms round our shoulders and said; *'well, boys and girls, are we ready?'* He then said; *'I wonder if that was prophetic?'* as Lucy was expecting our first child! It turned out to be so: the boys were David and Mervyn and the girls were Lucy, and the soon to be born Naomi. David used to speak in the bible studies in the early days of *Hollybush Camp*. We used to hang on to every word, and the presence of God was awesome.

Mervyn remembers an illustration from one of those messages. David had been having a siesta in the afternoon the day previously in his room at *Hollybush House* and a butterfly had come in through the open sash window. It was fluttering up and down trying to escape. As David was watching, he thought to himself, if it had flown down a little lower it could have escaped into freedom. In his illustration he likened that to us saying; *'if we would lower ourselves down onto our knees before the Lord we would be liberated into His freedom.'* Whenever David was in the house there were always great times of blessing because he always uplifted the name of Jesus.

Pastor Ivan Michael
(retired Elim Pastor)
Upperlands, Maghera
Northern Ireland.

I first met David years ago. We had a music group, my three brothers and myself, called; *'The Michael Brothers.'* We met at a Christian outreach coffee bar in Portglenone; we were ministering in song, and David was the preacher. He impressed me very much and it was a wonderful evening with many responding for prayer for different problems. Davy Anderson held those meetings and he thought the world of David's ministry.

My ministry took me to Cornwall and I didn't see David for many years until I returned home. I was ministering in Markethill, Northern Ireland, for about nine years and Steven Blevins started to fellowship with us. I once asked him if he knew David Greenow and he said *yes.* He invited me to lunch at his home. When I got there, I found he had invited David there also; and what a wonderful reunion that was! David remembered the group my brothers and myself had, and the meeting in Portglenone where we had first met, which I thought was quite amazing.

I met David just a few times after that and really enjoyed his company and our chats, which mostly were about God and our Glorious Saviour. He sent me his prayer letter for a few years, and when David took ill, Steven Blevins and myself visited him in hospital and prayed for him.

Mary and Francis Cunningham
Bride Christian Fellowship
Donegal, Ireland.

David Greenow was a very humble man. He was the only minister who, when coming into our home, would always say, *"peace and blessing be in this house, Lord let your peace rest here."* Also, when David would come to the fellowship, he would say; *"blessing, blessings, blessings to this place."* He met people where they were at, never lording it over them and always calling down blessings.

The first time we heard David sing *'God is love'* had a profound impact on our lives, because we had heard about the wrath of God, and that's what impacted our lives until David came and spoke about the love of God. We never forgot that message and it changed our way of thinking.

Initially we forgot his name but not his message of God's love; and so, we called him *'God is love.'* David will always be remembered for his gentleness, compassion and giving hope in the midst of any given situation.

Sandy Thompson[3] said "if I wanted my life to be measured to anyone it would be David Greenow!"

---

3 Itinerant evangelist and missionary, Northern Ireland.

David and Dorcas Willows
Evangelist
Northallerton
North Yorkshire, England.

I first met David Greenow during the 1960s in some of Henri's Glory meetings as he travelled as an evangelist. He had an apostolic ministry, operating in several gifts of the Spirit. His knowledge and understanding of the Bible gave him the ability to speak into lives from the platform or one to one. He was an encourager, a great mentor and example, because he was patient, gracious, loving and kind; never one to discourage or put one down in any way.

I once asked him if he believed in eternal security, expecting a discussion and reason why or why not. His answer was simply; '*I believe in mine.*' That was the end of the discussion!

He was always interested in the local church and church leadership. He also opened doors of ministry for me when I started to travel as an itinerant evangelist, and often asked how I was getting on. He came to stay in our home a few times on his travels. It was always a pleasure for us when he came to the house, whether it was a fleeting visit as he was passing to another engagement or staying for a few days if he had ministry in the area.

We reopened the small village chapel where we then lived, in Bathley, near Newark. David came and spoke at the opening. He spoke from Joshua 1:8-9, the title of his message was, from the last few words of verse eight; '*Thou shalt have good success.*'

We would meet at IGO (International Gospel Outreach) conferences, glory holidays, etc. He was always the same gracious, kind, patient, loving gentleman. He always had time to listen and speak with you.

It has been a great privilege to have known him and enjoyed fellowship together over many years. The great news is, we shall meet again in the new Jerusalem. Hallelujah!

Gwen Mills
(Family friend)
Lurgan, Northern Ireland.

There was widespread renewal in the Craigavon area in the early 70s, bringing many people into a new dimension of hunger for God and spiritual gifts. David Greenow showed up at many of these new *house group meetings*, teaching from the Word and praying for individuals using words of knowledge and prophecy in a way that was entirely new to most of us. We loved his teaching, his accordion playing and singing and his prayers which helped build us up and brought strength and comfort to everyone. He also prayed for those who were sick.

By this time his wife Emily was free from her responsibilities of caring for her elderly parents and could accompany David to meetings. He often asked her to share the Word, which she never failed to do. She must have endured many long evenings as people put great demands on David for prayer and counselling. As a couple they prayed for many families in their own time and had a remarkable recall of family names and situations.

David continued to build up the church, strengthening and encouraging believers over the next four decades. His character exuded graciousness and gentleness, but he was not afraid to give warnings and correction if he felt this was needed. He was often called in to settle disputes or give advice. He was keen for people to find a suitable partner and believed that a happy marriage was God's greatest gift after salvation.

David was welcome in many different churches and fellowships in the area, outside of the mainstream churches, and wanted to encourage leaders and individual believers wherever he found them. He was a disciplined man who spent mornings in study and prayer and then walking in his neighbourhood for an hour. He was well-known in the area and had prayer input into many people and families he encountered as he walked. David compiled leaflets and tracts and was meticulous in writing to thank anyone who gave him a gift.

Brian and Meryl Thomas
International Gospel Outreach (Ministers)
Swansea, South Wales.

Our memories of David Greenow are vivid ones. My wife Meryl and I remember the Swanwick conferences in the early nineties. These were two-week-long conferences at the Hayes conference centre; one in the spring and the other in the autumn each year. David was the convenor and always founded the conference on Calvary. David's ministry never moved away from this *sure ground* of the cross and the sacrifice of our Lord Jesus Christ – Christ crucified, died and rose again!

We first met David walking in the grounds of the Hayes. He knew we were new to IGO and he stopped to talk with us. We told him we were from a certain part of South Wales which evidently, he knew very well. David had ministered in fellowships in our area. He also said that he had been to the Apostolic conferences in Penygroes and knew ministers from the Apostolic Church, an International Pentecostal denomination. We learned David Greenow had studied at the Apostolic Bible School at Penygroes. David was delighted we had also been to these conferences, which were just a few miles from where we lived in Gwaun-Cae-Gurwen.

David was Pentecostal. He was a man of the Spirit of God and had a real and lasting impact on our lives, as did a number of the ministers at that time in IGO. One time he gave a personal word to me about '*nipping things in the bud*' which related to the deluge of negative thoughts that I was being bombarded with. It was a *good word* which I have built into my life and shared and passed on this advice to others over the years.

David explained to me that dealing with the accusations of our enemy quickly and early and not letting the desire get a foothold in our minds was the thing to do. It really helped to be speaking to David and also an encouragement to my wife and myself. He was friendly, even though this was the first time we met.

Again, in the early 1990s there was an IGO conference at Biggar in the Scottish borders. David Greenow led this conference in the anointing of the Holy Spirit. One meeting was memorable: David ministered, prayed and laid hands on all those present. He had a prophetic word for each one he ministered to. He had a personal word for Meryl and myself – Isaiah 50:4; '*The Lord God hath given me the tongue of the learned, that I should know how to speak a word in season to him that is weary: he wakeneth morning by morning, he wakeneth mine ear to hear as the learned.*' (KJV) I thank the Lord that over the years there has been a performance of this Word in our lives.

Matthew 10:41 says; '*He that receiveth a prophet in the name of a prophet shall receive a prophet's reward; and he that receiveth a righteous man in the name of a righteous man shall receive a righteous man's reward.*' (KJV) In 1 Thessalonian 5:20-21 we read; '*Despise not prophesyings. prove all things; hold fast that which is good.*' (KJV) Over the years we certainly confirmed David's word to us and the ministry the Lord has gifted. Praise His Name!

In 2007 at IGO Swanwick conference, Derbyshire, it was a privilege to be ordained as full-time IGO ministers by David Greenow and David Chaudhary. We always do think highly of David Greenow and senior IGO ministers, who have gone on to glory now. Those conferences in Swanwick and North Wales at The Oasis were special to my wife and me. The Lord did so much in our lives and meeting with brothers and sisters in the Lord who had walked many years like David Greenow gave us a real uplifting and encouragement in the Spirit.

We knew that under David Greenow's ministry, the *floodgates of heaven* would open and the Lord would pour out His blessing. Praise the Lord!

It is a real joy to us both to have fond memories of David and the way he shared his love in the Lord. Perhaps David never realised to the full how much he was impacting the lives of young believers like ourselves in those days.

Rodney Adamson
Evangelist
Waringstown, Northern Ireland.

David Greenow was a true ambassador of Christ and his desire was always to have others to be reconciled to God. As a teenager growing up in Knocknamuckley Boys Brigade, I have been blessed in going to camps each year. During this time God's Word and testimony would have been presented by faithful leaders. When the week of camp was over, the leadership would have held follow-up meetings. David would have been a main speaker at these events.

I recall him as a man who took time to listen to young people and give good advice. He gave me literature which gave direction in my life as a young believer. In recent years, being involved in mission in the south of England, I have come across people who appreciated David's ministry. On one occasion when in south Devon I was asked "Are you from Ireland?" The person went on to say the only man they knew from Ireland was a man called David Greenow! David has passed the baton on and we have the privilege to serve the King of kings today.

Pastor Derek Williams
(Retired Pastor)
Riviera Life Church
Torquay, England.

I first met David Greenow in the early 60s. I was the pastor of an Assemblies of God church in Penryn, Cornwall. My home church was Hockley, Birmingham, in the late 50s. We had a number of evangelists visiting our Saturday night revival meeting; David was one of the visiting speakers. These evangelists then became regular speakers at the little Penryn church.

David was a great help, imparting into the church a new dimension of faith, and to expect and enter into new heights of the moving of the Holy Spirit. Penryn Assembly of God became a little Hockley. Each visit of David Greenow was filled with excitement and expectancy. He always brought a refreshing word from heaven; God-given and Spirit-filled. The work grew; it became a strong Pentecostal witness in the whole of the south-west.

Dr Cecil Stewart O.B.E.
Senior Pastor, international evangelist
founder and director of CCN
Belfast, Northern Ireland.

It is a special privilege to have this opportunity to express my gratitude and appreciation for the amazing influence that David Greenow has had on my life. My first memory of meeting David and Emily was in a prayer meeting at Wallace's farmhouse in County Monaghan. Their passion for the Lord and their words of encouragement had a life-changing impact on me, especially when David spoke about the purpose of God and His call in our lives.

He prayed with me to be baptised in the Holy Spirit, which transformed my life forever. Through the years that followed, David and Emily continued to have a powerful influence on myself, and indeed my whole family. In 2003, when I received the worst news about my health, David was there and stood with me, along with Walker Gorman and others. Only eternity will reveal the immeasurable benefit of David's influence on my life. To God be the glory!

Claire Goudy Henderson
(Executive Director)
Helping Hands Healing Hearts Ministries
Philippines.

I loved David Greenow. He was always hearing from God and able to communicate it well to others. He and Emily are some of my real-life heroes!

Robert Foster
(musician)
Newton Aycliffe
Co. Durham, England.

My memories go back to Blyth, Northumberland as an eight-year-old and being filled with the Spirit, sitting on David's knee. I'm 64 now and still working in the church.

Wendy Dickson
Armagh, Northern Ireland.

(Daughter of late Victor Cunningham who was killed in the 1983 terrorist attack at Mountain Lodge Church) Armagh, Northern Ireland.

One thing I will always remember he said when he was taking the Lord's table was; *God always comes to His table.*

Drusilla Dougan
Keady, Armagh
Northern Ireland.

David had an encouraging ministry. I remember as a young Christian, he was always encouraging; and when he spoke you knew he had heard from God. A very sincere, wise man.

Tim Hayes
Lead Campus Pastor
Calgary, Canada.

David preached regularly at Mevagissey Revival Centre in Cornwall. During one Easter convention I can remember he kept using the phrase; '*It's Friday but Sunday's a coming*' in a way and with his unique accent that only David could. I remember his words every Easter and I remember David every time someone uses that phrase. He personally encouraged me and my wife Christine and our family in the early years of our ministry.

Paul Cocking
(Former International Development Coordinator)
Living Water, Adopt-A-Child
Glasgow, Scotland.

I came in at the end of David's era, but needless to say was blown away by the humility, acceptance and serving heart he shared with all. He really made you believe in yourself and what God wanted to do through you. A man wise beyond his many years and such an approachable father in the Lord.

Pastor Bill Partington
International evangelist, Itinerant minister
Stoke-on-Trent, England.

Back in the mid-1960s, when I was a teenager, my parents, Jim and Dorothy Partington, who both knew David well, would take the whole family down to the *Good News Crusade* Easter conference in

Ipswich. David was invariably one of the speakers, and much loved and highly esteemed by all the grown-ups in attendance. He would sometimes walk calmly and unassumingly down the central aisle, in-between what I recollect as 200-300 people, stopping to pray, speak or prophesy over whomever he felt to stop at. I was, in essence, just a kid in my mid-teens, so it was quite a shock to me to find that on at least two or three occasions over the next few years, David stopped to pray over me. All these years later I cannot remember anything of what he said, but I do remember the impact that he had on me. Looking back, I somehow feel that whatever he prayed or prophesied has been, is being or will come to pass.

Throughout my 20s and 30s, our paths crossed on a number of occasions when he spoke at small house groups or larger fellowships in our area. He seemed to be just as at home ministering to a small group as he was to a large crowd, and vice versa. What stood out to me was the gentleness of his spirit. Even now he is one of only three or four people whom I describe as someone who *oozed the presence of God*, someone with a sweetness of spirit that reflected the person of Jesus and a calmness about them one could feel.

One incident that stands out above all others was when we were at a small summer camp during my late 30s or early 40s. During the morning meeting, as the worship time was coming to an end, the morning speaker opened up the floor to give people the opportunity to move in the gifts of the Spirit. Although it was highly unusual for me, I gave a brief message in tongues. No one instantaneously interpreted it in any way, in fact the morning's speaker left a gap of perhaps 10 seconds before moving on to preach the Word he'd no doubt prepared. I remember feeling somewhat discouraged, especially as it was so unusual for me to move in this gift. However, David and his wife Emily joined my family for lunch in our on-site chalet. After lunch David and I retreated to the kitchen to do the dishes. While there I asked him if he thought what I'd given in the morning was a genuine message in tongues, thinking that he, as a neutral observer, may tell me that he thought I'd moved in in the flesh, so to speak. What he did though was pause, and then (I assume so as not to be critical of the morning's well-known preacher, nor to criticise me) he said; '*Well, I thought it was a gentle tongue, and perhaps our Brother could have given it just that bit longer before moving on.*' That spoke volumes to me in terms of David's wisdom; and somehow soothed the sting I'd felt from the morning's incident.

Chrissi Hailes Perillo
Missionary to the Philippines.

David Greenow had a big impact on my life. My parents were both ordained through IGO. Going to the Conferences in Oxford (Wycliffe) every year and listening to some of the powerful preachers in the 1970s had a great influence on me. I would get hold of the tapes and listen to the messages over and over. I grew up having such great respect for all of the preachers. David used to visit our church often as a visiting speaker. With regard to David: to me, he was not only a wonderful preacher of the Word, but he was a giant among gentlemen. In the 70s preachers often stayed over in our home (travel wasn't so easy in those days) and so I got to witness what the preachers were like when they were not in the pulpit but guests in our home. David was a gentleman when in the pulpit and in our home. He was such a lovely man.

I left for the Philippines in 1983, so I didn't get to see him as often from then. However, when Dondie and I were planning our wedding (to take place in Altrincham), Dondie had no friends or family attending. Knowing that David and Emily had no children of their own, we wondered if they would do us the great honour of standing as Dondie's parents at our wedding. We couldn't afford to pay their transportation costs, so we didn't really think that they would accept our request, but they did. That was a very great privilege for us as a couple. They were wonderful too. They really did take their position to heart and encouraged Dondie and had a few laughs with us along the way. It was such a joy for us. We had three IGO David's at our wedding. David Chaudhary led the ceremony, David Willows participated too, and David Greenow honoured us by sitting at the presidential table as part of our family. From that moment they continued to support us, and even to this day, Emily supports us financially.

David often helped us to get openings for speaking engagements in Northern Ireland and would come along to hear us. What an honour that was for me. I remember them coming to Mountain Lodge several times to hear us speak there. They were so, so supportive of us; as I have said, even to this day. Every time we are in Northern Ireland, we would pay a visit to their humble home. They are a couple that I held in high esteem from the first time we met to last. Consistently faithful to the Lord, in their life and service.

Pastor David and Sally Bell
Mountain Lodge Pentecostal Church
Darkley, Northern Ireland.

David Greenow first came to Mountain Lodge in 1953, when he and Bob Mullen, two young evangelists, conducted a mission that lasted for three months. During that time, he stayed with Thomas John Hunniford, the pastor of the assembly, and his family. While there, David became friendly with Thomas John's daughter Emily, whom he later married. David was greatly used in healing and words of knowledge.

David, a regular speaker at Mountain Lodge, was one of the first preachers I came to know and respect when I began attending the meetings. David always had a word of encouragement to people, no matter what age, young or old; and he spoke into many lives. He was a true friend, mentor, preacher and teacher. David would play the accordion and lead worship; the anointing would come down and then he and Emily would minister and pray with people to receive from God.

David often spoke of the importance of choosing a life partner, and frequently referred to a relationship that he was in when God called him into ministry. He quickly realised that the one he thought he loved did not share the same passion and he soon realised this relationship was not for him. God had someone who was His choice for David, and Emily proved a faithful companion and ministry partner down through the years.

David was such a help to us in Mountain Lodge, especially in the earlier years, when he conducted weddings, dedicated our babies and officiated at funerals for us. He moved in an apostolic ministry, going from church to church, giving godly wisdom and guidance and encouragement when he could. David was greatly used in healing and words of knowledge.

We recall that on one night at Mountain Lodge, David gave a word of knowledge: he said someone in the back of the church was making a decision and it was the wrong move. He urged them not to go down that road. That young man had just filled in an application for a job. He took the word to heart and did not proceed with it.

David and Margaret Bailie were just recently married when they attended a meeting in Mountain Lodge one Sunday evening. David Greenow had officiated at their wedding some time earlier. Margaret remembers that they were sitting about halfway up the hall, on the left-hand side. David Bailie had been suffering from regular and severe migraine headaches. Margaret recalls that on bright sunny mornings particularly he would return to the house, spending the day in bed and vomiting. That Sunday evening, David Greenow gave a word of knowledge, to which David Bailie responded. David Greenow prayed for him and all these years later, he still testifies to the healing he received that Sunday evening. The migraines were completely gone!

David always spoke of '*bringers*' and encouraged people to bring others to the meetings just as those in the Bible brought people to Jesus. Down through the years, David frequently ministered at the Lord's Table in Mountain Lodge. Often, he would remind us that *the Lord always comes to His table, so it is important for us to be there also*, fulfilling His request until He comes.

David wrote a lot of tracts and leaflets, freely distributing them to people to encourage them. He also gave us a set of Bible studies which he had obtained from America, which we have found to be a useful tool in ministry. When Christian television was quite new to a lot of people, David recorded sermons that really blessed him and regularly passed them out to others to uplift and encourage them.
David also told us how in 1969 (during the time of the Troubles) he was flying over Ireland and wondering what lay ahead for our country. He felt the Lord saying to him, that there would be a time of continual disturbance followed by a time of unparalleled divine intervention. We have had a time of disturbance, now we are waiting for a mighty move of the Spirit of God!

Tommie McCracken
Banbridge, Co. Down
Northern Ireland.

David seemed to turn up just at the right time. Of course, there were other times, but these 'right times' were very evident in my life then, and in my early journey with Jesus.

Back in the early 1980s I had become involved with a Christian organisation called Stauros. They ministered to people who had addictions, such as alcoholism. I had read John 4:38; '*I sent you to reap that for which you have not laboured; others have laboured, and you have entered into their labours.*' When I read this, I thought that was what the Lord wanted me to do. I was only saved about four to five years, and I was still trying to find my feet in what the Lord wanted for me.

One day as I was walking down the street in Portadown, County Armagh, I met David Greenow. I had met him on other occasions with my brother Billy, so I stopped to talk to him. He asked me how I was doing, and I told him about being involved with Stauros. I quoted the verse that I have already mentioned, and I told him that I believed that is what the Lord wanted me to do. David then said in his wisdom of the Word, and in his encouragement; '*And what about the ministry that God has called you to do?*' I was gobsmacked, as they say; but it made me think, that although I was involved in this ministry, it was not the ministry God had called me to do, as I found out later on in my journey with the Lord.

The next time was about a more personal thing. About two years after I was saved, my marriage broke up, mainly because I had become a Christian. About six years had gone by, and I had started to go to Banbridge Elim. I was still involved in Stauros, and I met Frances at Banbridge Elim when I was doing some painting. We became friends, but I struggled with the thought of being married over again. I knew the Word, and I thought that I would be disobeying the Lord. In 1984 about midway through the year I was walking down through Meadow Lane in Portadown, heading to a car part shop that was there. As I walked across the car park, David Greenow came walking from his car. He knew nothing of my struggle concerning this personal thing. We stopped and talked. The first thing he said, was *"How is Frances?"* Without waiting for an answer, he said, '*You know the innocent party in a divorce case has the right to remarry.*' That was about the height of our conversation; he went his way and I went mine. Frances and myself are now married, coming 35 years this year at the time of writing. What surprised me, was that David didn't know about this situation, and yet he came out with a wise answer that dealt with my struggle and settled my mind.

In passing, the things that I learned from David were in his teaching of the Word: that it was simple but carried depth. His attitude to people was one of treating everybody with encouragement and dignity.

Pastor Bill and Ruth Hopley
Sheldon, Birmingham
England.

My wife Ruth recalls that David would often come to preach at her church when she was a child. Her parents, Pastor George and Olga Hadley, led the Revival Centre at Aston in Birmingham. His ministry of the Word was always greatly appreciated, because he was a sincere, humble and gracious man of God. Many times, his dad and brother Glynn would travel from their farm in Hereford, once milking was done, to come and be blessed by the moving of the Holy Spirit.

David preached at our wedding in 1973 and memorably spoke about the Marriage of the Lamb. Later, when Bill began itinerant ministry,

David met us whilst he was a guest speaker at the Mevagissey Convention. He took time with us over lunch to pass on some valuable practical advice about the *do's and don'ts* of going into ministry. Such advice and godly wisdom have stood the test of time!

Norman and Pat McCleary
Lurgan, Co. Armagh
Northern Ireland.

I acted as an accountant on behalf of David for upwards of 35 years. His bookkeeping was so meticulous that I often wondered why he required an accountant at all. But he wanted to do exactly what was right regarding his taxation affairs, as with everything else in life.

David noted down in his books *every penny* which he received either as a gift or an offering, which says volumes for him both as a man and as a Christian. He did not care about the financial aspect of his calling but made sure that *every penny* was accounted for and declared to the revenue authorities and tax paid accordingly.

It goes without saying that David lived '*by faith*' and did not seek remuneration from any source whatsoever. It was a delight and, dare I say it, a privilege, to see that small silver-haired saint of God park his car and come down the driveway into our home. David really brought the fragrance of Jesus with him everywhere he went, not only because he was Spirit-filled and Spirit-empowered, but he oozed the personality of that Holy One both by his walk and by his talk. When he left our presence, he left the aroma: that sweet-smelling scent of the rose of Sharon; a tangible anointing of the Spirit of Christ. It is difficult to speak of David J. Greenow and not bring oneself into it because he was interested in the individual.

He was interested in what I was doing in the service of our Lord and Master; in how our church was faring in the battle. But when I asked him about his work for our Lord and Saviour it was like sitting at the feet of Jesus Christ. He just loved to speak about his Lord and Saviour, not about what David Greenow was doing but what Christ was doing throughout the British Isles and in the south of our land. David was a true evangelist, and this shone through in his talk about Jesus, as in his walk with Jesus and in his financial dealings as well.

Psalm 1 would adequately cover this man of God because after he had talked about God's work for perhaps an hour or more, he would pray God's blessings down on our home. I can truly say that David left a lingering presence of God in the home, and this was simply because of his close walk with Jesus.

Can I say at this point that I loved to hear him at a mission or an evangelical meeting or indeed at a '*wee meeting*' playing his beloved accordion and singing God's praises, and then exhorting, explaining, encouraging and preaching and teaching faithfully the life-saving, life-giving Word of God. While David has passed on to his reward, he left behind the blessing which God gives and to which He adds no sorrow.

It was an honour and a privilege to have known this saint of God. Anyone who knew the Christ-centred man of God could not but admit what a real Christian he was because he was the epitome of that same Christ.

Evangelist David Robinson
Mountain Lodge Pentecostal Church
Darkley, Northern Ireland.

What can one say about a man who was not just a friend but a friend indeed? What can I say to express the many blessings he poured out upon me and many others over the years? He was more than a friend; he was a mentor to me as a young Christian; one who delighted to encourage and guide me through my many questions about faith when I struggled against opposition in ministry.

His answers were always from God's Word and breathed by the Holy Spirit. To me he was a great encourager, one who saw beyond my youthful vigour and guided me in much needed godly wisdom.

I remember so well being awakened night after night with one word: '*Canada*'. I met David and asked him what to do about it; to which he simply replied; '*Go and you will find the answer when you get there.*' Simple answer: which brought God-inspired blessings as the Lord directed me to speak to a total stranger and gave him a direct word to '*return to Africa and finish the work.*'

In all my 30+ years of following Christ I can safely say I have never met a man quite like David. Every time we met my faith in God was raised, I was strengthened and found healing through his hands. When he spoke, it was always to encourage, to build and never to tear down, to inspire and never to discourage. He truly was Christ-like in nature, in words and in deed; and one who challenged people of all ages to fulfil their destiny in Christ.

A great friend, an imparter of blessings; I and many others owe him a debt for the growth we have experienced as he had such a love for the work of the Holy Spirit and simply introduced Him to all who wanted to know more of Christ.

His ever-parting words were always "*blessings, blessings, blessings.*"

Danny and Mary McCauley
(Family friends)
Portadown, Co. Armagh
Northern Ireland.

My memories of David Greenow were when he was introduced to us by Tom Somerville at a prayer meeting we attended. Though he only lived up the road, he was away ministering all over the UK and down in the south of Ireland. It was the late 70s when we really got to know this evangelist of Jesus Christ.

David was a very understanding, patient, generous, uncritical and flexible man. He did not need to speak: he had that anointing on him. People just knew he was a Christian. When he came to the prayer meeting, he taught us about the baptism of the Holy Spirit and the gifts. When David prayed you could feel the presence of the Holy Spirit, and people's needs were met.

I remember on one occasion when David and Emily were going to bed and two men broke into their home. David remained calm and he told the men about Jesus. That was the kind of man he was and even well after the event he continued to pray for their souls. In his latter years he loved to go out for walks and get chatting with the neighbours. Some of them got him to pray with them. One lady got him to pray for an eye problem and she was healed. He also prayed for other neighbours with leg problems and they professed their feet were a lot better. That was David, ready at all times to pray with anyone who had a need.

He taught us that in this world there will be trials, tests and tribulations; a constant spiritual warfare. He said you will have mountain-top and valley experiences; and we did find that out. He always said stand your ground against the enemy.

I can say this: we counted David and Emily as our spiritual parents. In times of need they were always there to help. One thing I know; David was welcomed home by His loving Father saying, *"well done my good and faithful servant."* As a group of believers, we thank God for all His servant David taught us. His door was always open for anyone in need.

Pastor Andy Paget
Trinity Tabernacle
Vice President, International Gospel Outreach.
Bristol, England.

How do I remember David? Many words come to mind. He was gentle, selfless, unassuming, patient, kind — a genuine servant and a man with a powerful anointing of the Holy Spirit. He would never have professed to be a dynamic orator, but the presence of the Spirit of God with him and in him brought us to our knees time and time again with a deep hunger to know more of Jesus and to serve Him better. A true father in the faith, David encouraged many, many young people and, in the mid-1960s, I was one of them.

I launched out into evangelistic ministry while still in my teens and David's unconditional encouragement at this time became part of my spiritual DNA. Inspired by T L Osborn's book *Soulwinning: Outside the Sanctuary*, and recently filled with the Holy Spirit, I was part of a group of young people determined to reach the unreached with the gospel message that had transformed our lives. Together with Bob Searle and several of those who were to become the founding members of IGO, David travelled to Kinson, just north of Bournemouth, where we'd rented a community centre for a coffee-bar-style outreach. I still recall with embarrassment how, on their arrival, we ushered them into a small room, and asked them to pray for us, afraid that these 'older guys' — David being the oldest — might scare our clients away! They complied so graciously and, from that evening onwards, continued to encourage us in each of our outreaches, including those to the huge Isle of Wight music festivals and to local Hell's Angels.

My wife Gay had known David previously through his visits to the Ringwood Revival Centre and she remembers the many occasions when he took time to chat to her. Later, during the IGO Swanwick conferences, they would walk and talk together around the lake. David never ceased to take a prayerful interest in our lives and, for both of us, spending time with him was a top priority during our visit to Northern Ireland a few years before his home-going.

As both evangelist and teacher, David made balance beautiful and integrity attractive. Because of his sensitivity to the Lord's voice, his words sometimes had a prophetic edge. No doubt he was bringing us words of wisdom or words of knowledge; but, being David, there was no need to label them as such. He prayed for my safety during my visits to a troubled Middle East and, before one particular trip in 1990, felt impressed to warn me not to take unnecessary risks. His warning was spot on. Bill Robinson had just been martyred in Lebanon and I wanted to visit his widow Barbara and their four sons, because one of Bill's closest friends, being an American, was unable to go. It seemed that every obstacle had been removed. A former Press Secretary to an Israeli prime minister volunteered to use his influence to get me across the border with my Canadian companion. We were eager to go but I remembered David's warning. There were two possible scenarios that would minimise the risk but, over the next few days, it became clear that neither of these would fit into our time frame, so we abandoned our plans. I learned on my return to the UK that, had we gone, we would have missed Barbara, who had been given safe passage by the South Lebanese army to Metullah, where she'd crossed the border into Israel to meet American friends. Our visit to Lebanon would not only have been unnecessarily risky but it would also have been futile!

All of us who have valued David's friendship and ministry owe a great debt to Emily who was willing to share him with us, although this meant many long periods apart from him. Her quiet godliness, and the many sacrifices she has made, are not forgotten.

Ken Parsons
(Retired Christian worker)
International Gospel Outreach
Co. Durham, England.

My wife Jeanne and I are among the countless people to have been blessed by the fruit of David's ministry, International Gospel Outreach. I used to hear him minister at the IGO conferences, and his impact, which we, this side of the Irish Sea, would never fully appreciate, is in the amount of healing he must have brought to Northern Ireland during the terrible time in its history. He was a pastor of the pastors, and a much-loved and wise man. He had a warm presence in conversation and was very unassuming.

Pastor John Scott
(Retired Pastor)
International Gospel Outreach
Bangor, Northern Ireland.

I first met David Greenow in 1977 at a Christian Camp in Portrush, Northern Ireland, and over the years he became a close friend. David and his wife Emily stayed in our home many times both in Londonderry and Bangor. David was not only a friend to me but was a mentor, which he also was to many younger men in this country and throughout the United Kingdom.

David laid strong foundations in the lives of individuals and churches wherever he ministered. He would pass on books, tapes, writings, ideas and all sorts of Christian material to bless, help and encourage people to serve the Lord.

On one occasion when we were talking together, he shared that he had asked the Lord how he could serve Him better. He felt the Lord impress him with; *'Live in the light of Deity, Calvary and Eternity.'* I felt that was worth taking on board. I had the privilege of ministering alongside David in churches and fellowships in the south of Ireland and England.

David was an anointed preacher and teacher of the Word of God and was an example to all in his love for God. He served God fervently, encouraging everywhere he went. David was a gentle-spirited man who lived his life with wisdom, honesty and integrity. He served the Lord in his generation and left a great legacy to those of us coming behind. I thank God for having known David and Emily, and for the many sacrifices they made over the years.

Babs D'Cunha
(Missionary in India)
Surrey, England.

David was a lovely man, very softly spoken with a quiet gentle spirit. He was a man of great wisdom and understanding; his messages were a great encouragement to me. They were always a word in season. He was talking to me once and, taking both my hands in his, he looked me straight in the eye and said, *'Dig the well deep.'* It was as if he knew something I didn't. I walked away and pondered on what he had just said. I think that was the last time I spoke to David before my beloved husband Danny Cherian died.

We all know that a well has to be deep to find the real source of water and not just surface water, or it runs out in times of drought. If it is deep you can always go to the bottom of the well and still find lovely fresh water to quench the thirst, and not collapse under the heat of the day or pressures of life. Spiritually, I have always known how important it is to have a deep, close relationship with Jesus.

When Danny died, I was out walking the dogs (a job he always did at night), almost mechanically moving across the dark compound of our little school in India. I could hardly believe it all. It was difficult to comprehend all that had just taken place. I had just left the dead body of Danny in the hospital 21km away, and here I was, totally alone.

As I walked, I was aware of another Presence. It was as if an angel or Jesus Himself had just joined me. We walked together into the orchard behind the school. It was at that time that I remembered the word that David had spoken; *'Dig the well deep.'* As I watched the dogs sniffing around, I remembered thinking in my heart; *'What now, God?'* I hadn't uttered a word; but as if in response to my silent question, I felt Jesus wrap a blanket of love around my shoulders. I was engulfed in a wonderful sense of His love and had a tremendous peace in my heart.

Danny was lying dead in the hospital; and here I was in this dark, lonely compound on the edge of the village: no-one but me and Jesus. But oh! what peace! It didn't make sense. The words, *'dig the well deep'* were resounding in my mind. I knew I could draw from that well of Living Water deep within me and be refreshed and continue to live in that desert-like place and serve my Lord. I was not alone. He was there with me.

Many times, I have wondered to myself, *'Did David have some sort of an inkling that Danny was soon to die and that it was important for me to draw my strength from the Living Water?'* Remembering his words was a real encouragement/help to me when I most needed it. I was not totally destroyed by the grief that engulfed me. I was indeed able to look away from my situation, draw from that '*well*' and drink and live. I continued to serve where Jesus had called me to be, much to the amazement of all around. Even now, I still remember David's words: such a means of strength and encouragement.

My word to all reading this is… *dig the well deep.*

David Hughes
(Retired Pastor)
Bourne, Lincolnshire
England.

I first met David when I was ordained into ministry with IGO in October 1973. David was the president of IGO, but he always seemed friendly, never aloof and always interested in each person. At that time, I was youth leader/assistant pastor of an Elim Church in Brighton but a few years later the Lord led me into full-time itinerant ministry. David encouraged me greatly as he sensed God's leading for me into this new ministry.

He willingly opened doors for me, especially in Northern Ireland. On my first trip he took the trouble of picking me up from the airport, driving me back to their home for a lovely meal prepared by Emily, and taking me to my first speaking appointment. From that start, many doors opened for me. I delighted in returning to Northern Ireland regularly, but I was always aware that it was David's reputation and his willingness to introduce me to churches that the Lord used to open that door.

Because of the distance, I only saw David either when I was in Northern Ireland or at the IGO conference; but he would always make sure that he spoke to me and my wife, Rosie, and was genuinely interested in what the Lord was doing in our lives.

We always looked forward to David's Christmas newsletter that also included scripture cards and short messages which were always encouraging and well worth holding on to. David was a quiet, unassuming man with a gentle yet powerful teaching ministry who never saw himself above others but exuded the love of Christ.

Don Double
Good News Crusade
Founder and Director
St. Austell, Cornwall
England.

David was a very faithful friend and a great encourager in the early days of my ministry. He was a very positive Holy Spirit man and a regular speaker at our International Easter conventions. His ministry was always very positive - full of faith, love and Bible-centred. He also conducted the wedding of my daughter Julia to Simon Matthews.

Margaret Evans (Hackett)
Co-pastor, *Oasis Church,* IGO
Beaumaris, Anglesey
Wales.

When I was a teenager, the Lord began a wonderful work in my family home. My father had gone to glory at a relatively young age, and my mother rededicated our home to the Lord to be used by Him. My mother, brother and I were really seeking the Lord for something more. We were members of a very good evangelical Anglican church, but had heard of the baptism of the Holy Spirit; and along with some other friends were seeking the Lord for this. It was back in the late 1960s when the baptism in the Spirit was mainly confined to the Pentecostal churches in England.

God graciously did baptise us, and a regular Friday meeting began in our home, where many people were ministered to and blessed. Through a visit to South Chard Church in Somerset, where God was moving powerfully, we met some people from London who had a *house church* - they met on Thursday nights, Saturday nights and on Sundays, both morning and evening. When they heard about what God was doing in our house, which was about a three/four hour drive away, they told us that when they had speakers coming they would be happy to bring them over to minister in our house on the Friday. This was such a blessing, as they were having International speakers and also IGO ministers.

One of the ministers who came fairly frequently was David Greenow. He became very special to us as a minister and also as a friend. At that season in his life, the Lord was greatly using him in personal prophecy, and usually he would go round the whole group and give them an extremely accurate word from the Lord. We always found his ministry very encouraging and learned a lot from him. We also went with him when he was ministering in other local places, and saw many others blessed too.

He had a lively sense of humour and we also had some fun. I remember one time he came and stayed for a few days when we were going to some special meetings in London with a visiting American preacher. Among our group was a newly saved rather down-to-earth Londoner who came along to the meetings with us. As a group we spent much time praying together and worshipping. The preacher was lamenting the state of Britain and declared that we had not been praying as we ought. Our newly-saved brother stood up in the large auditorium and declared loudly, '*Oh yes we 'ave!*' He got some surprised looks, and David could not stop laughing quietly - nor could I! In fact, it became a standing joke to say, '*Oh yes we 'ave!*' to restore the memory.

We learned much from him about the things of the Holy Spirit; and were extremely blessed by his teaching and stories of ministry he shared with us. It was at a season when we were learning so much about the moving of the Holy Spirit. He was a very important part of that.

George Jesze
Evangelist, Missionary
Nottingham, England.

Helen and I were very pleased to hear that a book was being written about David Greenow. I do not have any personal stories to tell, but I remember him as a kind, gracious and humble brother in the Lord. Through his recommendation, several doors of ministry were opened in Ireland for me, and David and Emily looked after me well when I stayed in their home.

We thank God for his big heart towards the whole Body of Christ, and for his understanding that people who minister interdenominationally often lack encouragement and support, which led to the vision and founding of IGO.

Pastor Kingsley Armstrong
New Life Baptist Church,
IGO President, Evangelist, Northallerton,
North Yorkshire, England.

I knew him as the most encouraging of men. He would often speak words of encouragement and would turn up when I was speaking at Emmanuel Church in Lurgan, Co Armagh. He smiled a lot and never said a bad word about anybody. He believed in the priesthood of all believers and would never cut anyone off. He worked with people who had failed and made lots of mistakes, but he always saw the best in everyone.

He loved seeing younger people enter the Ministry and would cheer them on. He regularly would give over the pulpit to younger men and loved to see them excel. So, I guess, the word '*encourager*' would best sum up David Greenow.

Pastor David Price
Bible teacher
Gosport, Hampshire
England.

I will always remember David's soft voice; but yet he had spiritual authority when he spoke, and has spoken much truth into my life at the International Gospel Outreach meetings. He often used to say that he thought that we were related as I think his mother was a Price.

I shall always remember the time when I was feeling particularly down. It is rare for me to be honest about such things, and David asked how I was doing. I told him how I was feeling, and he asked me a question: When was the last time you spoke in tongues? I must admit I was surprised at his question and thought that his advice was quite unhelpful. How wrong I was! I started to speak in tongues more than before. As I did, my attitude was lifted, and things began to change in my life. Obviously, a wise man and a true gentleman, his advice continues to impact me all these years further down the road. I appreciated him and his time.

Pastor Haydn Greenow
Emmanuel Pentecostal Church
Gateshead, England.

David and my father, Rees Greenow, were cousins, so I have known David all of my life. David was my dad's best man when he got married to my mother, Joy. My earliest memories are from when David used to come to Hereford to visit his father, Lloyd Greenow. He would often attend the Apostolic Church and preach. I also remember going to the Glory meetings he was involved in with his brother Glyn.

What I will always remember David for was the time we spent together in 1978. I had gone to Northern Ireland to spend a week in Dunmurry with a retired pastor and his wife that I knew from the Apostolic Church. I got in touch with David to say that I was in Northern Ireland and he offered to pick me up and take me out for a day. I recall his Mini car that he had at that time. He took me to their home which at that time they were sharing with Emily's parents, Mr and Mrs Hunniford. After some lunch we headed out to visit a few places including Bangor, Antrim, Armagh and Lough Neagh.

Lough Neagh was special, not only because of the place itself but because of what happened. David, knowing that I attended a Pentecostal church, challenged me in regard to my Pentecost experience, using the words of Scripture: '*Have you received the*

Spirit since you believed.' He was shocked when I replied no and immediately challenged me to seek for the filling of the Holy Spirit, praying for me there and then. Those moments with David were such powerful moments in my Christian experience that they have always lived with me.

As a result of the time that I spent with David (I was 18 at the time), we had regular contact in that he always sent me his annual newsletter and some copies of his up-to-date tracts. Whenever I saw him, he always sought to encourage me in some way. The last time that I saw David was in 2012, when I was able to get cheap flights from Liverpool to Belfast City Airport and was able to take my dad with me. Pastor Marcus Thomas very kindly picked us up from the airport and took us to David and Emily's home. He then picked us up later to take us back to the airport. I know David appreciated our visit, but I also know my dad was thrilled finally for the first time ever (and only) to be able to go to his cousin, his best man's home and visit.

Peter Brazier
Retired itinerant Bible teacher
Ammanford, South Wales.

Very gracious; very humble. Saw the best in everybody. A great encourager, especially to my wife and me in our ministry in Ireland. Believers in Ireland, both north and south, always spoke very highly of him. His preaching was always spot on and anointed, and such a blessing and a challenge.

He was a man of integrity and honesty, and straightforward. The phrase often used by others about someone such as David is *'a mighty man of God'* but I am sure David would say, *'just a man with a mighty God.'* I am pretty certain that the Lord used David to open doors for our ministry in Ireland, because it grew so quickly, although he never said so.

What a blessing to have known such a lovely man of God, who is now receiving his reward.

Doreen Moore
(Retired prayer coordinator)
International Gospel Outreach
Southport, England.

My memories of David Greenow are very precious. He was a wonderful man of God, gentle but strong in faith. After my husband died, I was invited to attend an IGO conference. Prior to my first conference, I received a rebuke from a brother I trusted, and had been happy to stand back and let him lead the small church my husband had started.

I was devastated and went to the conference to resign from membership. David talked with me, encouraged me, assured me it was a false accusation and advised me to leave the group before it destroyed me. I will never forget the peace and restoration his words and friendship brought to me. That was 1990. Over the years, as I met other IGO members and was invited to visit their churches, at home or abroad, David was always an encouragement.

The respect for him remained after he stepped down from being president and I met with him and his dear wife, Emily, perhaps for a meal out or a visit at their home. He was also a man of prayer and his prayers were answered – and will yet be answered. Brother David is still missed, but his advice and encouragement lives on.

Maurice Wylie
Founder of Maurice Wylie Media
Northern Ireland.

Sitting in a café in Ballymena, waiting to meet with Pastor Marcus, was just like another normal day to me, yet, in God, that day would join many dots together.

Over coffee, Marcus, whom I had not known previously, told about his connection with David Greenow and how God had led him to write a book on David's life. I sat listening intently to every word that came out of his mouth. It was not just his Welsh accent that was drawing me to listen, but it was the mention of names of pillars in God that had played big parts in my own life. Yet he was unaware of this as he told me who all he had been meeting and researching for the past few years for this book.

Then I said, "I knew David. I have known him for years; in fact, he would have visited me in my home!" It was just like the last piece of a jigsaw fitting.

David was one of the humblest people I have ever known. His meekness balanced with his understanding and power of the Spirit and I just would sit like a son at his father's feet, taking every word in, like a sponge to the water.

Although most of us never like to talk about the dark valleys in life, there is no doubt that we all go through them, myself included. But even in the midst of a dark valley, God would send David! He was like a healing balm, words that carried no loudness but weight, eyes that were ageing but saw the heart. He was one in many millions.

The last time he travelled to Ballymena to see me, we chatted and prayed together. As he was leaving, he looked at me and was about to say…. I interrupted him and said, "I know what you're going to say!" He said, "What am I going to say, Maurice?" I replied, "you're going to say, *do not despise the day of small beginnings!*" He said, "How did you know that?" It was then it hit me as I said to him… "You always tell me that every time we meet!" You see, David never wasted his words and for him to keep telling me something several times meant I was not taking heed. That day, the last time I saw him, I purposely decided that I would never see *small* as I saw it before, and to this day I have and will continue to do so.

Because of that one word, what would have looked *small* in my eyes years ago, I now saw as God opportunities, which have since grown into large harvest fields across the world. So many things have changed, so many doors have opened, all because David sowed the seed… "*Do not despise the day of small beginnings!*"

For the numerous names in the book that impacted me as a person, to David himself and his lovely wife Emily, to Marcus who spent the time researching the book, allowing us the honour to publish it; we are indebted to you all who have gone before us and stood before the God of David!

PART 2

The Life of David Greenow

'Thou wilt show me the path of life: in thy presence is fulness of joy; at thy right hand there are pleasures for evermore.'
Psalm 16:11

Foreword

Someone said that life is about living, loving and leaving a legacy. I believe that my uncle David did that. He had a profound effect on my family's life and calling, and for myself personally. He was probably the person that was the closest to being 'like Jesus' that I have ever known. He had an incredible ability to speak prophetically into my life at key times in my journey and ministry.

Once, when I was in a relationship that wasn't right for my future, he gave me some advice that I still remember over thirty years later, and another time when I was going through the darkest time of my life, he brought encouragement, wisdom, and incredible Godly insight that was truly life-impacting. I can immediately recall and reflect on the things that he said to me at those critical junctions in my life, that still resonate deep in my soul. I am so thankful for him, for without his influence, the story of my family would have been vastly different, and many lives would not have been impacted to the extent that they have. I believe that my family is still benefiting from the effects of his prayers and his godly influence.

I often suggested to my uncle David that he should write a book about his life and ministry. He would always respond, of course, with his characteristic humility and seemed surprised at the possibility! His writing, whether his sermons or his pamphlets, were always the outflow from his incredible relationship with his heavenly Father, so this book is very important.

In order to move forward, it's important to look back and say thank you: remembering the pioneers, the spiritual fathers, the heroes, who helped form the faith of so many. David Greenow, you were one of them; so, thank you for your service to Jesus, for your life, and for your incredible legacy.

May the story of my uncle David inspire you to live well for Christ in your own generation as he did. *'For David, after he had served God's will and purpose and counsel in his own generation, fell asleep and was buried among his fathers.'* (Acts 13:36)

Pastor John Greenow,
Lead Pastor, *Xcel Church*, Co. Durham, England.

CHAPTER ONE

David's early life

David John Evans Greenow was born on May 26, 1927 on a farm in an area called the Black Mountains, which is a group of hills spread across parts of Powys and Monmouthshire in south-east Wales and extending across the England-Wales border into Herefordshire. This was a remote, sparse, thinly populated area, where farming was the main occupation. Cows and sheep, making butter, making feeds, were the daily routines of the families in this part of the United Kingdom. The nearest town for the Greenow family was Hay-on-Wye.

David's parents were Lloyd and Ada Greenow. Lloyd Greenow was one of thirteen children. One of his brothers was Allen and one of his sisters was Florrie or Florence. Amazingly, looking at the family tree, these thirteen all married, so David had loads of cousins and uncles and aunties. From the information that I have been able to gather we know that Ada had a sister Emily and a brother William. The family name was Price.

Lloyd was a hill farmer: we can imagine the joy that there must have been over their first-born child. But within a month of David's birth, his mother sadly died of heart trouble.

In an article titled, '*An Extra-ordinary Visitation from Heaven,*[4]' we are given some insight into her death. It reads... "When she died there was a mighty 'rush' of the Holy Spirit into the bedroom. Her hair was

---

4 Author and publication unknown

swept into the air and brought down perfectly into place as if it had been brushed and combed. When the spectacular happens, God, in His sovereign grace, causes a movement of the Holy Spirit to manifest His working. By a gentle work of the 'Hand of God', her hair was set perfectly. These things were given for a purpose: a testimony to remember that; *'Precious in the sight of the LORD is the death of His saints.'*

"We are told that 'The LORD is righteous in all His ways, and holy in all His works,' and this work was a 'holy' work that displayed His handiwork. The hand of God crowned her very last moments on Earth. Her death was precious to Him. The timing was the moment of the penultimate degree of being changed from one degree of glory to another. She was fitted for the ultimate degree of change for which the body is still waiting: the moment when 'corruption' will be changed to 'incorruption' and 'mortality' will put on 'immortality.'"

To celebrate 30 years of his salvation, David wrote a leaflet on his life in 1972. The leaflet gives us some more background regarding his birth and family.

He writes, "I was born on May 26, 1927 of Welsh parents who knew and loved the Lord Jesus. At that time, they lived in a place called Dorstone, quite near to the Welsh border in Herefordshire England. One cannot fully estimate the value of having praying parents and the influence that those prayers have in shaping the lives of the children.

I am told that my mother dedicated me to the Lord's service before I was born. However, she was not spared to see the fulfilment of her prayers, for she died on June 26th, exactly one month after I was born. This great loss marked my life indelibly and was the cause of much unhappiness and questioning in my early years as I sought to adjust to this tremendous void in my life.

I am grateful to the Lord and to those who watched over me in those days; and thus, I was soon brought under the sound of the Gospel and became aware of my need of Jesus. I also had a strange awareness that someday I would give my life to the preaching of God's Word. I did not understand that this was the call of God in my life, but I somehow sensed, even before I was saved, that there was a Divine plan for my life. I can remember as a child having visions of crowds of people to whom I knew that I would, someday, preach the Gospel.

After David's mother died, two relatives stepped in to look after the new baby on the farm in Dorstone. David spent the first six years of his life at this farm. Firstly, Emily (married name Greenow), his mother's sister, looked after the new child for a period of time. Then, Florrie Greenow, his father's sister, came to live with her brother and looked after David. She absolutely doted on him.

When David was six, his father remarried and the family moved 25 miles away to Cott's Farm, Luggbridge Road, near Hereford, in 1934. David recalls walking through a field at this time and a man shouting at him; "What are you doing here? You shouldn't be here!" David's innocent reply came; "My daddy lives here." David later learned to walk his Father's fields as a travelling evangelist whose ministry stretched the length and breadth of the UK, to America, Canada and Scandinavia.

Lloyd's brother, Allen, also moved to a farm near Hereford in 1934. It was at a place called Tarr's Hill. This was a big move for the two brothers, because the Greenow family had a long association with the Black Mountains, dating back to the 1500s. So why did the two brothers move to be nearer Hereford? While we cannot be certain, one reason that has been given is that farming in the Black Mountains was restrictive and the family wanted to expand. Lloyd made the move first, and then his brother, Allen Greenow, followed.

The surname 'Greenow' was a common name in the area that David's family originated from in the Black Mountains. In the 1911 Census there were over 100 families in the United Kingdom with this surname. Seventy-four families lived in the Herefordshire, Monmouthshire, Brecknockshire area. (see www.your-family-history.com)

In David and Emily's Christmas letter 2006, David mentions a Greenow reunion that has taken place. David writing about his journeyings that year says, "Another interesting experience I had was to visit the Welsh Border area of Mid-Wales, near where I was born to meet with about 80 people of the Greenow family connection. We last got together 10 years ago when there were about 100 of us. Emily and I are the only two Greenows in the whole of Ireland that we know of; but there are hundreds in the family connection in the Herefordshire, Powys area and beyond. It was good to renew acquaintances again, and also to meet with some relatives I didn't know I had."

What does the name Greenow mean? I did some research and found that the name dates back to Anglo-Saxon times in Britain. Originally the surname derived from 'greene' as in village green but there is also a topographical influence on the name. It was given to someone who lived near a physical feature such as a hill, stream, church or a type of tree. So, we can see how the Greenow surname became common in the area known as the Black Mountains. I was told by someone who has researched the Greenow family that the name means 'green meadows.' Another variant on the name is 'Gronow.'

The article referred to earlier, "*An Extra-ordinary Visitation from Heaven*[5]," which was found by Allen Greenow's grandson, Pastor Hayden Greenow, gives us some insight into the workings of God in the Greenow family while they lived in the Black Mountains.

The article opens with these words: "Rising high, south from Hay-on-Wye, the peak of Hay Bluff (677m) dominates the end of a long

---

5 Author and publication unknown

ridge that borders England and Wales; to the west of the ridge stands The Twmpa. In between these two high places a road runs in through a gap that has been known for possibly almost two millennia as The Gospel Pass. The top hillside-fields of 'Blaendegedi' drop down from this narrow highway (Degedi was the name of a brook). It was there that William and Emily Greenow [Gren-ow] worked the land."

On the RAC website we have this insight about the Gospel Pass: 'This narrow lane snaking over the Black Mountains between Monmouthshire and Powys is the highest stretch of road in Wales.... Linking the towns of Abergavenny and Hay-on-Wye, this 18-mile lane snakes its way past historic Llanthony Abbey all the way up to the 1,801ft-high (549m) Gospel Pass – folklore has it that St Paul came this way taking the Bible to Wales.'

In the article, *An Extra-ordinary Visitation from Heaven,*' there is this comment about the Gospel Pass: "The Gospel Pass was given this name because along this road came preachers from South Wales long before there was any Christian settlement at Canterbury."

Emily Greenow, as previously highlighted, was David's mother's sister. She married William Greenow. This Greenow family was not related to Lloyd and Allen Greenow, David's father, and uncle.

The article tells us about a visit to the area by the renowned evangelist of the time, Stephen Jeffreys. A lady who had recently moved into the locality arranged for a tent to be pitched in a field and invited Stephen Jeffreys to come and conduct a series of meetings. The local families did have a Baptist chapel but predominantly the culture was religious and nominal in regard to Christianity. As we are told in the article; *'they had plenty of religion but no life.'*

Emily Greenow said how they felt being constrained to attend all the meetings. In order for her and her husband to attend the services it meant '*a journey on horse-back. It was almost a twenty-mile round trip by road, around Hay Bluff.*'

The article says, "He came and went. There was no one who answered any call of the Gospel. Mrs Greenow (Emily) never talked about the healing of the sick taking place. In short: 'Nothing happened.' She was quite emphatic in saying that."

But God did step in. The article does suggest that prayer was made during the mission for God to move in power. One woman who attended the services said, "We were not 'saved people' who prayed... (but)...God answered their prayers in a miraculous way." Some six months after Jeffreys' visit, there was a visitation of the Holy Spirit to the area. The article says, '*Nothing was there on the ground other than a dead religion,*' but there was a complete change of spiritual atmosphere in the locality.

The article tells us how, one morning, David's uncle, William Price, was out working 'butting and topping' swede. That is where he was converted. Mrs Greenow (Emily) was carrying milk to the dairy. After putting the pails down in the middle of the yard, she came to the Lord on her knees. On another farm, her sister Ada had a very powerful encounter with the Lord and was the only one amongst the saved company who had a 'Pentecostal' experience.

So spiritual life came to 'Blaendegedi' and to David's family in particular. Another Jeffreys brother came to minister in the area in the years following this visitation. William Jeffreys came and open-air preaching services were held annually on the lower parts of the Black Mountains.

I have already mentioned that following the death of David's mother when he was a month old, it was his aunty Emily who looked after him first. This article gives us this insight in how this woman took care of the new-born baby and her spiritual input into his life.

"A month before she went to be with the Lord, Ada gave birth to David Greenow... Mrs Greenow took him and nursed him through that very critical stage of bereavement which was deeply felt by all the family.

"This has been spoken of by one who knew the reality of the grief of those days. It was very hard for them all. It cannot be said how long David Greenow stayed at Blaendegedi, but it lasted until it was best for him to be put once again into the care of his immediate near relatives. I had never been in touch with David until writing these words, but I knew of him as someone for whom Mrs Greenow continuously and faithfully prayed."

"He was always 'remembered.' This was part of the workings that were the result of being incorporated into such a rich spiritual heritage, the beginnings of 'an activity' that is difficult to describe. The simple reason is that very few have known such a powerful work and working of the Holy Spirit. These workings of grace were wrought out of 'a refining within' by an anointing from above.

"Emily Greenow's 'taking' of this child was a most natural thing to do, but it has had a dynamic effect on the one who was taken for a season, not only for the days of his nursing, but for their duration. Emily Greenow 'remembered' him continually at the Throne of Grace."

David Greenow was bathed in prayer from his birth. I think of Timothy and the influence that his family had in his life and ministry. A prayer foundation was laid in David's life by his natural family. I don't think it is a coincidence that the baby who was nursed in a blanket of prayer went on to find power in prayer for his own life and be an example and encouragement to many others to pray. We must *thank God* for those who stepped in to show care and love for this new-born baby, David John Evans Greenow, who never knew his natural mother; and David always felt this loss.

In January 1979, when David's mother-in-law died, Emily was surprised to find David weeping uncontrollably in the bedroom following her funeral. He was weeping for the friend he had lost; weeping too for the mother he had never known. David felt the loss of his mother's love all his life, and it was this that drove him as a child to seek comfort in God.

When David entered heaven on 3rd May 2012, what a joy it must have been for him to meet up with his parents, but particularly his mother. What incredible blessing it must have been for Ada to see her son and hear about the blessing he had been to thousands through the preaching of the Gospel in the UK, Europe and North America.

But knowing David, as I did, I think after meeting his mother, he would have turned to Jesus and given Him praise and worship for all the answered prayers in his life. Prayers that had started with his mother when, before his birth, she had dedicated him to the Lord's service.

CHAPTER TWO

Early spiritual influences...

including a tribute from his brother Glyn...

When the family moved nearer Hereford, they attended the local Apostolic church in Hereford. David was six years of age when the family moved to Cott's Farm near Hereford in 1934. The family's link with the Apostolic church can be traced back to 1923 when the Apostolic church started meetings in Hay-on-Wye. This was a new venture for the Hereford Apostolic church. There were these reports about those early days in Hay-on-Wye: "*The work has been difficult.... There has been much opposition in this place through false reports.*"[6]

In 1924, some eighteen months after the meetings started in the town, the Apostolic church built a new meeting hall. David's father, Lloyd, his uncle, Allen, and his aunty, Sarah Ann Price, purchased the land for this new church building. The cost was £50.00.

David grew up in the Hereford church, and it was in this assembly that David's spiritual formation started. He was part of this local assembly until he went to Bible College in 1950 at the age of 23.

It was a remarkable church at the time that David attended it. Someone who has traced the early history of this Hereford assembly wrote, "*it (was) probably the home of the very first Apostolic church in the modern history of Christianity in the United Kingdom!*"[7]

---

6 The Apostolic Church Missionary Herald April 1925: Monthly Magazine.
7 Greenow, H. (2016) "The Apostolic Church in Hereford." (search "Our First Century: Apostolic Church UK 1916-2016).

The church was called Apostolic before it joined with the Apostolic church movement in 1920.

The leader of the Hereford church was Frank Hodges. He owned a gentlemen's outfitters business in Hereford. Prior to his conversion he described himself as *'a man full of the world, living without Christ.'*

He was converted under the ministry of Torrey and Alexander at a mission in London. Sometime after his conversion, "Hodges was prayed for and healed of an enlarged heart condition; something he was happy to testify to until his old age."[8]

Frank Hodges was baptised in the Holy Spirit in Wales and spoke in new languages in a house quite near to the home of the Welsh revivalist, Evan Roberts. He wrote of this experience at a later date: "I got a wonderful baptism in the Spirit. I had a Welsh tongue, and I spoke in Welsh...I was told what the tongue meant, in English, and everything has been fulfilled." This was truly remarkable because, before this experience he confessed to hating the Welsh but that after his baptism he "now loved them.[9]"

Prior to his experience of the Holy Spirit, Frank Hodges had attended a Christian mission in Hereford; but because of his Spirit baptism he had to break away from this fellowship. This resulted in his gathering a group of believers around him to establish a new church in the city of Hereford.

A certain Mrs Hambridge gave a plot of land for this new work and a church building was erected. This took place in 1908; and after the building was completed, this new group of believers asked the Lord for a name to be given for them. Frank Hodges visited a woman in Cardiganshire, west Wales who had a gift of prophecy and it was through direct revelation that the name 'Apostolic Church' was given. The building was in Monkmoor Street and was still used for services

8-9 Worsfold, J.E. (1991) 'The Origins of the Apostolic Church in Great Britain.' New Zealand: Julian Literature Trust)

up until the early 1990s. The building is still standing and is now used by a funeral director.

A few years later, Frank Hodges heard about a convention being held in Wales and that those holding the convention were also called 'the Apostolic church.' He went to the convention and gave an invitation for the brothers Pastors D.P. and W.J. Williams to come to Hereford. On their arrival they were amazed to see the name Apostolic Church over the door, and after many confirmations and ministries of the Ascension gifts, the Hereford assembly decided to join fellowship with the work in Wales, this taking place in 1920.

The work in Hereford began to expand quickly and in mighty ways. Because of the growth of the work, in 1926 a new building was opened in Canal Road just a couple of hundred yards down the road from the original building in Monkmoor Street. At one period of time there were 35 Churches connected to the Hereford Church, as it became the centre for the Apostolic church work in the Midlands with six apostles, many pastors, elders, evangelists, deacons and deaconesses.

There is a story about Pastor Frank Hodges which I want to mention. One day, he was sitting on a train waiting for it to leave. Shortly after he sat down, two young men came in and sat down also to await the train. He could not determine what they discussed as they sat there, for they were speaking in the Welsh language. Strangely enough, in a very short time, the Spirit of God quickened him and he felt he must speak out to them. As he spoke out in a 'tongue,' the two men stood and stared in amazement at him until he had finished. Speaking in English, they asked him if he knew what he had said. Pastor Hodges explained to them that he was Pentecostal and that he had spoken in tongues but did not know what he had said.

It was then his turn to be surprised, when they said to him, 'You spoke to us in perfect Welsh language. You told us what our profession was, where we were going on this trip, and how to go about our mission, which, you assured us, would be successful. You then told us that we should buy a large tent and that you would give us the down payment for it.' Brother Hodges took out twenty pounds, gave it to them, wished them God speed, and they parted. The two men were Stephen and George Jeffreys.[10]

Pastor Frank Hodges was David Greenow's pastor. He was a man who had a testimony of Jesus being Saviour, Healer and Baptiser in the Holy Spirit. The Hereford church also had prophets who spoke out God's word. This reminds me of the multi-faceted ministries that were in the church in Antioch in Acts chapter 13. In the Hereford church, under Frank Hodges and others, David Greenow was nurtured and encouraged in his walk with God.

During his years in Hereford, David would have come under the ministry of men who had experienced the God of Revival and the God of the Miraculous. The Apostolic church had a yearly calendar of conventions for their local churches. David would have heard men speak at the conventions in Hereford who had experienced revival and the miraculous in different parts of the world and in the UK. So, we see the threads of the ministry that God had for David in later years being weaved into his life while he was part of the Hereford Apostolic church.

Frank Hodges was a full Gospel man and he led churches that were full Gospel churches: Jesus - Saviour, Healer, Baptiser and Coming King. David Greenow was a full Gospel man, too, and I don't think it was by accident that these truths gripped David's heart. He saw them in the local church, he saw them in the leaders of the local church. It was under the ministry of Pastor Frank Hodges, others in the Hereford Apostolic Church, and visiting speakers, that David was trained and matured in the Christian faith. All these influences helped to shape and weave God desires and dreams into the young

---

10 Cathcart, W. (1979) "The Glory of the Christ Revealed in Charismatic Ministry". USA: Vantage Press

David Greenow. He allowed these truths to soak into his own heart; they became a great part of his ministry in the years following. Right up to the end of his life, David continued to speak about 'Calvary love' and the blessing of the fullness of the Holy Spirit.

When David spoke of 'Calvary love' he had something particular in mind; something more than the experience of salvation. David never forgot or lost the thrill of his salvation. In his Christmas letter 2008 he wrote, "On May 25th, 1942, I received the Lord Jesus as my personal Saviour, a wonderful and blessed day. I came to know the Saviour under the ministry of a Scottish Pastor, W. Massie, in the city of Hereford."

But what other truth was gripping David's heart about 'Calvary love?' The Greek word that is used in the New Testament is 'agape.' The English language is so limited in regard to the word love. We have one word which covers a huge range of meaning, from loving our wives to loving food. In the Greek language there were words to describe physical love and family love.

R.T. Kendall writes;[11] "The Greek word agape was not largely used in ancient Hellenistic literature. It was the Christian faith that brought it in and made it well-known...Agape was used to describe God's love in giving his one and only Son. It is self-giving love. It is unselfishness."

When David talked about 'Calvary love', he was encouraging us to live in the thrill of our salvation experience; but also, he was challenging us to live 'Calvary love' out to others. Our love for family and friends is good, but this Calvary love can break down barriers and bring reconciliation, which would be impossible for any of the natural loves. For David, 'Calvary love' was spiritual; it was God's love. Through this love, God took the first step towards us. This love was demonstrated *while we were still sinners.* This love didn't depend on our response or our acceptance. God just loved us. For David,

---

11 Kendall, R.T. (1997) "Just Love. The Most Excellent Way". Scotland: Christian Focus Publications Ltd.

'Calvary love' motivated him to take first steps to all, whatever their church denomination. For David, 'Calvary love' encouraged him to believe that whatever breakdown there was in relationships, this love would overcome all barriers. In Ireland, where David ministered, 'Calvary love' would bring Catholic, Protestant, Loyalist, Republican, terrorist and non-terrorist together and share fellowship under Jesus.

David did practise this. I can remember a particular moral issue in someone's life, that I had to handle. There was a family broken over it. I asked David to come alongside me to seek a resolution for the situation. When David and I met the person, I can remember how David's influence and presence brought a calmness and a loving care to the discussions. David brought 'Calvary love' into the situation.

When David talked about 'Calvary love', he was encouraging us to live this spiritual love out in our relationships, to our natural enemies, to our church 'competitors' and to whosoever.

His brother Glyn...

As a result of the marriage of Lloyd, David's father, to Laura, two boys were born. David's two step-brothers were Fred and Glynn. David had a big spiritual input into Glyn's life, but Glyn also helped David. It was Glyn who taught David to play the accordion. I can remember David, at one particular service in the church that I led in County Armagh, playing and leading us in the song, "He has healing hands. The hands of Jesus are healing hands." They shared ministry together through IGO and Glyn became a recognised minister himself within the Christian Pentecostal circles in the UK and Europe.

The following is Glyn's tribute to his brother...

I consider it a privilege and an honour to share a tribute to my brother David. I was born and raised in a Christian home and it was expected that I attended the church services on Sunday morning and evening, and also Sunday school in the afternoon!

However, at the age of 13-15 I went through a period of teenage rebellion, which meant that I preferred going to the cinema, and to keep company with my teenage friends who were not Christians. I did make a commitment to Christ at the age of 15, but there was still a sense of emptiness in my heart which I believed could only be satisfied by following worldly pursuits.

In August 1959, When I was 16-years-old, my brother David, who lived in Northern Ireland and was travelling as an evangelist, came to visit our home, which was a farm, three miles from the city of Hereford. During his visit, he invited me to accompany him to what were then known as Glory Meetings. I was somewhat reluctant, not quite knowing what to expect, but was persuaded to attend.

We travelled to Evesham in Worcestershire and attended the afternoon and evening services. I found them quite different from that which I had been used to attending. There was a great sense of joy and freedom, which, at first, I found quite overwhelming. The following day, Sunday, we travelled to Newark-On-Trent where we attended the afternoon and evening services.

There was a large banner across the front of the platform which said, 'You will never be the same again,' which certainly proved to be true! That day I received the Baptism in the Holy Spirit with the evidence of speaking in tongues. And I was never the same again!

I returned to Hereford and attended house group meetings where again there was a real and evident sense of God's presence and blessing. From that time forward I continued attending Glory meetings in addition to the local church meetings. I also continued working on my parents' farm; until there came a point where I knew that God was calling me to full-time Ministry.

My brother David had a huge impact on my life. He was the one who was pivotal to my decision to leave the farm and pursue a full-time ministry call. It seemed a huge step; but I know it was God's plan and purpose for my life. I continued to travel, and in the following years visited Sweden, Norway, Finland and Denmark. There was a great sense of fulfilment and joy in doing God's will. Then I was invited to visit America, where I travelled with a friend. We ministered in many different churches and experienced great blessings. Also, during that time I visited Kenya - where again great blessing ensued.

After that, I also became the pastor of the Full Gospel Church in Newton Aycliffe (Now Xcel Church), alongside my wife Pamela, and serving Pamela's parents, Jack, and Pansy Dickenson. This was throughout the 1980s and 1990s, until I handed the church to my son John and his wife Lisa.

During this time David and Emily would come and visit and David would minister in our church with incredible grace and anointing; 'strengthening' our church and being an amazing blessing to our children and our family. He will never be forgotten and left an amazing legacy for all of us.

In the tribute, written by Glyn, he mentions "Glory Meetings". These were meetings organised by a Pentecostal group of people called "The Glory People."[12] I have written more about this movement and David's involvement with them in later chapters.

Let me just quote something about Glyn's experience with "The Glory People". "There were amazing blessings in those days. The meetings were fantastic. People were prayed for and were just laid out on the floor. I remember being carried out of many meetings, and I

---

12 For more details about "The Glory People" see www.glory-people.org

remember Ann Searle dancing around the hall with her eyes closed. In one of Cecil Stewart's meetings in the Isle of Man, David Willows (nephew of Henri Staples) and I went across from Fleetwood on a fishing boat. The meetings were amazing. I recall getting prayed for and falling backwards into a piano accordion case, where I stayed for the rest of the meeting."[13]

In Glyn's tribute to David he mentions about travelling to Sweden, Norway, Finland, and Denmark to minister. In the Glory News no. 36[14] there is a full report of Glyn's visit to Scandinavia. The article is headed, 'LOVE is the Key in Every Land,' and the opening sentence was: 'Brother Henri often says, "This Gospel works", and we are praising the Lord from the depths of our hearts for the way it has worked in the lives of so many men and women on our recent visit to Scandinavia. Glyn was joined on the trip by Roy Turner (see section 'The Glory Way') and only knew two people over there and we could never have imagined the mighty way in which God was going to lead us.'

Glyn and Roy ended up spending one hundred and five days in Scandinavia. "We held one hundred meetings in the four countries, travelled 6,500 miles, which included five boat trips and two air flights; and we ministered to over 20,000 people." Let me just highlight some of the testimonies that the Glory News received following Glyn and Roy's ministry in Scandinavia.

Vivi Mehlum, from Norway, wrote, "There was a wonderful spirit of love in the midst and it melted my heart. I received such a wonderful love as Roy and Glyn ministered, that I wanted immediately to beg all my friends' forgiveness. Oh Jesus, Jesus, Jesus!"

Enoch Carlson, from Sweden wrote, "We do praise the Lord for sending our dear brothers Roy and Glyn to us here in Gothenburg

---

13 Armstrong (2007), "IGO International Gospel Outreach The First Forty Years". Manchester: Barratt Ministries Publications)
14 Magazine published by "The Glory People."

with a wonderful side of the Gospel we are longing for, namely the Love of God. We were in a lack of real love, and we received what we were longing for – a wonderful renewal in our lives and a new love for our Bridegroom and Friend Jesus."

Vivian Martensson, from Sweden said; "I shall never forget the first meeting when these two brothers, filled with love and faith in the Holy Ghost, stood and testified of our wonderful Saviour. The wonderful love of God just melted my heart and transformed me. I realised that this was the thing I had been longing for."

Henny Jorgensen, from Denmark wrote, "Brother Roy and Brother Glyn from England came along to have meetings in our country, with their interpreter sister Gyda. At the first meeting we felt a heavenly atmosphere while they were singing and playing, and we could see the love of God shining through them. At a meeting a few days later, God met me in a wonderful way. The Holy Spirit came over me in such a way that I felt I was lost in the love of God. My mouth was filled with laughter and my body was shaking under the power of His love, while our brothers were singing and testifying."

Just like Andrew went and found his brother Simon to introduce him to Jesus, so David Greenow came to the family home, just outside Hereford in August 1959, and introduced his brother to the fulness of the Holy Spirit. Andrew's brother Simon went on to carve his own experience of the will of God in his life. The same happened for Glyn Greenow. That story is still to be written.

CHAPTER THREE
His spiritual experiences...

David was *born again* on 25th May 1942 at a Whitsun Convention with the Hereford Apostolic church. The meetings were held in a tent on the Greenow's farm. David wrote, 'I came to know the Saviour under the ministry of a Scottish pastor, W. Massie, in the city of Hereford, England. Later I met with his daughter in Bible College in Wales. Barbara Massie had an effective ministry in several countries including Ireland and not least in the USA.'

His cousin Rees Greenow was also saved at the same meeting. Actually, David was *born again* the day before he celebrated his 15th birthday on 26th May 1942.

In an article that David wrote about his life, he mentioned some of his early spiritual experiences in the Hereford church. He had first come under the convicting power of the Holy Spirit when he was 13 years old: "I came under conviction of sin as the Holy Spirit sought to show me my need of Jesus, as my personal Saviour.

At 14, I opened my heart to the Saviour; and my young life was forever changed. At 15 I was baptised as I obeyed the scriptures regarding water baptism. I also had the joy of pointing my first person to Christ as Saviour. At 16, I received the mighty baptism of the Holy Spirit, our Divine Helper in the Christian life. At 17, I began to proclaim the Word of God. I am most grateful for those in the local church in which all these experiences took place, for all their help, encouragement and guidance. At 18, I had a very real experience of the sanctifying Power of God that let me know God's Holiness was real for my life. At 19, I was planning on marriage, but the Lord intervened with a question, 'what about My call in your life?' My plans were superseded by the Lord's and I went into training for Christian ministry in Wales."

I now want to give some more details about the challenge David received from the Lord when he was 19 years of age. David wrote, "Like every normal young person I had ambitions for my life and one great and cherished desire was to be married as soon as possible and have a home where I would be loved and possess the happiness I felt I had missed in life. So, at 19 years... God challenged me again regarding His call in my life, and finding God a difficult Person to argue with, and having a loving respect in my heart for Him, I abandoned my ideas and sought to walk in the path He was opening up before me."

In a recording of David telling something of his Christian experience we can see the pain of this surrender at 19 years of age. He was engaged to be married but it was broken off. They were 'in love' said David. Remember David had lost his mother when he was a month old. This is no reflection on those who loved him and cared for him, but he really wanted to have his own home and family. Listening to David telling this story, you can hear the cry in his heart for someone to love. He repeated the words a number of times; "we were in love, we were in love, boy, we were in love." They were making plans for married life together, but God stepped in and challenged David with these words; "What about My plan for your life?"

I did wonder whether this challenge came through prophetic ministry in the local church in Hereford. Like Antioch in Acts chapter 13, the assembly did have some powerful prophets. They were involved in the leadership of the local church and the other churches that were in relationship with the Hereford church. David responded to God by saying; "Sorry, I was busy with my plans." The engagement was broken off. The young woman said, "You go your way, and I'll go my way." "There were tears." David said, "there were tears, there were tears."

David wrote something further about this surrender: "God did not forget the surrender I made to Him at 19 years of age when I began to make Him responsible for providing me with the life partner of His choice. God is no man's debtor, and when we seek first His kingdom and righteousness, delighting ourselves in Him, He will give us the desires of our hearts (Psalm 37:4). God gave me a wife who had known Jesus since she was 12 years of age and who was willing for God's purpose to be always first in our lives whatever the cost."

At 19 years of age David fully surrendered his life to God, with the sacrifice of a broken engagement. David was always grateful for the 'strength and urge of God's call to service' in his life.

David, in later Christmas letters or testimony leaflets, would often refer to those early spiritual experiences in Hereford and their impact on him. Each time David wrote about those early experiences he gave some additional insights about how God was working in his life. In his testimony tract, '*The Goodness and Grace of God in My Life*,' he wrote: "About the time I reached my teens I was strongly convicted of my need to receive Jesus as my Saviour. I endeavoured to improve my life and dropped off some bad habits, thinking I could silence the voice of the Holy Spirit who was causing me to feel my spiritual need. It seems that as the Holy Spirit seeks to lead us to Jesus, we, by our own good works and religious endeavours, often seek to stifle His work; but there is no substitute for coming to Christ in repentance, faith and surrender. I discovered that all attempts to make myself acceptable to God and obtain peace within were utterly futile. Gradually I realised my own spiritual bankruptcy and came nearer to the moment of truth: which was that I was a sinner, and that only Jesus could save me. Acts 4:12. Then there came those times when I sincerely prayed for salvation but seemed to receive no answer because I made the mistake of looking at my feelings instead of God's Word for assurance that He had accepted me. On the morning of May 25th 1942, I distinctly remember praying, 'Lord; let this be the day that I shall look back upon all my life as the day in which I gave my heart to You.' God answered that prayer, and that very afternoon I responded to the Gospel invitation. I was pointed to Romans 10:9 and asked if I believed that Jesus was alive; if so, would I confess Him as my personal Lord and Saviour. This I did and immediately experienced assurance as God fulfilled the promise in the verse, *'thou shalt be saved.'*

My life was changed, Jesus became real, the Word of God had worked and the peace of God wonderfully witnessed in my heart, a peace that has not waned in 65 years, (David was writing in 2007) but rather increased. How thankful I am that I came to know the Lord as a young person, for He has saved and kept me from so much evil in this world and from hell in the next. Jesus saves, keeps and satisfies."

Continuing to quote from the leaflet, 'The Goodness and Grace of God in My Life,' David tells us how those experiences changed him.

"With my conversion there came new spiritual desires, and soon I discovered that I now possessed a very real desire for God's House and for His service. Also, there was a deep love for God's Word and for His people. I began to testify of what Christ had done for me and it was not long before I was pointing souls to the Saviour. What a joy it was to lead my first soul to Christ! My understanding of God's plan for my life became increasingly clear, and it began to dawn upon me that God was calling me; that I would never be able to live my life as I pleased, if I was going to obey Him. What I had strangely sensed as a child now became a strong conviction in my heart.

I sought to obey the teaching of the Bible and was baptised in water on July 12th, 1942. Mark 16:16. I was baptised in the Holy Spirit in October 1944, and with this experience came a new challenge regarding God's will for my future. I wanted to obey Him, and yet like every other normal young person I had my own plans and ambitions, but finding God a difficult person to argue with, I fully surrendered my life to His will for all my future. It was not easy to abandon cherished desires for God's way, but I knew then, and I have proved over these many years, that God's way is always best."

The early years in Hereford Apostolic Church were foundational for the plans that God had for David Greenow. He acknowledged that when he wrote, "I am most grateful for those in the local church in which all these experiences took place, for all their help, encouragement and guidance."

A particular challenge that David would have come under while in Hereford was the call to evangelism. The Apostolic Church in Hereford were fervent in evangelistic outreach and church planting. As was mentioned above, David led his first person to Christ when he was 15 years of age. The church had been donated a caravan and during the summer months, women would take the caravan around the outlying villages of Herefordshire to preach the Gospel.

David was called as an evangelist in the Apostolic church towards the end of the 1940s. It was again at a Whitsun Convention in Hereford. Having read and written about the early history of the Apostolic Church and the way God moved in their different Church conventions, it is very likely that this calling came through prophetic direction at the Whitsun Convention.[15]

I only knew David in the latter days of his life. From the stories he told me of the past and knowing what he was still living for in his end years, those key spiritual experiences never left him. He continued to

15 Thomas, D.M. (2016) "The God of Our Fathers". Belfast: Ambassador Books and Media.

exude a love and passion for the Gospel, and he sought to encourage people to live with the same fervency. He would often talk about 'Calvary love.'

He was baptised in the Holy Spirit when he was 16 years old, but it was still an experience he sought for his life: to be continually filled with the Holy Spirit, evidenced by spiritual languages. At 19 years old he surrendered to the call of God in his life. The thrill of that call never left him.

On one occasion he was heard to say, "I am still learning how to be the best channel for the Holy Spirit." There was other evidence of the Holy Spirit in his life: words of knowledge and wisdom, gifts of healings and a strong prophetic ministry.

In an article, in the Glory News no 16 'Revival Fires are Burning in my Soul,' David mentions something about his conversion and early Christian life and the struggles he faced. (This article must have been written sometime before May 1960.)[16] "I received Christ as my own personal Saviour nearly 18 years ago. I shall never forget the experience. From that day the Lord has never failed me, and He has become increasingly precious. Praise Him! Within about two and a half years of having received the Saviour, I had followed Him through the waters of baptism and had also received the mighty promised baptism of the Holy Ghost. Truly, obedience brings blessing. Several years of my Christian experience, however, were in a great measure spent in defeat, discouragement, and unbelief. I did not seem to be making any progress with God and yet my heart yearned to please Him. Then came the year 1951 when God began to move in my life in a new way. Praise His Name."

Let me mention a principle of Christian ministry. I do wonder if this principle was working in David's life. Selwyn Hughes would have talked about the death of a vision and then a resurrection. How many

---

16 Magazine published by "The Glory People".

times does God take us through wilderness experiences and, after a time, new life springs up? This is a period of time that tests our faith and grows our trust in God. Without jumping too far ahead of the story, David did experience a renewal of heart in 1951.

Reflection...

Before going on to the next part of David's life, I think it would be good to pause and ask the question: what spiritual truths can we draw out, for ourselves, from the early life of David?

The first thing is this: God wants us to experience Him and know that it is Him who is moving in our hearts. Christianity is not 'head knowledge' but something to be experienced on the inside that makes us know that we are in relationship with our Heavenly Father.

The second truth is this: We mention how Jesus died for us. We need to also say that we have died in Jesus. We see how in the early steps of David's walk with God, he was challenged to lay his hopes and plans aside for the call of God in his life.

The final thing is this: Today the Gospel is often presented in a way that it seems we are doing God a favour by accepting Jesus. The presentation is often couched in what God has for us and how He has a good life for us. When God calls us to salvation, it is a call to follow Him and to obey whatever He says.

CHAPTER FOUR

Training for His Master...

David attended the Apostolic church Bible school in Penygroes from 1950 to 1952. He studied under two particular giants of the Apostolic church at the time. The first was Dr Greenaway and the second was Pastor Rowlands.

Dr Greenaway had spent a number of years in New Zealand pioneering churches. God had really used him in this ministry. He pioneered his first church within four months of landing in New Zealand and in his first year, God used him to pioneer with the Maori population of New Zealand. He came back to the UK in 1948 to take charge of the re-opened Bible school in Penygroes. It had been commandeered during the war for use as a military hospital and it was released back to the Apostolic church in 1948.

He returned to New Zealand at the end of 1950. Although he spent only two years as the Principal, '*his scholarship and expertise laid a sound theological basis for the post-war period of the School.*' [17] (In the picture across, David is standing on the far left and Dr Greenaway is standing fourth from the left.)

17 Riches of Grace,1960. Monthly magazine published by The Apostolic Church.

The woman, standing on the right of Dr Greenaway, in the picture, is Barbara Massie. We will mention more about Barbara a little later.

David only spent approximately six months under the tutorship of Dr Greenaway but his influence on David can be seen in the leaflets that David produced later in his own ministry. I have copies of the lectures and study books that Dr Greenaway produced for use in the Bible College. They were Bible-based, thorough in their application to Scripture, and were structured around headings and sub-headings. The same can be seen in the writings and lectures that David produced in his later ministry years.

Dr Greenaway's successor was Pastor William Rowlands or '*Willie*' Rowlands. He was known for his love of God's Word and had a unique ability from God to both teach and preach God's word. Pastor Rowlands was the Principal from September 1950 to September 1956.

(In the picture across, David is standing on the right and Pastor Rowlands is sitting on the right. The picture was taken in the lounge/library area of the Bible College.)

The following tribute was given of Pastor Rowlands on his death: "He was a theologian... His knowledge of theology and Christology was immense. His tongue was like the pen of a ready writer, revealing a mind that was profound in knowledge, penetrating in its search, clear in its comprehension."[18] I mention these two men just to highlight the influences that David was coming under in his early Christian walk.

---

18 Riches of Grace, 1981. Monthly magazine published by The Apostolic Church.

In part 3 of this book I have included details of what David taught on particular Bible topics. In part 4 examples of some of the leaflets and bookmarks that David produced are included. David was a prolific writer of pamphlets and leaflets and the one thing that stands out about them all is this: David had a theological foundation in his life. He was Pentecostal in belief and practice and there was a Biblical basis to all that he wrote and said. David had a strong and vibrant Christology. I have no doubt that he learned this from Pastors Greenaway and Rowlands and the other lecturers at the Bible school. The Apostolic Church were known for the strong message they preached about the Lord Jesus Christ. David would have first heard this message in the local church in Hereford and the message was further expanded as he sat under men in the Bible school.

There were some upbeat titles to the leaflets, but they were written on sound beliefs that came from God's Word. David's time in the Bible school prepared him for his future life in word and deed.

I have been able to look at David's photo album from his years at the Bible College. In addition to Pastors Greenaway and Rowlands, David came into contact with some amazing men during his years at the Bible College. Their names were unknown in the wider church circles but their influence on David must have been special. These men carried something of God's anointing with them; they would have been able to share with David and his fellow students some amazing stories of how God works to fulfil His purpose in the lives of people dedicated to His service.

In May 1951, two Apostolic Church Pastors visited the College. Pastors Evans and Poole had spent some years ministering in Canada and the USA and had been greatly affected by what was then called 'the latter rain anointing.' David writes, "These brothers visited the Bible College to share their hearts with us, both students and staff; and we experienced the Holy Spirit in a latter rain visitation in a way never to be forgotten. After they had ministered God's Word, we felt a tremendous brokenness, and a deep repentance toward God and each other. We came forth from that time with an awareness of the current moving of the Holy Spirit in revival on the earth."

Barbara Massie, who I mentioned earlier, was at that meeting which took place in the lounge of the Bible school. She had attended the Bible school as a student when it had reopened in 1948 and finished her studies, and left, in 1950. On this occasion, Barbara was coming back to the school for a visit and this is what she wrote about this visitation at the Bible school in 1951.[19] "The previous night, some of the students had attended a meeting at the local Apostolic church where Pastors Poole and Evans were ministering. The students saw some amazing things that night. There was a row of 25 or 30 people up front who had been seeking the baptism of the Spirit for ten, twenty, thirty and forty years. Real *chronics* (Barbara's description) I called them. I never thought they'd receive; neither did they. That's why they didn't! Pastor Poole was walking down the line of people and talking to them quietly. I could hear what he was saying. He was telling them that it was their lips, their tongues, their mouths that would be speaking the glory of God; and to just lift their hands and begin to praise God. As he touched the first one, I said to myself, 'He's got the most difficult one up there!' He put his hands on her, and when she opened her mouth and began to speak in tongues, I nearly fell over! Then down the line he went, not missing a one. Each person received the baptism just like starting a car that had all its points and plugs ready to fire. A row of deaf people also suddenly received their healing."

What about the next day in the Bible school? Barbara Massie writes: "The (meeting) was held in a big student lounge, and Fred Poole was speaking. I was the only girl there. He told us about the visitation that started in Saskatchewan, Canada, and then spread to Detroit and Philadelphia. He spoke of revival taking place in the churches day and night, and of people falling on their faces before the Lord as

19 "O River of God: A Tribute to the Prophetic Life and Ministry of Barbara Massie." 2008.

the Holy Spirit would minister. He gave us first-hand news of what God was doing in America, and what God had done in his own heart. While he was speaking, I noticed some in the lounge turning around in their chairs, getting down on their knees and beginning to cry. I had tears in my eyes; but was trying to hide it! The Spirit of God was now dealing with us. Some in the room began falling off their seats as if in agony. Pastor Poole just went on talking about the visitation. He knew what was happening to us; he knew the Spirit of the Lord had come in! Some people turned their faces to the wall; some went on the floor, and some went under the table or under their chairs. It was weeping you couldn't stop, and you couldn't explain. God was dealing with every life in that room, and every life would be changed, absolutely transformed!"

Barbara also received a mighty touch from the Holy Spirit in the meeting. She also dropped to her knees; "I turned my seat to the wall for I didn't want anyone to see the mess I was in."

Let me just continue a little more with the story. Barbara writes: "During that meeting in the lounge, a young man from London who usually didn't prophesy opened his mouth and said, 'Thus saith the Lord...' The word was that the students were to kneel down at a certain place and the brethren were to lay hands on them... A chair was placed in the middle of the room, but no one moved; everyone was in their corner weeping. The fear of God was in that place and the weight of His presence was tremendous. Gradually, after a long spell, as we felt ready, we came and knelt by the chair; and the brethren gathered round and prayed."

The visitation continued into another meeting the students attended that day. At this service one of the students was preaching, and the theme was, '*I believe God.*' The Holy Spirit moved in again: there was groaning, crying out to God. "We slipped off our seats and onto the floor. Soon the preacher couldn't be heard over the groans from around his feet. But he kept saying, 'And I believe God; I believe God!'"

During the night, Pastor Rowland's wife had a dream from the Lord. Barbara, who was staying somewhere else in the village, came back to the school the next morning to say goodbye. "Walking into the school, I saw the students were not in their classes but around the piano singing, dancing and praising God. The principal's wife came up to me and said, 'Oh, I'm so glad you came by.'" Mrs Rowlands shared the dream with Barbara. The dream contained some personal guidance for Barbara, which I am not going to repeat. Mrs Rowlands said to Barbara, "I had a dream. I saw the school as a tree of glory. The branches were life sparks going out from the tree and there were names on the sparks."

Who were these sparks?

In David's photo album there are pictures of his fellow students who were at the Bible school at this time. Did the dream of Mrs Rowlands come to pass? Who were these *sparks?* Let me mention a few by name. Barbara Massie was one. Barbara went on to be used by God in a powerful way. The book '*O River of God*'[20] is a tribute to the prophetic life and ministry of Barbara Massie. But there were others also. One student was Luther Philips. God used him mightily in church planting and spreading the message of the full Gospel in Italy in the sixties. Another student was Parry Selby. Parry, with his wife Kitty, became missionaries in Nigeria and stayed in the country during the dreadful years of the Biafran War. These names may not be familiar with the wider church in the UK, but they were known by God; and God used them.

---

20 "O River of God: A Tribute to the Prophetic Life and Ministry of Barbara Massie." 2008.

David Greenow was also one of those sparks. David was in those revival meetings in Penygroes. I trust, as we continue to tell the story of David Greenow, we will see the spark that David became in the hands of God.

David often talked about this experience with me. It remained fresh in his memory; but most of all, it did not become a monument in his life. In the 1950s David experienced 'latter rains' in Northern Ireland, the UK and Europe. This visitation at the Bible school went on for weeks. Classes were stopped and time was spent seeking and experiencing the presence of God.

Mentioning again David's article in the Glory News no 16[21] 'Revival Fires are Burning in my Soul,' he wrote this about that experience in the Bible College: "More than ever before, I realised the reality of God's power, the necessity of faith and the significance of God's purpose for my life and for the world in these last days."

In the final paragraph of the article, David, looking back over all his experiences and no doubt the visitation he experienced in Bible College, wrote: "I thank God for all the experiences of the past; but I am not living back there, for I am rejoicing in a continually renewed experience with God that is fresh every day. I feel His wonderful presence and power now."

I have a few audio tapes of David speaking and he mentions some of his own testimony. In one tape he highlights something of his experience between 1942 and 1951. He says that he knew Jesus was alive and that God was real and, no doubt because of the prophetic teaching he was hearing, he thought things were just going to get worse and worse until Jesus returned. His parents would speak about the 1904 Welsh Revival and David thought he had missed out; but the experience he had of the 'latter rain blessing' at the Bible school

---

21 Magazine published by the "The Glory People."

between May-July 1951 changed his thinking. David said, "The Spirit came, and I was never the same again. I understood that God has a plan for these last days. Things are not going from worse to worse, but revival is coming. The build-up is on."

David's advice was, "Find out about what God is doing. This is our day. Christ is in His Church in our day."

David came out of Bible school with theology: with skills to divide the Word properly; but he also came out with an experience. The Word and the Spirit had come together in his life but, also, he came out of Bible College with purpose regarding the times in which he was living. The latter rain movement took truths and practices that had been laid aside for many years and renewed them into people's lives and into the Church.

"The movement was characterised by many reports of healings and other miraculous phenomena, in contrast to the preceding decade, which was described by Pentecostals as a time of spiritual dryness and lack of God's presence. It stressed the imminence of the premillennial return of Jesus Christ, preceded by an outpouring of God's Spirit, which was expected in accordance with the 'former rain' and the 'latter rain' of Joel 2:28."[22]

This outpouring of the Holy Spirit did not only include a Spirit baptism of power with the evidence of new languages, but also the laying on of hands for the impartation of spiritual gifts. For David, and others, the latter rain was God restoring the Church to the days of the Acts of the Apostles. I think it is worth mentioning that the latter rain movement was one of the catalysts for the charismatic renewal of the 1960s and 1970s.[23]

---

22 Burgess, S.M. and Van Der Maas, E.M. (2002, 2003) 'The New International Dictionary of Pentecostal Charismatic Movements. Revised and Expanded Edition.' USA: Zondervan
23 Burgess, S.M. and Van Der Maas, E.M. (2002, 2003) 'The New International Dictionary of Pentecostal Charismatic Movements. Revised and Expanded Edition.' USA: Zondervan

Cecil Cousen, who was a pastor in the Apostolic church and who experienced this new move of God in the 1950s, was instrumental, with Michael Harper, in establishing the charismatic movement, Fountain Trust, in the UK in 1964.

David came out of Bible College with three things. Firstly, a sound theological foundation for his life and future ministry. Secondly, a purpose: God was restoring to the Church the days of the Acts of the Apostles. Times of refreshing were coming from the Lord (Acts 3:17-21). Thirdly, an experience of the Presence and the Power of the Holy Spirit.

I would suggest that as you read further in the book, you will find these three threads being revealed in the life and ministry of David Greenow.

CHAPTER FIVE
His call to Northern Ireland...

In 1952, The Apostolic church made an appeal across the UK asking for evangelists to come to Belfast. David and a man from Glasgow, Bob Mullan, responded to the appeal. They moved to Sandy Row, Belfast. A local businessman, David Ferran, financed these two evangelists. David Ferran owned a tug-boat business and was very generous in supporting evangelistic work in the Apostolic church. He would purchase gospel vans for evangelistic teams to use in the Apostolic church. He also financed a holiday home in Bangor, Northern Ireland, that Apostolic church families could use.

The pastor in Belfast at the time was Philip Williams, who originated from South-east Wales. When David first came over, he stayed with Pastor Philip and his family, before moving into accommodation in Sandy Row, Belfast. This man had an amazing testimony of salvation. Philip had been a heavy drinker and boasted that when 'he was drunk he feared no man or devil.' He was a bare-knuckle fighter, but because of his drinking, brought his family into poverty. He saw his wife come to faith and healed. This challenged him. He said; "The Lord wonderfully healed her, both in body and in mind, and it was this great change which I saw in her, in such a short time, that made such an impression on me."

Two weeks after his wife became a Christian, Philip gave his heart to the Lord. People in the community of Beaufort were amazed. With God's help in the subsequent months, Philip paid off all his debts, and he became a powerful witness in the Beaufort and Ebbw Vale areas. While living in this part of south Wales and being involved in the church, he would have witnessed God moving in powerful ways in salvation and healing in his community. He would also have experienced the God who speaks prophetically, guiding and directing the church.

Again, we can see God continuing to bring David into contact with and under the influence of men who had seen God move powerfully in their own lives and in their communities. I am reminded of a poem entitled 'The Divine Weaver.' The poet who is anonymous uses the image of God as a *Divine Weaver*, weaving the tapestry of our life in time, but to an eternal pattern and design that He has purposed.

The Divine Weaver

Man's life is laid in a loom of time to a pattern he does not see.
While the Weaver works and the shuttles fly till the dawn of eternity.
Some shuttles are filled with silver thread and some with threads of gold;
While often but the darker hues, is all that they may hold.

But the Weaver watches with skilful eye, each shuttle fly to and fro,
And sees the pattern so deftly wrought, as the loom works sure and slow.
God surely planned that pattern, each thread – the dark and the fair –
Was chosen by his master skill, and placed in the web with care.

He only knows the beauty, and guides the shuttles which hold,
The threads so unattractive, as well as the threads of gold
Not till the loom is silent, and the shuttles cease to fly,
Shall God unroll the pattern, and explain the reason why.

The dark threads are as needful, in the weaver's skilful hand,
As the threads of gold and silver, in the pattern He had planned.

God uses our experiences, bad and good; He brings people and opportunities into our lives; He leads us to different places. All the time, He is shaping us to be the minister and servant He has destined us to be. He never stops this work and, as we continue with the story of David Greenow, we will see how God continued to weave His image into David.

One person I spoke to had the distinct memory of David attending the Easter Convention in Belfast in 1952. Easter Sunday in 1952 was on April 13th. David and Bob Mullan were on the platform. They had come to Northern Ireland to do evangelistic work. This would involve door to door work, as well as conducting meetings and tent campaigns in Belfast and beyond. By way of example, David and Bob spent nine weeks at Moore's Hill, just outside Lurgan; six weeks at Battlehill, just outside Portadown, where they stayed with the Proctor family; and three months at Mountain Lodge, Keady.

In David's Christmas letter 2007, he gave this insight into his early work in Northern Ireland...

"This has been another year when I've been busy for the Lord in the work that He called me to as a young Christian. I wondered how it could possibly work out for a farmer's boy to become a full-time worker in God's Service. I remember praying desperately that He would do something regarding His call in my life which I became increasingly aware of; thus it was that after two years in Bible College in Wales, I arrived in Ireland 55 years ago this past March. So it was that a shy, introverted farmer boy was found witnessing on the streets and knocking on doors to tell the Good news of the Lord Jesus. We had a 12-week mission that first summer with meetings for children and adults nightly. This was followed with a four-week mission accompanied with ten days of prayer and fasting. Then there was a six-week mission, and next a nine-week mission; and so, it continued."

David wrote this about those first years in Northern Ireland...

"I will never forget those early years of Crusades in Ireland when the meetings continued for anything from four to twelve weeks at a time and God worked wonderfully in salvation, healing, and blessing as we sought to tell of Jesus. We used open-air services, tract distribution, door to door visitation, children's meetings and the nightly salvation services in the church or Gospel tent. All this was backed by nights of prayer and days of fasting, and eternity alone will reveal the results; for when you work for the Lord it is not for time alone."

A magazine called "The Apostolic Herald" carried this headline in the December 1952 issue: 'Campaigning for Christ. Bros. Greenhough and Mullin conduct successful Evangelistic effort in Belfast.' (Please note: both surnames were spelt wrongly.)

The report said, "During an Evangelistic campaign held in Frankfort Street, Belfast, from September 14th to October 12th, 1952, the presence of the Lord was manifest in power. It is never easy to put into words just what one experiences in such meetings, but in the hymn and chorus singing and in the preaching of the Word, the leading of the Spirit was manifest to all. Many of those who attended have voiced their sorrow at the closing of the mission; but as *Brothers Greenhough and Mullin* were needed elsewhere, we had very reluctantly to say 'goodbye' to these two dear young servants of the Lord. Despite the small congregations and opposition outside from the enemy, they faithfully preached the Word and visited almost 3,000 houses, inviting people to come to Jesus and to attend the services. We are praising God, in the Name of Jesus, for 25 children saved, whose ages ranged from 9 – 13 years; also, for five adults and one backslider who were restored. Three women testified to instantaneous healing, also a little girl. One woman, who confessed to being bound by Satan in unbelief, was delivered when the demon was rebuked in the Name of the Lord Jesus Christ. We have learned much by these meetings which we believe will be of value to us in the future, as the drops increase to a shower and the shower to a deluge. There was definite proof in all the meetings, especially the closing one, of the power of conviction upon sinners and backsliders, but many went away refusing to surrender. We are still continuing in prayer that the Lord will move in a mighty way to fulfil His promises and will in this part of the Vineyard. Elder A. Bradsaw."[24]

In the early part of 1953, David and Bob Mullan were sent for mission to an Apostolic church just outside Lurgan in County Armagh. A particular group of young men attended the mission and amongst them was a young man, Tom Gilchrist. On the final night of the mission, David turned to Tom and said, "Young man, you have been here every night, (the mission lasted nine weeks) Isn't it time you made a decision?"

On the final night of the mission, Tom Gilchrist made a decision to follow Jesus. Tom, with his cousin, Fred Douglas, made their way back to the Gilchrist's family home but it was very late. Tom's father (also Tom) was waiting for him, but his cousin stepped in and said, "It is alright uncle Tom, Tom got saved tonight." Tom went on to serve the Lord faithfully in different Pentecostal churches in Northern Ireland.

Entering the bandit country…

Later in 1953, Bob Mullan and David Greenow went to a Pentecostal church at Mountain Lodge to conduct a mission. The mission lasted three months. The story of this mission is told in the next chapter because for David, this visit to Mountain Lodge in 1953 proved strategic for the future direction of his life and ministry. He had a real encounter with God during the mission. An encounter that changed

---

24 "The Apostolic Herald December 1952." Monthly magazine published by the Apostolic Church.

the whole direction of his future ministry and Mountain Lodge would become an Antioch for David.

Mountain Lodge is situated on an 'unapproved road' in south Armagh, near the villages of Keady and Darkly, and just one and half miles from the border with the Republic of Ireland. During the years of the troubles, south Armagh was known as '*bandit country.*'

The connection with the Apostolic church was through its leader, Thomas John Hunniford. Mr Hunniford had previously been part of the Apostolic church at Battlehill, just outside Portadown. This church had a dramatic spiritual birth in 1923. It all came about with the visit of Apostle Dobson Hunniford from Philadelphia, USA. He was in the UK undertaking some itinerant ministry with the UK Apostolic Church. Dobson had been born in Battlehill but had not been back to his birthplace for 37 years. (He was no relation of Thomas John Hunniford. The Hunniford surname does seem to have been popular in this part of County Armagh)

Gordon Weeks wrote this about Dobson Hunniford's visit to Battlehill: "His testimony in a Methodist meeting about the baptism of the Holy Spirit resulted in sixteen people seeking the experience the same night and twelve received the baptism. This was the start of the Apostolic church in Battlehill."[25] Thomas John Hunniford attended this Methodist church but I was unable to confirm whether he was present at this meeting.

Thomas John Hunniford became part of this new Apostolic Church plant in Battlehill, until he, and his family, moved to live and work at Mountain Lodge, County Armagh in 1949.

---

25 Weeks, G. 'Chapter Thirty Two – part of.' Barnsley: Gordon Weeks.

CHAPTER SIX

Amazing works at Mountain Lodge...

The Hunniford family had moved to Mountain Lodge, some twenty miles away from the farm that the family had near Portadown, in the early part of 1949. The estate consisted of a gentleman's large residence, with a gate lodge and some 260 acres of land or farmland, some 800 feet above sea level.

The house is described as having 'twelve-foot-high corniced ceilings; an arched window on the landing; white Georgian windows and a grand entrance consisting of three sandstone steps flanked by wrought iron railings on either side.' It was a very impressive building. It was rumoured to be haunted; but for the time that the Hunniford family lived in the house, there were no ghostly apparitions.

There was no Pentecostal church in the area, and Pastor David Bell in his book, *'Fire on the Mountain,'*[26] gives us an insight regarding what Thomas John did regarding church. Initially, "Thomas John (travelled) back to Portadown at weekends, to fellowship with the believers at the little Pentecostal Hall at Clonroot.[27] During the week, he also started to attend a number of Faith Mission meetings in the local Keady area and, before long, he met other Christians in the locality, to whom he offered encouragement and inspiration in all things concerning the scriptures. It wasn't long before Thomas John began to arrange prayer meetings in the front drawing room in Mountain Lodge House. These were meetings filled with the Holy Ghost and full of the presence of God.

---

26 Bell, D. (2013) "Fire on the Mountain. The Story of the Darkley Church Northern Ireland."
27 This was the Apostolic Church at Battlehill.

According to Thomas John's daughter Emily, who would eventually marry David Greenow,[28] 'nobody went home until everybody had an opportunity to pray.'"

The meetings quickly moved from the drawing room of the 'big house' to the Gate Lodge, 'a peculiar hexagonal-shaped building, sporting living quarters with a pony house attached to the rear,' at the entrance of Mountain Lodge House. Thomas John demolished the internal walls and the back wall between the gate house and the pony house. He built benches from a disused wooden hen house on the farm. The benches didn't have any backs so there was no chance of anyone falling asleep, 'not that anyone would have been afforded the privilege of sleeping in those early Holy Ghost meetings anyway.' There were two paraffin oil lamps to give light, and a pot-bellied stove to give some heat; "On occasions, the old stove would smoke them all out of the hall!"

Emily recalls: "There was no clock on the wall and no finishing time. Most people came on bicycles, there weren't many cars in those days. There were a lot of bicycles around the Gate Lodge every night."

David Bell writes: "Some people began to come from further afield, from over the border (the Republic of Ireland) in cars. Some nights they would leave the meeting so full of the Holy Spirit, they would have to stop and 'sober up' before crossing the Customs Post!"

He also writes this about the visit of David Greenow and Bob Mullan to Mountain Lodge in 1953: "(It) was a tremendous time of visitation and blessing. The meetings were packed each night. The gospel was preached, and the sick were prayed for. Mrs Mullan made cushions stuffed with hay to soften the impact for those kneeling in prayer on the floor. Emily (Thomas John's daughter) remembers the

---

28 David and Emily married in October 1956.

condensation rising out of the cushions each night, once the stove got fired up. No double glazing or central heating in those days!"

David stayed with the Hunniford family, making use of the gate lodge during the day as he prayed and prepared for his ministry. He prayed in the fields around Mountain Lodge. He prayed, on one occasion, in his spiritual language, non-stop for four hours. In these early days as a missionary, David would often fast for a week or ten days. On one occasion Thomas John Hunniford declared; "If that young fellow does any more fasting, he will be green by colour as well as by name."

One story from the mission at Mountain Lodge concerns a man from Darkley, called Bob Flanagan. Bob was a Christian but attended a church who did not believe in divine healing. David and Bob Mullan were preaching about signs, wonders and miracles.

After one meeting Bob Flanagan went up and challenged the preachers, "Do you believe what you are preaching?" "We certainly do," they said.

"Well then, prove it to me!" Said Bob. "I have a girl at home dying of asthma. If you pray for her and she is healed, I will believe."

The two men followed him to his house, just as Jesus would have done. The men entered the room and saw the girl gasping for breath. They laid hands on her rebuking the asthma and the next breath went straight to the bottom of her lungs and she was perfectly healed! Bob and his wife were amazed.[29]

The following Sunday, Bob Flanagan and his wife were at the Mountain Lodge meeting. Bob was a Godsend to the assembly for he was a man who could preach and teach, and he taught in the Sunday school for nearly 20 years.

---

29 see www.MountainLodgePentecostalChurch.co.uk/history

Just as an aside, David Bell writes; "During the months (and years) that followed, much more was seen of the young evangelist David Greenow as he continued to frequent the meetings long after the mission ended! Romance was blossoming with Emily Hunniford."[30] David and Emily married in October 1956 and lived with Emily's parents at Mountain Lodge.

After this first visit to Mountain Lodge, and following his marriage to Emily, this Pentecostal assembly became David's home church. Although the Hunnifords and the Greenow's moved away from Mountain Lodge in 1969,[31] David and Emily continued their link with this Pentecostal assembly on the Irish border.

The place where he had given himself to so much prayer and fasting in 1953 became a place where he was a blessing and where he received blessings from the Hand of God. This did not stop even when David and Emily moved to live in Portadown in 1969.

It was while David was on mission at Mountain Lodge that he received clear direction from God to make his ministry available to all churches and Christian groups. The challenge was to leave the security of a denomination with all the resources, contacts and opportunities it had; and to step out in faith, believing God for opportunities, finance and ministry.

David wrote this about the experience he had with God while on mission at Mountain Lodge: "In the summer of 1953, whilst staying in a certain home in Northern Ireland, Christ came to my side one afternoon. I had such a vital experience of His presence and power that my Christian life was completely transformed and I've never been the same since that day. Glory to God! Jesus is so wonderfully real and I love Him with all my heart."[32]

---

30 Bell, D. (2013) "Fire on the Mountain. The Story of the Darkley Church Northern Ireland."
31 David and Emily moved with Emily's parents to Portadown.
32 "The Glory News no 16." Magazine published by "The Glory People."

In a testimony leaflet written by David, he gives us further insight into this experience and the challenge that it brought: "In 1953 God told me to make the ministry He had given me available to all who would receive it without any denominational label attached." As we know, that is what David did. He left the Apostolic church and, as the charismatic renewal movement came into Ireland, David was available to give teaching and instruction in the things of the Holy Spirit. In the years after 1953, few people had the openings into so many churches, mission halls, conferences, revival campaigns and homes as David. As different house meetings and church groups sprang up on the island of Ireland, David was there to exercise an apostolic and prophetic ministry for the building up of the Church.

David gave this insight regarding the change that the Holy Spirit brought into his life as a result of the experiences he had in 1951 and 1953: "Christianity is God living in us. The apostle Paul says, 'Christ liveth in me.' I discovered that I had limited the life of Christ in me to certain traditional religious ideas that had no real scriptural basis. I had tended to substitute a weekly religious routine for living faith and constant union with Christ. God has provided ABUNDANT LIFE for us and not a dead religion. Glory to God!"

In the years after 1953, David became increasingly recognised by the Body of Christ in Ireland, as an encourager, someone who built up and as a man who walked with God. His counsel was sought. His judgement was valued. One leader told me; "If there was any trouble; ring David Greenow." He connected different ministries and churches together. His heart was the heart of a shepherd. He fulfilled an apostolic role over many independent fellowships. He was there to advise and not 'lord it' over these churches. He didn't establish any network where he was first. He was a father who cared for the flock and the under-shepherds of the Chief Shepherd, the Lord Jesus Christ.

CHAPTER SEVEN

His partner in ministry and life...

David received a challenge from God at Mountain Lodge regarding his ministry and at Mountain Lodge, God brought Emily Hunniford into his life. Earlier, in the story, we mentioned how at 19 years of age David experienced a broken engagement and how he gave God the responsibility of finding the life partner of 'His choice.'

It was here that Emily, Pastor Hunniford's youngest daughter, first heard David speak. Emily was a young woman who was full of life. In recent years, Emily would have come with Pat and me when we went to Mountain Lodge for meetings or conventions at the church. Emily would tell us story after story about how she rode a bike in the lanes around Mountain Lodge, Darkley, and Keady. She was fearless coming down the hills and going around corners; even though sometimes she fell off her bike. She thought nothing of cycling eighteen miles to visit her aunt at Battlehill, outside Portadown, attending two meetings at the local mission and cycling eighteen miles home to Mountain Lodge in time for milking.

Emily describes her first date with David as follows…

She had not attended that evening's meeting and was standing on the kitchen table, wall-papering, when David burst in and told her to hurry up and take off her apron and come for a walk with him before her father returned from the meeting. They dated secretly at the beginning and would court for nearly three years before they were married in the local Presbyterian church in Keady, in October 1956. On the day of her marriage Emily remembered being "a nervous wreck." During their years of courtship, David was not always around. As a result of leaving the Apostolic Church in 1953, David made himself available for ministry wherever he was invited. On one occasion, during the courtship, David was away for three months in England and Emily remembers writing to David about the visit of the American evangelist, Keith Iverson, to Armagh and Mountain Lodge. Without going too far ahead in the story, from February 1955, David was based in Portadown, Northern Ireland. He initially stayed with a couple in Lurgan called Mr and Mrs Hill. Emily was unable to go to the meetings in Portadown because she was working on the farm and the family had no car. David's involvement with these meetings in Portadown stopped just prior to his marriage to Emily in October 1956. As I have already mentioned, after their marriage, David and Emily lived in the Hunniford family home at Mountain Lodge.

Following the direction that David had received from God about his future ministry in Mountain Lodge in 1953, he continued with his travelling ministry after his marriage. In the years following October 1956, God opened doors for David to minister all over the UK, to Scandinavia, America, and Canada. Emily did not often accompany him as they could not afford the extra fare. David and Emily lived by faith. While David was away, Emily stayed at home and worked on the farm and supported David in prayer. As Emily's parents grew older, she became their main carer.

 In David and Emily's Christmas letter December 1967, we get an idea of the travelling David was doing. "Every Christian worker," David writes, "has a tremendous privilege of doing something of a spiritual value, and that will last for eternity. Praise God! The following are some of the places I have been privileged to visit for ministry this year: Par, St Austell, Newquay, Mevagissey, Downinie, Plymouth, Southampton, Ringwood, Boscombe, Portsmouth, Wimborne, Reading, Chard,

London, Ipswich, Norwich, Banbury, Leamington Spa, Birmingham, Hereford, Bream, Pontypridd, Treharris, Wolverhampton, Lancaster, West Auckland, Newton Aycliffe, Blyth, Peterhead, Isle of Man, Belgium, Holland."

David listed another thirteen places he had visited in Ireland. David wrote; "The Gospel works in whatever part of the world we may be, and through these months it has been my joy to see the power of God save souls, heal bodies, and fill the lives of believers."

In 1969, Mr and Mrs Hunniford, David and Emily all moved from Mountain Lodge and continued living together at Wayside, Ballydougan, Bleary, near Portadown. (Before leaving, Emily's father placed a hymn book in Bob Bain's hand, appointing him as the Pastor of the Mountain Lodge assembly.)

Often David would be away for weeks and Emily did not always hear from him. One long silence was caused by a three-week postal strike in Canada, when David's letters did not reach home. Emily was kept busy keeping house and caring for her parents and, no doubt, praying that God's anointing would be upon David.

When Emily's parents died in 1979, she asked David if he wanted to move back to England. The thought had never crossed his mind.

Prior to Emily's parents dying, David and Emily were thinking of moving house. Emily heard about a house further along the Bleary Road which was on the market. When Emily mentioned the house to David, he asked if there was land with the house. They discovered there was half an acre of land, so David needed no further encouragement to move; but it took about 18 months for it to become a reality.

When he had time, David loved to garden. His love of cultivating the soil and memories of his earlier farming never left him. He took pride in his small County Armagh orchard, grew blackcurrant and gooseberry bushes, potatoes, and all kinds of vegetables and flowers. Over the years I enjoyed many of their cooking apples, picked straight from the trees when leaving after visiting. His greatest delight was to have Emily work alongside him in the garden: David would turn the soil over and Emily would plant the seeds. This trait also marked their spiritual ministry. He and Emily both prayed for people both publicly and in private. David often asked Emily to share from the Word of God at the beginning of meetings and she never failed to have a definite and relevant message for each group.

David believed that every child of God should learn to play a musical instrument. Typically, David would lead a meeting in praise and worship playing an accordion. Then he would preach and often pray for every person in the room, giving detailed and specific prophetic words to people and encouraging them in their faith. He particularly liked to identify and encourage developing gifting in young believers and persisted in nurturing their calling.

David was disciplined in his studying and prayer ministry. He walked for at least a mile every morning after breakfast, greeting neighbours and getting to know their needs and interests. He exercised a caring ministry to those who lived around him, counselling and praying for them. He had a genuine interest in people and remembered names and details of family situations with amazing accuracy.

People knew they were covered by his and Emily's prayers. His mornings were spent in study and prayer. He also wrote extensively, creating tracts and pamphlets and he also corresponded with a wide circle of people. Any gifts received were acknowledged straight away by a card and a personal message.

After David died, I discovered more and more the spiritual ministry that God had given to Emily. I remember organising a meeting of Spirit-filled ministers from across different denominations in County Armagh. Our heart was for the Pentecostal message to be again taught and experienced in the Body of Christ. Emily was at the meeting. In the midst of all the discussions Emily shared a prophetic word. One of those present, Donald Buchanan said; "After all our talking it was Emily who brought some clarity to the discussions."

Another story concerns Emily being used in healing in the local church that I led for many years in Northern Ireland. I remember one Sunday night being led by the Holy Spirit to invite people forward for prayer. A man by the name of Raymond McSherry came forward. He had a very, very large cyst on one of his eyes. It had been present for 36 years. I called Emily forward to pray for Raymond. Nothing happened straight away but some 10 days later, Raymond woke up one morning with his eye feeling funny. He asked his wife, Ann, to take a look at it. Raymond blinked and liquid came out of the cyst but there was still a sack of skin on his eye. Seven days later, when Raymond was wiping his eye, the sack of skin came away!

I also recall a lady called Gladys, from Waringstown, Northern Ireland. Gladys was born-again and was faithful in her witness and service for the Lord, but she had never been filled with the Holy Spirit. She had asked and sought God for this experience for many, many years.

Emily and I were attending a prayer meeting at the Highways and Byways Ministry Centre just outside Waringstown. This centre is run by Donald and Shirley Buchanan. I felt led to pray with Gladys for the baptism of the Holy Spirit. I called Emily forward to pray with me. I prayed and then moved from Gladys to pray for other people but Emily stayed and continued to pray over Gladys and she was filled with the Holy Spirit and spoke in a spiritual language for the first time and continued to speak for hours after this filling from Heaven. Gladys is still living in this experience.

David never had a wage coming in and he and Emily lived by faith. Emily told me that they never wanted for anything. During the summers David would be away for anything up to seven weeks at a time. He would have moved between different Christian camps from Cornwall to Scotland.

Once he returned to Bleary in high spirits to find Emily anything but elated. She had carried out the responsibilities of caring for two elderly parents and the home for two months, without any respite.

Emily told David she needed a holiday, sent for her sister to take over the care of her parents and packed the suitcases, off they went on holidays for the well-deserved break.

In a testimony leaflet, David wrote, "In October 1956, Emily and I were married, and I am appreciative of the Lord's gift of a dedicated and devoted wife over all these years. Thank you, Lord."

In our time in Ireland when Pat and I grew in our friendship and love for this couple, it was always 'David and Emily.' It was never just 'David and his wife.' That was the introduction situation with some speakers I met during my time in Northern Ireland. This was not with the Greenow's: it was always, 'David and Emily.'

During 2002 and 2003, they were both ill at different times. In 2002, David wrote about his period of sickness, "(Emily) carried breakfast to bed for me for about three months." In 2003 Emily fell and broke her wrist. "Now it is my turn to do the same for her," wrote David.

In David and Emily's Christmas letter 2006, David wrote, "We visited my brother Glyn's home and church on the occasion of our 50th Wedding Anniversary. We were treated royally by the family and church, and we say a most sincere thank you to them all." They celebrated their 50th anniversary not in a hotel or with a party; but with family, natural and spiritual, in the setting of a church where they both could minister, and they did.

Reflection...

Before going on to the next part of David's life, I think it would be good to pause and ask the question: what spiritual truths can we draw out, for ourselves, from the relationship between David and Emily?

What can we learn from this couple who were married for over fifty years?

David cherished the gift of a wife that supported him unflinchingly and faithfully over many years.

Emily stood by David through months of separation when she was looking after her parents. Emily lived to fulfil the commandment of 'honouring her father and mother' but also cleaving to her husband, although apart.

CHAPTER EIGHT

Fire on the mountain...

We have already highlighted the importance of Mountain Lodge in David's early life. It was while David was on mission at this assembly that God further opened up the call that was on David's life. As already mentioned, David found his life partner, Emily Hunniford, at this Pentecostal assembly in County Armagh. This assembly became a base for David and Emily. Paul had Antioch; David had Mountain Lodge.

David Greenow, until his death in 2012, was closely associated with this assembly throughout his ministry in Northern Ireland. He worked with the assembly in the appointing of elders. He introduced to the assembly many Spirit-filled Bible teachers and evangelists from Northern Ireland and Great Britain. He presided at marriages, dedications and funerals as requested by the church leadership. His message and ministry were centred on the Five-fold Gospel, and the continuing work of the Holy Spirit in the church. Full Gospel meetings were held, where people experienced the laying on of hands for healing and the baptism of the Holy Spirit, and received personal words of knowledge and encouragement.

We must remember that David had spent three months on mission at Mountain Lodge in the early 1950s. During those months he had spent many hours in prayer in the fields at Mountain Lodge. On one occasion he had prayed in tongues in the fields non-stop for four hours. David sowed many hours through prayer, and saw God use him to reap in Mountain Lodge. David was blessed with his links to this Pentecostal church and, something that he would have always desired, he was a blessing.

The assembly had moved out of the Gate Lodge into a new hall in 1959. The hall suffered an arson attack in July 1971 and another hall was built on the same site. This new building opened on 24th June 1972. David Greenow was one of the guest speakers and his scripture was Haggai chapter one verses 3-15. David emphasised that, just as the Old Testament temple was completed on the twenty fourth day of the sixth month, so the members and friends of Mountain Lodge Pentecostal Assembly opened their new building on the twenty fourth of June!

David was also there at the 'cutting of the sod' for a new building in June 1989. He was a guest speaker, with his brother-in-law, Emily's brother Robin, when the new brick building was opened in August 1990. The building suffered an arson attack in September 1994 and David officiated at the reopening of the church complex in August 1995.

I met a number of people from the assembly, to talk about David's influence and input into their lives. Everyone said that David was always positive, an encourager and a worshipper. He would play his accordion and lead people into praise and worship before he would speak. He would seek people out to develop their spiritual gifts. Pastor David Bell spoke of how David introduced him to the challenge of taking funerals.

One person told me how David stood with him through depression. David would visit him in hospital and give him Biblical promises to believe for his life. He did overcome the depression and he made this comment about David: "David was special; you thought that you were his son." The same person spoke about David giving a word of knowledge in a service; the revelation was, 'Young man on my left, you are about to make one of the biggest decisions in your life, don't make it.' The revelation was for him and he obeyed this word of direction.

There was a tragic event in the life of this church in 1983 that touched and sickened the hearts of people across the world. In 1983, the assembly was meeting in a wooden hall and the leader of the church was Pastor Bob Bain. The Mountain Lodge Pentecostal Church website gives this insight about what happened on the 20th November 1983; "God's hand of blessing was on the meetings in this hall and Sunday nights saw an influx of young people come into the church. What a shock it was therefore, when on 20th November 1983, terrorists entered our church during the Sunday evening service, killing three of our elders and wounding seven of the congregation. In spite of all this, God's hand was upon us and the lives of all those in the main building were preserved.

In addition to adults, there were possibly thirty young people and children in the meeting and none of them were hurt. Pastor Bob was badly shaken by it all for he did not believe such a thing could happen in a house of God.

It was all over in a few minutes, and the gunmen fled. Pastor Bob was praying for the wounded when he noticed a young man in the back seat badly injured. This young man had been shot through the door and five bullets were lodged in his stomach and bladder. It looked like he wouldn't make it as he was bleeding very badly. Pastor Bob laid hands on him and commanded the bleeding to stop, which it did immediately! This man, who is now well and strong, testifies to this day that but for the prayers of Pastor Bob, he never would have made it to the hospital.

After this tragedy, Pastor Bob received over 700 letters from people across the world, encouraging him to keep going. Many sent donations to help with the work. "During the dark days that followed, the saints were strengthened by the word of God, and the prayers of God's people, and were convinced by God's Word that this door would not be closed because God had opened it."

The three elders who were murdered were Harold Browne (59), David Wilson (44) and Victor Cunningham. (39) There is a memorial plaque in the church honouring the sacrifice of these men. In addition, a group of Christians from Dublin planted three trees in Israel in memory of these three men.

Let me quote an extract from a poem titled *"The Three Martyrs"* written by John J. Somerville, about this tragedy.

"Everyone was seated, 'cept three elders by the door;
Soon two were lying lifeless, shot to death upon the floor.
A third though mortally wounded staggered in to warn the flock,
But another burst of gunfire caused pandemonium and shock.
That third Christian life was ended in the twinkling of an eye,
As God called His murdered martyrs to His mansion up on high."

Gunmen kept on firing both from within and from outside
Leaving men and women lying wounded side by side.
Little children screamed in terror, not knowing what to do
As they watched their stricken parents blood-spattered in the pew.
Three souls dead, seven wounded, little children scarred for life
Just another chapter in fourteen years of hideous strife." [33]

Responding to the crisis...

David and Emily were in Bangor Northern Ireland when they received a phone call regarding the massacre. It was too late for David and

---

[33] Bell, D. (2013) "Fire on the Mountain. The Story of the Darkley Church, Northern Ireland."

Emily to go directly to Mountain Lodge, but the next day, David was there with people who were hurting. Not only were three families to be comforted at the sudden loss of fathers, husbands and sons, but there were seven people in hospital with serious injuries. For weeks, on a daily basis, David and Emily visited these people to comfort, pray and support them.

Because two of the three funerals took place on the same day, David was not involved in all of them. The great and the good were represented at the funerals. Senior Northern Ireland politicians and churchmen, from many denominations across Northern Ireland, attended the funerals. There were up to 1000 people at each funeral.

At Harold Browne's and Victor Cunningham's funerals, David spoke in the family homes. In the Cunningham home, David said that he was praying for the killers, for *miracles of divine grace again, again and again* and encouraged the mourners to pray for the government, for those in authority and for the bereaved and suffering relatives.

Towards the end of the 1960s, despite David receiving a Word from the Lord about trouble coming to the land, I suspect that furthest from David's mind were the troubles that would come to Mountain Lodge Pentecostal Church: two arson attacks, and a deplorable terrorist attack. In 1997, David gave a prophetic word to the church to hold on and trust God for their visitation. The church is still believing for the latter rain of the Holy Spirit; a visitation from Heaven.

On Sunday 22nd January 1984, just two months after the terrorist attack, the people returned to hold a morning service in the building where three of their leaders had been shot dead, where others had been injured and all shocked by the attack. The following is an extract from one newspaper report… "Pastor Bob Bain took his place on the podium, and in the front seat sat David Greenow. If there was any feeling of apprehension, it did not show, and the congregation's fervent responses and spirited singing of the hymns displayed that their strength of faith was undiminished."

Another newspaper report included this: "Describing the three men as born-again Christians who had been cut down, Evangelist David Greenow said; "The worst a gunman could do to a Christian was to send him to Heaven. They had been ready to cross the great divide because they had put their trust in Christ."

Pastor David and Sally Bell from Mountain Lodge wrote this tribute about David Greenow: "David, a regular speaker at Mountain Lodge, was one of the first preachers I came to know and respect when I began attending the meetings. No matter what age, young or old, David always had a word of encouragement and spoke into many lives. He was a true friend, mentor, preacher and teacher.

"David would play the accordion and lead worship; the anointing would come down, and then he and Emily would minister and pray with people to receive from God. David often spoke of the importance of choosing a life partner, and frequently referred to a relationship that he was in when God called him into ministry. He quickly realised that the one he thought he loved did not share the same passion and he soon realised that this relationship was not for him. God had someone who was His choice for David; and Emily proved a faithful companion and ministry partner down through the years.

David was such a help to us in Mountain Lodge, especially in the earlier years, when he conducted weddings, dedicated our babies and officiated at funerals for us. David moved in an apostolic ministry, going from church to church, giving godly wisdom and guidance and encouragement when he could. David was greatly used in healing and words of knowledge.

David and Margaret Bailie were just recently married when they attended a meeting in Mountain Lodge one Sunday evening. David Greenow had officiated at their wedding some time earlier. Margaret remembers that they were sitting about halfway up the hall, on the left-hand side. David Bailie had been suffering from regular and severe migraine headaches. Margaret recalls that on bright sunny mornings particularly he would return to the house, spending the day in bed and vomiting. That Sunday evening, David Greenow gave a 'Word of Knowledge,' to which David Bailie responded. David Greenow prayed for him and all these years later, he still testifies to the healing he received that Sunday evening. The migraines were completely gone!

David always spoke of 'bringers' and encouraged people to bring others to the meetings just as those in the Bible brought people to Jesus.

Down through the years, David frequently ministered at the Lord's Table in Mountain Lodge. Often, he would remind us that 'the Lord always comes to His table,' so it is important for us to be there also, fulfilling His request until He comes.

David wrote a lot of tracts and leaflets, freely distributing them to people to encourage them; he also gave us a set of Bible studies which he had obtained from America, which we have found to be a useful tool in ministry." He also told us how in 1969 (during the time of the troubles), he was flying over Ireland and wondering what lay ahead for our country. He felt the Lord saying to him that there would be a time of continual disturbance followed by a time of unparalleled divine intervention. We have had a time of continual disturbance, now we are waiting for a mighty move of the Spirit of God!"

CHAPTER NINE
Bleary – David's Jerusalem...

As I have already mentioned, in 1969, David and Emily moved with Emily's parents from Mountain Lodge to Bleary in Portadown. Emily was the main carer for her parents.

In 1980, David and Emily moved further along the Bleary road from the house that they had shared with Emily's parents. Their new address was "Cartref", Bleary Road, Portadown. This was their first home together since they had married in October 1956.

Their new home was in the townland area, Ballygargan, known as 'the place of the little stones.' I just wondered: in the way that the boy David took an innocuous stone out of his bag to slay Goliath, how many Goliaths have been defeated through the prayers of David and Emily from their small bungalow on the Bleary Road, and have continued to be defeated by Emily's intercession from the same home.

David did a lot of travelling from both homes in Bleary Road and was often away for long periods of time. When they lived in 121, Bleary Road, Emily was not always able to travel with David because she was caring for her parents. Although David would often be away, he didn't forget the community that he lived in; his Jerusalem.

Mary and Danny McCauley lived near David and Emily and they sent this tribute about David, 'the Reverent,' as Danny called him:

"My memories of David Greenow began when he was introduced to us by Tom Somerville at a prayer meeting we attended. Though he only lived up the road, he was away ministering all over the UK and down in the south of Ireland. It was the late 70s when we really got to know this evangelist of Jesus Christ.

David was a very understanding, patient, generous, uncritical and flexible man. He did not need to speak; he had that anointing on him. People just knew he was a Christian. When he came to the prayer meeting, he taught us about the baptism of the Holy Spirit and the gifts. When David prayed, you could feel the presence of the Holy Spirit; and people's needs were met.

I remember one occasion when David and Emily were going to bed and two men broke into their home. David remained calm and he told the men about Jesus. That was the kind of man he was; and even well after the event he continued to pray for their souls. In his latter years he loved to go out for walks and get chatting with the neighbours. Some got him to pray with them. One lady got him to pray for an eye problem and she was healed. He also prayed for other neighbours with leg problems and they professed their feet a lot better. That was David, ready at all times to pray with anyone who had a need.

He taught us that in this world there will be trials, tests and tribulations; a constant spiritual warfare. He said you will have mountain-top and valley experiences; and we did find that out. He always said that we should stand our ground against the enemy. I can say this; we counted David and Emily our spiritual parents. In times of need they were always there to help.

One thing I know; David was welcomed home by his loving Father saying, "Well done, my good and faithful servant." As a group of believers, we thank God for all that His servant David taught us. His door was always open for anyone in need."

But there are some other stories regarding their neighbours, Mary and Danny, that need to be told. Mary had suffered from asthma from a child and had been in and out of hospital for injections during her childhood and her married life. In 1988, Mary had a very severe attack and ended up in the intensive care unit of the local hospital. David and Emily, with some local Christian friends and neighbours, led intercessory prayer meetings for Mary's recovery and, according to the Bible, laid hands on her for healing. After some period of time, Mary came around and returned home.

In 1990 Mary had another attack and was again admitted to the intensive care unit of the local hospital, where a machine was breathing for her. Again, prayer meetings were started, and David identified the spiritual battle that was involved in this sickness. David, Emily and some local Christians got into some intense spiritual intercession for Mary. In one of the prayer meetings, Danny told me that 'the Spirit took over.' Emily, after taking a few deep breaths, said; "It is now over, Mary will come back."

From that day, Mary started to improve and has not suffered an asthmatic attack since. Danny, at one stage, thought that he had lost Mary; but believing prayer changed the situation.

Another story was regarding the time when Mary was diagnosed with breast cancer. Again, the prayer group, led by David, swung into action. Mary was operated on and the lump removed. The cancer was proved to be malignant and Mary only had radiotherapy; she did not receive chemotherapy. They both acknowledge the power of prayer in the situation.

When Danny and Mary first met David they were not Spirit-filled people, but with David taking them to different meetings and teaching them about the fullness of the Spirit, they eventually received the Spirit baptism in a Full Gospel Business Men's meeting. Danny and

Mary attended a local Church of Ireland church, but David always encouraged them to stay in the church. David called it 'the mother church,' and it was a source of blessing, even when they received the power of the Holy Spirit in their lives. Danny and Mary freely acknowledge the Bible teaching that David gave them which helped them to live a Spirit-filled life.

Another couple who lived near David and Emily were Valerie and Norman Davidson. They were two of the local Christians who were involved in the prayer meetings for Mary, as told already. They spoke of how David led a praise night for Mary during one of her periods of sickness. Valerie and Norman would have had meetings in their homes for young Christians, and David would come when he was available. "David would always be an encouragement, whatever was going on," said Valerie and Norman.

A young man from that youth group has gone on to serve the Lord in full-time ministry. Valerie and Norman told me how David 'raised their level of belief' and taught them important Bible themes like spiritual warfare and deliverance.

They also told me about a Catholic man who lived near David and Emily. When David was out for his daily morning walk, he would say, if Patrick was out; "still praying for you" and then stop and talk to him.

They never associated David with the word 'if' when it came to the promises of God. David was 'approachable and accessible' to the local community and would call prayer meetings as needs required. If there was anything troubling them, they 'knew they could go to David.' They described David as a 'gentle giant' who had been a tower of strength when Norman suffered a stroke a few years back. When that happened, David gave them Isaiah 41:10 as a promise to hold on to.

These two local Christian couples, Valerie and Norman, Danny and Mary, knew that David Greenow was there for them. Both couples grew in the things of God under the ministry of David. His teaching and his example were an inspiration for them to live for all that God had for them. David, they said, "practised what he preached."

Jesus said to his disciples in Acts 1:8; *"But you will receive power when the Holy Spirit comes upon you. And you will be my witnesses, telling people about me everywhere—in Jerusalem, throughout Judea, in Samaria, and to the ends of the earth."* (NLT)

David's Jerusalem was his local community. In the eyes of the world he was a *'little stone'* living in the area known as *'the place of the little stones.'* No doubt many, many people, over time, would have driven past the both homes on Bleary Road and not been aware that there was a *'gentle giant'* living on the road who, with the support of his wife Emily, was slaying spiritual giants in the locality. I have heard that some evangelists who have visited the UK over the years are totally unknown in their own countries. That could not be said for David Greenow. He had an effective ministry in the community he lived in and this is demonstrated by the fruit that was revealed.

CHAPTER TEN
Who is David Greenow...

Another local Christian couple from the Bleary area that David influenced were Barry and Maggie Hodgen. Barry sent me this tribute...

"Who is David Greenow? A question I had asked myself on more than one occasion; the reason being that I had recently obtained gospel tracts that had been written by David, and these tracts really blessed me and encouraged me in my walk with the Lord as a young believer in Christ. Some of these tracts I still have today such as *Bible Salvation Benefits*, *The Cross Of Christ*, *Strength For Your Day* and *Seven Steps To A Miracle*. David, being the Spirit-filled and mature Christian that he was, not only explained so much in these tracts, but also gave other Scripture references in them that a hungry young Christian could turn to in a desire to know more of God's Word on these and other biblical subjects. How blessed I was as I read and started to live out these great truths in my life! Already having heard other things about David, the more I read, the more I wanted to meet this man so that I might speak with him and learn more of the things of God from him.

At that particular time in our lives my wife Maggie and I attended a local church, Knocknamuckly Parish Church. (The church, in fact where I was convicted of my sins and I came to faith in Christ, led through the 'sinner's prayer' by the Reverend Jim Mc Master) It was Reverend Mc Master who encouraged me in my faith in various ways in those early days of my Christian walk.

As well as attending Knocknamuckly Church Sunday morning and Sunday evening, we were invited to attend a Wednesday evening meeting which took place in Tom and Jean Sommerville's house in Portadown. It was at these meetings where we heard many wonderful talks on God's Word from many different preachers, and, praise the Lord, one of these speakers turned out to be David.

Many people attended these meetings, including some Catholics who, disillusioned by the various problems in the Catholic church and having heard of the biblical teaching and the moving of the Holy Spirit in these meetings, came along; and like so many others were truly blessed in what they heard and saw. It was at these meetings that Maggie and I witnessed for the first time the moving of the Spirit of God in His various gifts; tongues and their interpretation, prophecy and healings.

This meant so much to me, as just six months after my conversion to Christ I was diagnosed with Hodgkin's disease (many tests confirming that that was indeed the illness I was suffering from), and the Lord God by His grace and power completely took that illness away from me and healed me with no operation or medicine involved.

Having experienced that supernatural healing in my life it was then that I started to ask the question; "If God still heals today, then are there other gifts of the Spirit for today as well?" Something that I really wanted to talk to David about, which I eventually did. I can only say that over a period of time, as I both came to know and went with David to various meetings that he was preaching at, that I witnessed first-hand the Holy Spirit moving in power in his life and the life of others, and I came to realise to my delight that the Spirit of God was indeed still moving in power in this day and age.

As we got to know each other, David and his wife Emily took an interest in the work that God had called Maggie and me to do. (The Lord lay upon Maggie a real burden for young people known as

Goths, and I helped her in every way that I could to reach out to them.) We were witnessing to the young people in Belfast city centre, and over some weeks we had a difficult time trying to approach them and make God's love known to them. As we gave out tracts to them, they either ripped them up in front of us or actually put the tracts in their mouths and ate them. This troubled both Maggie and myself; and so, we got to praying about the situation. The Lord revealed to Maggie in a dream in a very vivid way just exactly what we should use to reach out to these lost teenage children.

It was the words of a poem that the Lord gave to Maggie that night. A poem that spoke of a youth's wasted life through drinking, drugs, being involved in witchcraft and Satanism, and it was a poem that really touched the lives of these young people, because many were involved in some of those things themselves. Some told us later that as they read the poem it was as if it was written about them and their lives, and that God knew all about them. (Which of course He did!)

But something else was lacking; yes, we were going to speak to these young people, called by God to do just that, but were doing so in our own abilities and power. So we talked with David about the work God had called us to and how we felt about the reception we had received and upon hearing all we had to say, he told us that the power that was lacking in our lives was the power of the Holy Spirit. After much discussion, a date was arranged for Maggie and me to meet with both David and Emily in their house so they might pray for us that we would receive the baptism of the Spirit.

That day soon arrived. Maggie and myself found ourselves sitting on two dining room chairs in David and Emily's living room. Emily was standing behind Maggie with her hands on Maggie's shoulders; David was doing likewise with me. They had explained beforehand that because of the work we were called to do, and because we were trying to do that work in our own strengths and abilities and only succeeding so far, that what we needed in our lives, what we needed in our walk and work for the Lord, was the baptism of the Holy Spirit. Of course I, like all other Christians, had read many times that portion of Scripture from Acts 1:4-5 when the resurrected Christ commanded the believers to remain in Jerusalem and wait for the promise of the Father, and then added; *'but ye shall receive power, after that the Holy Spirit is come upon you: and ye shall be witnesses unto me both in Jerusalem, and in all Judea, and in Samaria, and unto the uttermost part of the earth.'* And so, we find that they went into that upper room and continued with one accord in prayer and supplication.

The Scriptures declare; *'And when the day of Pentecost was fully come, they were all with one accord in one place. And suddenly there came a sound from heaven as of a rushing mighty wind, and it filled the house where they were sitting. And there appeared unto them cloven tongues like as of fire, and it sat upon each of them. And they were all filled with the Holy Ghost, and began to speak with other tongues, as the Spirit gave them utterance.'*

As I said, this is a portion of Scripture I had read many times. I was amazed as I came to understand that these believers, who were hidden away in an upper room with windows and doors locked for fear of the Jews, were empowered for service to the Lord when the Holy Spirit came upon them, and with a boldness they had never before known. They were made strong and fearless; before they had been weak and timid. I realised that this was what was missing from our lives: Holy Spirit power and a new boldness to be witnesses for Christ.

And so, David and Emily, laying hands on us, began to pray. Almost immediately the Holy Spirit fell upon us both and we began to speak in new tongues. I can remember feeling a great sense of joy and elation that the Lord would choose to bless Maggie and myself in such a mighty and wonderful way, and empower us for service: to witness, to speak to those who were lost in this world, to make Christ known, and all that He had accomplished.

It's a work that continues in our lives to this day in one way or another. From time to time we get that calling to pray, to act and to witness; and yes, we are so thankful that God has used us in such a way. We will be forever grateful to Him. We are also thankful that it was our dear friend David who realised what was required in our lives and decided to pray, and act that we might receive that power, that boldness, which was so much needed for that work in our lives. And what a difference it made to know that we were now no longer relying on our own strengths, intellect or experience, but rather knowing that we had been empowered by the Holy Spirit to serve the Lord in this way. We used to meet with these young people with some trepidation and anxiety; now we had a boldness, an inner strength to witness in a way that we never had before. This led to many interesting and deep conversations with these young people. We came away from every encounter knowing that a seed of God's truth, a seed of hope, had been planted in every teenage heart. Where once they had ripped up tracts, now they actually read the poem that we used, and we were able to share with them who Christ was and the great love He had for them.

David was also a Christian man who did not like to see believers (whether saved for years or newly) saved and stuck, stagnant in their growth as a child of God. Rather it was his desire to see them not just baptised in the Spirit, but studying God's precious Word and applying those biblical truths to their everyday life. Hence the gospel tracts that he had written himself, tracts written not just for the unbeliever to know more about Christ, His death and resurrection and what that meant for all people everywhere; but also that Christians might better understand all the blessings they have in Christ.

One tract entitled; '*God's Bible Ultimates,*' helped the person reading it fully to understand who Christ is and the life-changing experience that one has as they come to faith in Him. It made a real impact on my own life back in those early days.

I have included just some of the points made in this tract, so that those who come to read this book will better understand the knowledge of God's Word that David had, and hopefully be blessed themselves as they search out these particular Scripture passages..."

➤ **No Greater Person Ever Lived** (The Lord Jesus Christ)
   Colossians 1:14-20, Philippians 2:5-11, Hebrews 1:1-12, Revelations 1:5-8; 18

➤ **No Greater Event In Human History**
   (Christ's Calvary Sacrifice For Sinners)
   John 19, Isaiah 53, 1 Peter 2: 24; 3:18

➤ **No Greater Message Ever Told**
   (Good News Of Christ's Full Salvation Blessings)
   Romans 1:16; 10:15; 15:29, 1 Corinthians 15:1-3

➤ **No Greater Gift Ever Offered**
   (Eternal And Abundant Life In Christ The Saviour)
   John 3:16, Romans 6:32, 2 Corinthians 9:15, Romans 8:32

➤ **No Greater Life Change To Be Experienced**
   (Passing From Spiritual Death To Life Through A New Birth)
   John 1:12; 3:3-8; 5:24, Acts 26: 15-18, 2 Corinthians 5:17

➤ **No Greater Assets Can Be Acquired**
   (Incalculable riches in Christ Jesus)
   Ephesians 1: 3, 7, 8, 11, 3:8, 1 Corinthians 3: 21-22, 2 Corinthians 8:9

"I trust you will come to see through these few Scripture passages just how deeply David had studied, understood and lived out the Word of God in his life, and the salvation benefits that he had experienced and which he wanted all believers to experience; and live their lives in victory. May your life also be a victorious life lived in the freedom that Christ has won for you.

One of my other precious memories of David was when we travelled down to the townland of Burt in Co. Donegal. This we did once a month or so for about a year. We were asked to speak in a house which belonged to two sisters, Louise and Rosemary Marshall, and the meeting was attended by approximately twenty or so people who were hungry for the teaching of God's Word.

Some were local people and others had come from Letterkenny and Stranorlar, but all knew the Lord as their own and personal Saviour and were so eager to spend time in His Word. I had, on quite a few occasions, spoken at that meeting by myself. (I had been asked down by Louise and Rosemary after the death of Tom Sommerville, who led meetings there once a month for quite a while. I was asked if I would carry them on, to which I wholeheartedly said yes.) I had told the girls about David, and after a few months asked if I could bring him along with me. They, already having heard of David, agreed, and what a blessed decision that was.

Not only was David a Spirit-filled preacher, but he was also someone who could play the accordion; and how he loved to play it and sing God's praises, always singing about God's wonderful love for mankind: God's love, which he always referred to as Calvary Love. I should say that David had already known that I was taking these meetings, because when I had been invited down to Donegal, I spoke to him about it. He prayed with me and then, smiling, gave me this advice: 'Barry, Donegal time is not our time.' I soon found out what that meant because the very first meeting I took was supposed to start at 7.30pm but didn't start until an hour later. A fine dinner had been prepared for Maggie and me about 7 p.m. As people started arriving for the meeting, they just pulled up a chair, grabbed a plate and began to fill it with the beautiful food on the table; so, the meeting didn't actually start until 8.30 p.m. The people there were so laid back, so relaxed and so happy just to be in one another's company.

This took me completely by surprise on that first night, and as much as I enjoyed the dinner and the company, all I wanted to do was begin to teach from God's Word. '*Relax, Barry,*' someone said, (I think he realised that I was wondering would the meeting ever start!) '*Preaching is hard and thirsty work. Relax and enjoy the food and this time together.*' I did, smiling and laughing inwardly as I suddenly remembered what David had told me, about Donegal time not being the same as ours!

That continued most months when we went down to Donegal, accompanied by Maggie and Emily, and every night ended in people coming forward for prayer. We decided the best thing to do was for David and me to go into one of the upstairs bedrooms, and that those who had need of prayer could come up one at a time. This was a very wise decision as it turned out, because some of those who had attended the meeting opened up to us about various problems, spiritual, physical and other problems that they were experiencing at that time. What a delight it was to pray for brothers and sisters in Christ, praying, believing that He who knows all things would come to their aid in His way and His time! Indeed, it was reported back to us that the Lord God had moved in the lives of these people; and we were all blessed to know that.

It was usually about midnight or later before we actually finished, but what a blessing it was for David and me to be part of that, and what an encouragement it was for me to be with someone who spoke in the power of the Spirit about the God he loved so much to the people he cared so much about.

David was a man who took a considerable interest in me and my walk with God. I will be forever grateful to the Lord that his path crossed with mine in this life and grateful to David for his advice, guidance and impact in my own life. I will never forget him".

CHAPTER ELEVEN
1954 Revival in Belfast...

There were four major Pentecostal revival waves during the twentieth century. David Greenow experienced three of them. The first wave was at Azusa Street, Los Angeles in 1906. David wasn't born until 1927.

The second Pentecostal wave was the "Healing Revival" which occurred in the late forties and fifties in America. William Branham, Oral Roberts, Jack Coe, A. A. Allen, T. L. Osborn, W. V. Grant, Don Stewart, David Nunn and Kathryn Kuhlman were among about ninety healing evangelists who preached this message of healing and hope. It brought a new harvest of converts and renewed hopes of national revival all over the world. In 1959 David Nunn came to Belfast and Armagh and saw the power of God manifested in healings, salvation and deliverances. David had books by W.V. Grant, and I remember him telling me about attending T.L. Osborn and A.A. Allen crusades in the UK. David attended revival meetings with Kathryn Kuhlman when he was in the USA.

The third wave was the less known "Latter Rain Revival." This movement originated at Sharon Orphanage and Schools in North Battleford, Saskatchewan, Canada. George Hawtin led the movement which began in a Bible school when students experienced an amazing outpouring of the Holy Spirit on February 12th, 1948. David experienced this blessing when he was at Bible school in 1951, which I wrote about in chapter 4.

The fourth wave was the charismatic renewal movement. David would have been involved with this wave through various inter-denominational and independent house groups that he attended over the years. (acknowledgements to Revival-Library.org for this oversight of twentieth century Pentecostal waves).

The 1954 Revival in Belfast was part of the "Healing Revival" wave of the late forties and fifties that started in the USA and spread across the world. The evangelist who came to Northern Ireland was a man by the name of James White. In the USA he was known as the "Irish Evangelist." He was part of the Gordon Lindsay, Last-Day Sign Gift Ministries group which published "The Voice of Healing" magazine. David was an avid reader of this magazine. You can find the song book that James White used in his revival meetings on the Amazon website.

Who was James White?

The White family were originally from Donegal and had moved to America. James was a professional heavyweight boxer before being converted in 1931. In 1949, White had a vision of a large building and a prominent statue. As it turned out the building was The King's Hall in Belfast and the statue was of King George, which stood outside the hall. In 1952 Pastor Joseph Smith, the Divisional Superintendent of Elim in Ireland, met James White when he was visiting Los Angeles. I cannot confirm whether James White shared the vision he had received with Pastor Smith, but an invitation was given to come to Northern Ireland. James White came to Belfast in July 1954.

Keith Malcolmson gave me this insight to the Revival in Belfast in 1954...

"There are many revivals down through church history that have never been recorded. I believe that a number of these revivals have carried the same marks as that in the book of Acts, but, sad to say, their written record has been lost to us in this present hour.

"As a child, I grew up hearing about a Pentecostal Revival in the city of Belfast, Northern Ireland. The preacher God used was James White. I have talked with preachers and believers who were eyewitnesses of these meetings. My own father and mother were witnesses of the after-effects of this outpouring of the Holy Spirit over into the 1960s."

The meetings started in a small tent on York Street, Belfast. After a few weeks, as a result of an invitation, James White went to the Revival Centre in Ballymena.

David Greenow attended the first service but, due to other commitments, he was away from Northern Ireland for a time.

The meetings in Ballymena lasted six weeks with 300 professed conversions and many healed. In the first week, a man who wore leg irons was healed. Later, a girl who was deaf and dumb was healed. Many others were miraculously healed. They had to move the meetings a number of times because of the crowds attending. Keith Malcolmson wrote; "They were forced to move from the Revival Centre to the Town Hall. So many crowded into the Balcony that it cracked!"

Towards the end of 1954, White moved back to Belfast and several venues were used: firstly, the YMCA in Wellington Place, after which the meetings then moved to the Ulster Hall, where White spoke from the boxing ring. Hundreds were turned away with people travelling 150-200 miles from Mayo and Donegal, to get to the meetings. They moved to the Grand Opera House, where a banner was placed on the wall with these words; "Bible Days Are Here Again!" Finally, the meetings moved to the Kings Hall; an auditorium that could seat 12,000 people, and where there was a statue of King George; exactly

Kings Hall, Belfast.

as James White had seen in the vision in 1949. I was told that at one meeting in the King's Hall, fifty people were healed and left their wheelchairs.

Keith Malcolmson wrote; "Meetings were also held in other centres around Ulster, e.g. Portadown and Banbridge. In Banbridge a building was secured for one night that could hold up to 3,000. In Lisburn, people were queuing two hours before the meeting."

By the time James White had moved back to Belfast towards the end of 1954, David had returned to Northern Ireland and attended the meetings. David was very complementary in his comments about these meetings in Belfast. David said things like; *'there was a hunger for God;' 'the awesome presence and power of God was felt, you could cut it in chunks;' 'angels were seen on the platform;' 'James White would stretch out his hand and people would fall under the power of God;' 'the atmosphere was laden with the manifest presence of God;' 'faith would rise;' 'God's unseen hand' was over the congregation.'*

One story that David told was that at one meeting he was sitting by a lady and her two children. The children were cross-eyed. White spoke to the congregation and encouraged them to lay hands on the sick beside them. Hands were laid on these two children and they were instantly healed. On another occasion, while David was sitting in the gallery, an usher went out and brought five children into the service, all with crossed eyes. They were prayed for and, again, instantly healed.

In David and Emily's Christmas letter of 2005, David gave some of his memories of this God-given revival in Belfast; "During the year '54 we witnessed a remarkable move of God here in Ireland. It was estimated that about 3,000 souls came to Christ during the period, multitudes were healed and baptised in the Holy Spirit and many experienced the power and blessing of God. People saw visions of Jesus, angels, and other interesting things. Sinners were convicted and arrested by the power of the Holy Spirit. A lasting impact was made in many lives. I was there to see scores of people struck down by the Power of God."

About 2-3,000 people professed salvation in the Ballymena and Belfast meetings that James White held. Some of those saved in Ballymena went on to serve the Lord in full-time ministry: men like Roy Kerr and Billy Mullan. In the Belfast mission, two of the converts were Frank Bray and Alex Scofield. David would in later years share Gospel preaching with both these men, but I must mention Frank Bray. He was saved when the James White meetings were held first in a tent in Belfast. Frank was a professional gambler and owned a number of betting shops in Belfast. He came into the tent one night and saw a crippled child being healed. He left the meeting and went home but he couldn't sleep because of what he had seen. He returned to the meetings and gave his heart to the Lord. He walked away from his previous life and established a church in Dromore, County Down. Earlier, I mentioned the visit of David Nunn to Northern Ireland in 1959. It was during these meetings that Frank Bray was commissioned to go and establish a revival centre in Cork. There was money left over after all the costs of the Nunn meetings were covered; this money, over £550.00, was left to support this endeavour in Cork.

David and Frank, in the years following Frank's salvation in 1954, became partners in the Gospel of the Lord Jesus Christ. They would often have ministered together whether at the local church in Dromore; evangelistic missions in Dublin; supporting the work in Cork or in meetings in Northern Ireland.

In 1955, White came back to Ulster and held further meetings in the Ulster Hall. David attended as he was able. Sitting on the platform one night with other preachers sitting around him, White turned to him and said you are preaching tonight, which he did. Emily said to me; "James White did David good. He saw the miraculous happen." In later years when David was on a preaching tour of North America, he visited James White.

David has had a few interesting years in his life. In 1951, he experienced the wave of the latter rain while attending Bible school in South Wales. In the years 1952 and 1953, he experienced something of the power of the Holy Spirit in his ministry, especially during the mission in Mountain Lodge. In 1954 David saw a Gospel explosion; signs and wonders and a harvest of the Kingdom through the ministry of James White. But in 1955, God was going to use David to bring revival to a town in County Armagh.

CHAPTER TWELVE

1955 Revival in Portadown...

In early 1955, David was asked to continue a mission at the Plaza ballroom in Portadown that had started on 30th January 1955. The newspaper headline was *"Portadown Healing Revival."* The guest speaker, at the beginning of the mission, was a healing evangelist called Eric Butterworth. Eric was a missionary with the Church of God in Bombay, India. His wife, Margaret (née Anderson) was from Armagh. She had trained as a nurse and Eric, an Englishman, had spent time in the British Army.

In the Portadown Times, 29th January 1955, there was a brief article about Eric Butterworth. Let me quote the final paragraph: *"Many are the thrilling stories this servant of God relates to of life on the mission field. Mr Butterworth claims the experience of speaking in unknown tongues, as did the early disciples, and tells of an instance when his interpreter deserted him in the heart of the jungle. Finding himself surrounded by a people whose language he did not understand, Mr Butterworth prayed and received an anointing of the Spirit of God under which he began to speak to these people in their own language."*

The Butterworths, while home on leave from India from 1954-55, spent time leading different healing campaigns in Northern Ireland. Prior to coming to Portadown, Eric Butterworth had been involved in healing missions in Belfast and Armagh. Pastor James McConnell remembers the meetings in Belfast. He was a young man at the time, and said they were good. People were saved, and there was evidence that God was working. The advert for the meetings in Armagh which started on Sunday 2nd January 1955 at the Scout Hall, The Mall, made this claim for the Belfast revival meetings: *"HIGHLIGHTS of recent Butterworth Revival in Belfast:*

"OVER 1,000 ATTENDANCE"

"MIRACULOUS HEALINGS OF DEAF & DUMB"

"MENTALLY AFFLICTED, CROSS EYES"

"SCORES RECEIVE HOLY GHOST"

"LOST COUNT OF NUMBERS CONVERTED"

I was told regarding the Armagh gatherings that Eric Butterworth gave testimony that he heard angels singing as he would come to the meetings.

In the Portadown Times, Friday 28th January 1955, announcing Eric Butterworth coming to Portadown, they carried the same report as was publicised in Armagh. News was spreading about the high attendance and the miraculous healings that were taking place. The Times published; *"Butterworth returns to India shortly... NOW is Portadown's opportunity to see this Powerful Evangelist in action!"*

Butterworth was described to me as *'a character.'* He patterned himself on the healing evangelists from the USA who were around at the time. He also had a white suit. I was told how he would prophesy to himself while calling on God for his ministry. He finished his ministry in Portadown on 11th February 1955. Butterworth's ministry was anointed during his time in Portadown. I was told about a deaf and dumb speaking and hearing for the first time. Also, some deaf people received their healing also.

There was one final meeting for Butterworth, in Armagh on Monday 28th February at the Armagh City Hall. The advert said, "*Come and hear what God is doing in India.*"

David Greenow started to preach at The Plaza, Portadown from 13th February 1955. The Portadown Times announced "Evangelist David Greenoe (England)" would be at the Plaza. The headline was "*POWER FALLS IN THE PLAZA.*" The headline in the other local paper, the Portadown News was "Baptism of the Spirit for Believers: Deliverance for the Captives." In the advert in the News David's surname was spelt, "Greenoo." By the second week David's surname was being spelt correctly in both papers, "Greenow."

I must add something before continuing with the story of the revival at the Plaza. I spent time looking at the church adverts that appeared in the two local papers in 1955. The town was spiritually alive and seeking God. The two mainline Pentecostal denominations in the town also held healing and revival meetings during the early months of 1955. An advert for one of the churches which appeared in the Portadown Times on 21st January 1955 said: "*A FULL GOSPEL CAMPAIGN*" and the visiting speaker was identified as a '*Revivalist Evangelist.*' There was also a continuing evangelistic thrust in the town from non-Charismatic groupings. Within the first few months of 1955, Billy Graham's mission meetings in Glasgow were being beamed into Portadown. The town was spiritually alert and open for more of God.

Let's get back to the Plaza and David Greenow. Instead of the planned two weeks, the mission continued for twenty months. The blessing of God came down; many people were convicted of sin and filled with the Holy Spirit. There were many healings. David wrote, "The presence and power of God … was manifest night after night." One young man's badly injured hand was healed and later he gave his heart to the Lord. Another young man was healed of a serious illness. He later emigrated to Canada. It was twenty years later that David learned about that healing. David rarely spoke about the healings he had witnessed, believing that it drew attention to the person who prayed rather than to the Lord.

In David and Emily's Christmas letter of 2005, David gave some of his memories of this God-given revival in Portadown: "We had two services nightly for weeks. Souls were saved, backsliders restored, people were healed, baptised with the Holy Spirit. Marriages were restored and lives impacted for God. One brother tells me he came to the Saviour along with six others one Sunday night, was baptised in the Holy Spirit on the Tuesday night and I baptised him in water the following Sunday. The move of God was on for many lives."

I spoke to Elizabeth Orr who had attended the Plaza meetings with Eric Butterworth and continued going to the services when David came to preach. She was 12 years of age and attended the meetings with a friend. Elizabeth was saved when she was 6 years of age at a Methodist mission. Her testimony was: "she fell in love with Jesus." Elizabeth was filled with the Holy Spirit during the meetings at the Plaza.

Elizabeth told me about the impact David made on her and her family (Richardson): "David came into our lives in 1955. We went to the revival that had broken out in Portadown at meetings held in a former dance hall, the Plaza. My parents got saved, my mother healed, and we were all filled with the Holy Spirit. Not only were our lives changed, but the good news spread. Dad went to all the family to tell them that they needed to be saved. He led some of them to Christ. Some only repented on their deathbeds but Dad was there to lead them to the Saviour.

"Mum's family too were impacted. Many of her sisters, nieces and nephews gave their hearts to the Lord and many were healed through prayer." Elizabeth told me about the sense of God's presence that was in the town and as you crossed the river bridge to walk to the Plaza God's convicting presence was heavy and people would just call out to God.

Elizabeth told me how her mother, Elsie, had been diagnosed with cancer, and given only six months to live if she was not operated on. She was at the revival meetings in the Plaza the night before she was to go to Lurgan for her operation. In that meeting, David Greenow had a word of knowledge for her. The word was, "*You shall not die but live to declare the works of the Lord.*" The next day, Mrs Richardson made her way to Lurgan hospital. She asked to see the consultant and expressed a wish for another examination as she told him; "I have been prayed for and I am healed." The consultant was not prepared for this delay. Mrs Richardson walked out of the hospital. The consultant followed her to the bus stop, imploring her to come back into the hospital. She didn't go back, and she didn't take up the offer to phone if she changed her mind.

(In picture: From left: David, Mrs & Mr Richardson)

Some eight years later, Mrs Richardson was ill again. But, after examination by a doctor, the diagnosis was exhaustion. Mrs Richardson lived into her eighties.

David became a close family friend of the Richardson family. Elizabeth told me a story about her younger brother, William, which happened a short time after David had finished leading the Revival meetings in Portadown. The family were together in their home and William came in and said that they must pray for David Greenow. David was away in Ballymena and the family were not aware that anything was wrong. The family prayed. On David's next visit to the home, they mentioned to him the urgency that William had felt to call for prayer for him. David told the family that on that day that they prayed he was not feeling well and felt unable to lead a meeting in Ballymena in the evening, but God stepped in and he was healed. He led the meeting that evening in Ballymena.

Elizabeth received her baptism at the Revival meetings and she saw God work wonders in the life of her family. By the age of 14, Elizabeth was preaching the Gospel with Frank Bray on the streets of Cork. From the day of her salvation she felt a strong desire to serve God and doors opened for her. In her late teens, she went to Bible school in Devon and went on to minister in Ireland, Great Britain, Denmark, Germany and Italy. Elizabeth openly acknowledges the blessing that David was to her personally, and to the Richardson family, in the years following the Revival.

I spoke to another Elizabeth who attended the Plaza meetings. Although only a child of 5 years of age, she told me that the meetings had a profound influence on her life, although just a child. She remembered the power of God being evident, seeing the gifts of the Holy Spirit in operation and witnessing healings. Elizabeth told me about someone, who was crippled being healed and walking. Remember, Elizabeth was just a young child and would not have been at all the meetings but the ones she did attend left a mark on her life: "those times in God's house were mighty."

Billy McCracken, who was from a Church of Ireland background, visited the Plaza meetings. It was all so different from what he was used to and, also, from what he had been taught; but the Plaza changed him. He was water-baptised, Spirit-filled and also received a gift of faith; all of which transformed his Christian life. He became known as 'bouncing Billy.' He couldn't stand still whether preaching the Gospel or praising the Lord. In later years, Billy was a great means of encouragement and ministry in the Mountain Lodge Church, after the terrorist attack.

Another story from these meetings concerns a lady who was in a meeting and just shouted out; *"Can you not see it?"* She was asked; *"What are you seeing?"* *"The cross on the wall,"* was her reply. The wall was black; and the Lord spoke to that woman about going to full-time service for Him. And that is what she did.

In 2005, I had the privilege of being involved in the 50th anniversary services of the Plaza Revival. The meetings were held at the Apostolic Church, Jervis Street, Portadown. The lasting memory I have of these anniversary services was how many people who had experienced the power of the Holy Spirit in the 1955-56 meetings were still living and knowing the touch of God upon their lives some fifty years later. That is testimony to the good work that God did through David Greenow in those eighteen months that he spent ministering at the Plaza Ballroom.

One of the speakers at the 50th anniversary services was Cecil Stewart. He had attended the Plaza meetings with friends from Monaghan. The story is told in the next chapter.

Top left; David and Emily reading the scriptures together. Top right; Starting out as a married couple. Bottom; A photograph of David's family (from left to right) stepbrother Fred, David's father, Lloyd, stepbrother Glyn, stepmother, Laura and David.

Above: A day out with Emily's parents, Thomas John and Margaret Hunniford.
Right: David during the Portadown revival.
Bottom: David's business card.

Jesus Christ the same yesterday and to-day and forever
(Heb. 13 v. 8)

Evangelist
David J. Greenow

(In fellowship with International Gospel Outreach)

"Wayside", Ballydougan,
Portadown, Co. Armagh, N.I
Tel. Craigavon 41852

p16.

Revival in Portadown

Top photo is The Revival Team at the Plaza, Portadown in 1960.
Above photo is Evangelist's Mr Vallery, Mr Greenow and Mr Robinson at open-air meeting, Mountain Lodge, 1956.
Left: David preaching at the revival.

Above; (Left to right) Glyn Greenow, Roy Turner, Ronnie Duddy and Cecil Stewart.

Below; (Left to right) Roy Turner, David Greenow and Glyn Greenow.

Top; David preaching at the
Revival.
Above left; The newspaper
cutting advertising the event.
Right; David and Emily on
their 25th wedding anniversary.

Photographs captured
on their 50th wedding
anniversary.
Below right; David and
Emily with an
anniversary gift
Bottom; The
anniversary note that
was posted to family
and friends.

Celebrating 50 years of marriage

David & Emily Greenow
23-10-1956 — 23-10-2006

Emily and I are deeply grateful to our
Heavenly Father for His caring and
faithfulness across these 50 years of
married life together. Also we sincerely
thank all the Lord's people for all the
encouragement prayer and support
we have received. Thankyou for
continued prayer on our behalf. May
God richly bless you.

Lord, for all the years
Your love has kept and guided,
Urged and inspired us
Cheered us on our way,
Sought us and saved us
Pardoned and provided
Lord of the years
   we bring You thanks today.

IGO NEWS

June 2012

International Gospel Outreach, (Reg. Charity 252872)
The Oasis, Dwygyfylchi, North Wales, LL34 6PS Tel: 0044 (0) 1492 623229
email: mail@igo.org.uk Web-site: www.igo.org.uk

IGO — RECOGNISING THE WHOLE CHURCH & REACHING OUT TO THE WHOLE WORLD

David Greenow 26th May 1927—3rd May 2012

David Greenow, IGO Honorary President and original President and Trustee, went to be with the Lord on 3rd May 2012. David had been in hospital following a fall whilst out walking alone and continued exercising on discharge from hospital. He died whilst on another walk by the river Bann.

David was a farmer's son from Hereford close to the English/Welsh border. One of 3 brothers, he was born in 1927 and found Christ at the age of 14. In his late teens he felt a strong call from God to enter full time Christian service and later went to Bible College. He moved to N. Ireland in the early 1950's and became prominent in local evangelical circles as a preacher of renown. In the mid 50's he was involved in a campaign in the Plaza Ballroom in Portadown which continued every night for 18 months non-stop. His ministry was much in demand and he travelled widely across the UK, Europe, Canada and the USA.

On 23rd October 1956 he married Emily Hunniford, his ever loyal companion and support for 55 fruitful years. David's extremely large funeral was held on Sunday 6th May in Knocknamuckly Parish Church (kindly granted) and the sheer numbers in attendance were a reflection of the huge esteem in which from far and near he was held. The service was conducted by Pastor Gary Anderson (Armagh) and Pastor Marcus Thomas (Lurgan) at the graveside.

Fulsome and heartfelt tributes were paid by Pastor Glyn Greenow (brother), Pastor John Greenow (Nephew) and a lifelong friend, Evangelist David Chaudhary, all from England. David Greenow will be sadly missed.

(Excerpts of Obituary from 'The Portadown Times', submitted by Gary Anderson)

Henri's Revival
Evangelistic Association

Come, see and feel Revival in operation NOW

Lives Changed : Sick Healed
Souls Saved

Blessing for Everybody

Expect a miracle today.
You will feel better for coming and you'll never be the same again

FOR ALL PEOPLE OF ALL CHURCHES

Hear Roy Turner
on Hammond Organ

Announcing
GREAT HOLY GHOST GLORY MEETINGS
commencing Sunday, 15th August, 1965, for one week nightly at 8 p.m. in the Big Tent, Armagh Road, Monaghan, Eire

ENQUIRIES TO
CECIL STEWART
PHONE
BELFAST 650558

Cecil Stewart   Roy Turner   Dave Greenow

AND REVIVAL PARTY

CHAPTER THIRTEEN

There are no borders with God...

David believed and taught that there was a distinct and separate experience of the Holy Spirit for Christians. This experience was for all who confessed Jesus as their LORD and Saviour. This experience has no borders as Peter found with Cornelius in Acts chapter 10. In the context of this book, the experience of Spirit baptism was for all Christians, north and south of the border.

David wrote in the leaflet, *Be Filled with the Spirit: Ephesians 5:18*; "*The Baptism and Fullness of the Holy Spirit is a definite God-given spiritual experience, promised in the Scriptures, ministered by Christ subsequent to the new birth, for the empowering of all New Testament Believers. It is vitally important to our Christian obedience, service and character that we seek and receive the gift and fullness of the Holy Spirit.*"

The story is told of a group of men, from Monaghan, Eire, coming to the meetings in Portadown, when David Greenow was the preacher. This was not their first visit to the Plaza. The group had first come to the meetings when Eric Butterworth was the evangelist.

They were brought to the Revival meetings by a man called Sam Wallace. Sam was from a Church of Ireland background and a farmer in Monaghan. He held prayer meetings in his farmhouse for the purpose of seeking and knowing the power of God. One of the young men who came to the meetings in Portadown was Cecil Stewart. Cecil was also from a Church of Ireland background.

Cecil remembers Eric Butterworth having an "unusual accent" and would be saying to people, "something's coming brother." "He looked wild and hyped and wound up," Cecil told me but there was something that stood out for him: the enthusiasm that was in the meetings. This group did know something of the Presence of God in the house meetings in Sam Wallace's farmhouse, but Cecil said, "this was something different." Please remember, this would have been something completely new for these Christian visitors from Monaghan.

The same group of men came back to Portadown when David was leading the meetings. Cecil told me that when he came into the meeting, he saw a man on the platform and there was a fire behind him. The congregation was singing, "let the fire fall." Cecil told me that there was shouting and "high" singing. The atmosphere was fantastic and the meeting was a little crazy.

He actually left the meeting for a time and when he returned discovered that two of the group from Monaghan had been filled with the Holy Spirit. Cecil said that they were intoxicated and were singing and speaking in their new languages. They were 'drunk in the Spirit.' When it came time for the group to go back to Monaghan, Sam Wallace was concerned about the border crossing. He knew that the border guards would give a thorough check of the car and its occupants. So, they held back for a time until the individuals had 'sobered up' a little.

Through the connection made at these meetings in the Plaza, David started to visit the house group at Sam Wallace's farmhouse. It was at these meetings that David met Cecil Stewart. Cecil remembered the praying, the fasting and the prayer walking David did around Monaghan.

David wrote this about the first time he met Cecil (1957 approx): "We were having a time of worship at the Wallace's house in Monaghan when Cecil arrived with his big brother Herbie. I could see he was naturally a reserved lad, but, before evening was over, my wife and I knew without a doubt that God had a great future for both of the brothers."[34]

Another story from Monaghan concerns the time when David and Alec Schofield were holding meetings in the Corlea Hall, Monaghan. Mrs Stewart, Cecil and Herbie's mother, was desperately ill with duodenal ulcers. She was skin and bone. She was living on milk and biscuits. Herbie told his mother about the meetings. She was taken and helped forward to receive prayer. Mark 16 was spoken out and Mrs Stewart believed the promise of that scripture. She went home and ate a fry and suffered no after-effects.

Cecil remembers a meeting in their family home which Herbie had arranged, sometime in in the late 1950s. He invited David Greenow to come and bring some recordings of the American evangelist Jack Coe to listen to. Herbie also invited some neighbours to come. During the meeting Mrs Stewart fell to the ground. There was no pulse and Cecil said, '*it looked like she had gone.*' David and Herbie prayed over Mrs Stewart and rebuked death to leave and commanded Mrs Stewart to rise. That is what happened.

Cecil Stewart received his Spirit baptism through the ministry of David Greenow. Cecil recounts the story in a Christian magazine: "One night in County Monaghan, Eire, where I lived at that particular time, some of the folk and I went along to a meeting where brother David Greenow was ministering. It was there I received the Baptism of the Holy Ghost and spoke in other tongues. I shall never forget that experience, for I was drunk in the Spirit."[35]

Cecil gave further details about this experience in his biography: "I went forward to receive the Baptism in the Spirit. I cannot begin to describe the experience. It was incredible! It was as though an electric power surged through me and I felt a new strength."[36]

34 Wylie, Lorraine. ((2007) "What do you mean it's impossible: The Cecil Stewart Story".
35 The Glory News no 37. Magazine published by The Glory People.
36 Wylie, Lorraine. ((2007) "What do you mean it's impossible: The Cecil Stewart Story".

David was used by God with another member of the family. Victor Stewart recalls… "One night in Brother David Greenow's meetings, I said 'it is now or never;' so I took my stand with the redeemed. I lost some friends, but God gave me better ones and a much richer joy and peace. Praise His Name forever!"[37]

When Cecil came to live and work in Belfast for his brother Mervyn, David was instrumental in encouraging Cecil in ministry in local churches. When Cecil went into business, David was there to advise and counsel. Cecil said that the first thoughts whenever he was facing challenges were to ring David Greenow. David took Cecil to Sweden on ministry and Cecil was there when the International Gospel Outreach was established. When Cecil was diagnosed with cancer in 2003, it was David who stood by him in prayer over many months. Cecil said this in his autobiography; David Greenow was his *"spiritual father and a man who… deposited more of God's Word and character into my life than anyone else."*

What happened to Cecil Stewart? Cecil went on the establish the largest privately-owned nursing business in the British Isles, for which he received an OBE from the Queen. He also founded a church in Belfast and an International Ministry and a Christian Television Station that has reached thousands across this world. David and Emily's insight that God had a great plan and purpose for this young man when they first met him in 1957 has been proved to be correct.

Reflection…

Before going on to the next part of David's life, I think it would be good to pause and ask the question: what does the Bible teach us about the infilling of the Holy Spirit and how did David move so freely in these things?

---

37 The Glory News no 36. Magazine published by The Glory People.

I have already quoted what David wrote about the baptism of the Holy Spirit in his leaflet, "Be Filled with the Spirit" at the beginning of this chapter. There are stories and testimonies in this book about the power of the Holy Spirit both in individual lives and in congregational meetings. The Presence and Power of the Holy Spirit in our Christian life and in our congregational meetings makes all the difference. Sad to say, many substitutes for the presence and power of the Holy Spirit have been introduced and, as a result, we see a weak Christianity being lived and demonstrated. We can have all the hype and motivational statements going but it is the Holy Spirit who brings the reality. When did you read the Acts of the Apostles last? Read it, it is absolutely thrilling.

David saw this experience of the Spirit as part of our inheritance now in Christ Jesus. He didn't see it as a one-off experience for us to tick off on some to-do list; but as an ongoing and increasing experience for our lives. David walked this truth himself; and the evidence is demonstrated in his prophetic words, gifts of healings and words of knowledge.

We have been given a huge commission by the Lord Jesus Christ: "All authority in heaven and on earth has been given to me. Therefore, go and make disciples of all nations, baptizing them in the name of the Father and the Son and the Holy Spirit, teaching them to obey everything I have commanded you. And surely I am with you always, to the very end of the age." (Matthew 28:18-20 NIV)

The filling of the Holy Spirit, the gifts of the Holy Spirit and the fruit of the Holy Spirit are absolutely necessary for you and me and our churches to fulfil the mission Jesus has given us.

The baptism and the subsequent filling of the Holy Spirit is a work of the Lord Jesus Christ. Peter, when he preached on the Day of Pentecost said; "Exalted to the right hand of God, He (Jesus) has received from the Father the promised Holy Spirit and has poured out what you now see and hear." (Acts 2:33 NIV) The Day of Pentecost was a work of the Lord Jesus Christ and continues to be his work in our lives. David wrote, "We are to be filled with, yield to, depend on, and walk in the Holy Spirit."

CHAPTER FOURTEEN
Ministry in Northern Ireland...

Saintfield...

Following the meetings in Portadown, which continued into the latter months of 1956, David became involved in the move of God that was taking place in the small village of Saintfield, County Down.

The story I want to highlight is of a married couple, Stanley and Lena Morgan. The spiritual stirrings in Saintfield had started as a result of the visit to Belfast of the American evangelist James White. Saintfield is approximately 11 miles from Belfast. A shop owner in Saintfield, Mrs Jones, paid for buses to take people from the village to the revival meetings in Belfast. Mrs Jones was not a Christian but she could see the transformation in people's lives who attended the Belfast meetings. Mrs Jones did eventually become a Christian herself.

The stirrings in Saintfield continued through a number of nightly house meetings in the village. One of these nightly house meetings was in the home of a Mrs Cunningham who lived in the Pound area. David Greenow, with another evangelist, David Vallery, came to Saintfield to hold meetings in the local picture house.

Prior to one of the evening meetings, the two Davids were in prayer in Mrs Cunningham's home. David Greenow had a vision of a tall man with dark black hair and a white silk scarf walking down the aisle of the picture house to the front. On the night of the meeting, the man that David had seen in the vision walked into the meeting. The man's name was Stanley Morgan. David recognised the man and, following the preaching of the Gospel, Stanley responded to the invitation for salvation and became a follower of Jesus Christ.

That is an amazing story but let me give you some background which I trust will further demonstrate what a mighty God we serve. Stanley Morgan was a merchant seaman and would have been away from his family for three to four months at a time. Stanley's wife, Lena, was a Christian and there were four children. The family home was one of the homes where house meetings were held. Stanley was home from sea and didn't like his home being used in this way and tried to stop the meetings. He didn't want his wife and family to be involved in any of the Christian services going on in Saintfield. On this visit home the meetings were also taking place in the local picture house.

Things came to a head in the family home. Stanley gave Lena an ultimatum; if she didn't stop her involvement with the services, then he would leave the home and the family. Lena did not bow to this pressure. One of the children remembers their dad sitting in a chair, rolling a cigarette and saying to his wife, in a very angry way, *"I'm going."*

He got up, filled his kit bag and left. Lena begged him not to go but he did. Lena didn't know what to do. She was left with four children, not knowing where her husband had gone. Broken hearted, but not willing to deny her Christian experience, she got the children ready to go to the meeting. The meeting started at 7 p.m., but before leaving for the service, Stanley appeared at the home. He agreed to go to the meeting with the family. What an amazing turnaround in attitude in just a few hours. He put on his navy coat and a white silk scarf. Lena did not know anything about the vision that David Greenow had. The family went to the revival service and David recognised Stanley as the man he saw in the vision. When the call for salvation was given, Stanley responded.

Prior to meeting and marrying Lena, the only Christian input there had been into Stanley's life was when he went to see the film '*The Robe.*' The film had a dramatic effect on him, but he didn't have any knowledge of Christianity to progress further. He was *a man of the world* who had suffered rejection in his early years as a result of his father's remarriage. He, with his four siblings, were not wanted by their new stepmother. The children were put into orphanages.

His son, Lindsay, remembers the night his father was born-again. Lindsay said, "My father came home very confused and very broken. He didn't understand what had happened to him. Next morning, when eating his breakfast, something slipped from his plate on to the floor and my father burst into tears. He cried non-stop for three days and three nights. The Cross scenes from the film 'The Robe' came back to him and he saw blood pouring down from Jesus. I now know that my father was having a revelation of the Cross. As a young boy at the time, I couldn't understand what was happening to my father at the time. I watched him crying for three days and three nights but, looking back, I can say that was the start of a different father and husband in the home."

I read this quote recently, '*Our error today is that we do not expect a converted man to be a transformed man, and as a result of this error, our churches are full of substandard Christians.*' [38] For Stanley Morgan, that night in Saintfield was a transforming experience. Lindsay told me how his dad would talk to anybody and everybody about Jesus. His passion was for people to come and know Jesus. Stanley said, "*A love was put into his heart for God and others.*" Such was her husband's experience that Lena doubted her own experience. Stanley had a real agape experience from God when he was born again. Lindsay told me, with tears in his own eyes, that his father never lost the reality of the Cross or the brokenness that he had experienced at his conversion. Lindsay said, "*Whenever my father thought of the Cross, he would just cry.*"

---

38 Tim Totten: source unknown.

Stanley never went back to sea and got a job at ICL, Castlereagh. He stopped smoking instantly and, as Lindsay said, '*we got our father back.*' Stanley became part of a local church but would also go to churches and mission halls sharing his testimony of transformation by the Gospel of Jesus Christ.

What about Lena Morgan? She had been given a prophetic word that she would be '*a help to the reapers.*' Initially she couldn't understand what this meant; but after some years of opening the home to visiting speakers from the UK and overseas, she saw how God had used her with a gift of hospitality to bless visiting speakers, who in turn, had been a blessing to the family and an influence on the children. The family have continued this gifting although their mum and dad have passed away. Where did it all stem from? Lindsay was very clear with his answer; "David Greenow and the vision that God had given him."

David Greenow became a friend of the family and was a regular visitor to the Morgan home, staying overnight with Emily at times. In November 1961, Stanley and Lena's daughter, Shirley, came to faith under the ministry of David Greenow. She was subsequently baptised in the Holy Spirit in August 1962.

Dungannon...

In writing this book, I spent some time with a lady from Lurgan called June McCollum. She told me a story that happened to her in 1964 when she was 16. She attended the Baptist church in Lurgan and had a friend in Dungannon. This friend was a Christian. Her whole family were Christians. June was asked to go and stay in Dungannon for the weekend.

She didn't know what church her friend's family attended, so she went with the family to church that Sunday morning. The church was called '*The Upper Room*' and the preacher for the day was David Greenow. June had never heard of David Greenow. After the morning meeting June was in shock. She had never been in such meetings with clapping. She put her hands to her face and asked the Lord to forgive her and that she would not be back. This was a completely new experience of church for June. Being a guest of the family, she had no means of getting home, so she went to the meeting at night. David Greenow was the speaker again.

At the end of the evening message David asked, "is there anyone who wants to go further with God?" He didn't mention the baptism of the Holy Spirit or speaking in tongues. June wanted to go further with God. She went out for prayer. David prayed over her and laid hands on her and she was instantly filled with the Holy Spirit and spoke in tongues. There was no waiting and no tarrying: instantly. June is still living in that experience some 50 years later and continues to tell the story.

Portadown...

In 1967 David held a Crusade in Portadown. This was David's report: "One sister was healed… of an internal complaint from which she had suffered for 11 years. Another sister tells me that after prayer she has been certified clear of the dreaded disease of multiple sclerosis which had threatened to destroy her life. Yet another sister tells how, when I called her out for prayer, she was instantly healed of a serious spinal complaint. Her child was also wonderfully healed after prayer. Hallelujah! It thrills me to know that the God of miracles lives today. He is still answering prayer."

Battlehill...

For many years there was a house group meeting held at Battlehill, a townland just outside Portadown in County Armagh. We have already mentioned in an earlier chapter that Emily Greenow's parents were originally from this area of Northern Ireland. The fellowship was run by Bertie McAfee. He said, "Because of our background and our inexperience in the things of the Spirit, we were in need of a steadying hand. David provided this for us. I had met David through our local Chapter of Full Gospel Businessmen's Fellowship, and he was a real father figure to us in those days. He came alongside us in a very quiet, unassuming way. Sometimes we invited him other times he and Emily would just arrive and join us, always bringing words of encouragement and exhortation for us as we sought to grow in Christ.

"David would often bring the accordion, which helped our worship in those early days as our young people were light in musical skills but full of enthusiasm! David was never pushy, never tried to take over, never asked for money, all attributes which we as a small group really appreciated as he just wanted to see us grow in the things of God.

"I never remember him criticising or bringing a word of rebuke. I'm sure in those early days there was much that he could have criticised but that was not the spirit of the man. Despite his wealth of experience in the things of the Kingdom, he was willing to draw alongside a small group, insignificant in the eyes of the world but very significant to David. We appreciate all that he sowed into our lives in those days. The fruit is still apparent with some of that group having gone into full-time work as pastors, worship leaders, Church elders and others becoming good church members and Godly parents. We are very thankful for his input to our lives and, as David would say when he was leaving you, 'Blessings, Blessings, Blessings.'"

One person who attended this fellowship was Stephen Blevins. He told me a story from the early 1980s. Stephen went to the fellowship one night. God had started to speak to Stephen about divine healing prior to the meeting. No one knew about this. It was something personal and private between Stephen and the Lord. On the night in question, David was at this particular meeting and as the service was going on, David came over to Stephen, in a quiet and unassuming way, and said God wanted to open up a healing ministry for him. David did not know that God had been stirring Stephen's heart about divine healing. David prayed with Stephen. The question is – what happened as a result?

Stephen told me a number of stories, from his life, about how God had used him to minister healing, in the name of Jesus. One story was about a 25-year-old man who had been deaf since the age of five. Stephen laid his hands on his ears and prayed over him in the name of Jesus. Just as he was being prayed for, "he leaped two feet in the air," said Stephen, "squealing and shouting, "I can hear, I can hear!"

The prophetic word that David gave to Stephen in the early 1980s has come to pass.

Other stories from Northern Ireland...

When David started to minister freelance in Northern Ireland in 1953, the message that he carried was not held by the majority of believing Christians in the country. The three mainline UK Pentecostal movements were present in Northern Ireland and God had really used these movements to build His Church but the prominent teaching in the country was the evangelical, reformed faith of Presbyterianism. It was in the 1950s that the Free Presbyterians under the leadership of the Rev. Ian Paisley came into prominence in Northern Ireland. They took Northern Ireland by storm; but they were anti-Pentecostal in belief and practice.

Another dimension of the church scene in Northern Ireland, in the 1950s and 60s was the Charismatic Renewal movement and their message regarding the things of the Holy Spirit and divine healing. In later years this message was further promoted in Full Gospel Businessmen's meetings held around the country. Some in the Protestant community not only found the message difficult to accept but also the involvement of Catholics in these church movements. Added to this was the increasing influence in Northern Ireland of the healing revival evangelists from America.

David started his freelance ministry in Northern Ireland in a situation which was mixed; some were open to the full gospel message that he carried, but the majority would have been against it. So, in stepping out, David demonstrated much courage and faith to pursue his vision of Christians living in the abundance of God. As I wrote earlier in this book, in the years after 1953, few people had the openings into so many churches, mission halls, conferences, revival campaigns and homes as David in both Northern Ireland and Great Britain.

Pastor Billy Irvine from Ava Street, Belfast, told me of being at a meeting in Lisburn and David was the speaker. He gave an appeal for people to come forward to be baptised in the Holy Spirit. Billy said that he went forward and was filled instantly. Pastor Billy is still living in the experience and has encouraged many over the years to seek for the same.

During my research for this book, I spent time with Lexi Johnson who met David at the Revival Centre in Ballymena in 1958. This church came out of the Revival meetings that James White had held in the town in 1954. Lexi told me how faithful and committed David was to the Revival Centre in the ministry and teaching he brought to the fellowship.

On one occasion David came to the fellowship for six months, preaching in every Sunday and mid-week service in that period. On one occasion, Lexi remembered David speaking on the '*eyes of our understanding*' being opened by the Holy Spirit. Lexi was personally challenged by the Word and prayed, and God answered his prayer.

During some further meetings that David was having at the Ballymena Revival Centre, a need for leadership was identified in the Bethel Temple, Portglenone. This was in 1968. David approached a couple and asked them to go and lead the prayer meeting there. They went and the church is now led by the son of that couple, Pastor Norman Worthington. Pastor Worthington said this about David: "He never compromised with the Holy Spirit. He brought Pentecost into smaller churches in Northern Ireland and it was accepted." Pastor Worthington openly acknowledged that David imparted something into his life and that this has been evidenced with the way God has used him in ministering healing. On one visit to Cuba, Pastor Norman, after praying in the name of Jesus, saw a blind person healed and someone come out of their wheelchair.

David would visit this church in Portglenone at different convention times. Pastor Norman told me of a personal experience he had of the Holy Spirit at one of these convention times; "David was speaking, and the Holy Spirit came down. It was an awesome experience. It was like liquid silk, coming right down over me."

Emily told me about another meeting at Pastor Worthington's church in Portglenone. At the end of David's ministry, he called the young people out for prayer. From that meeting, as Emily said, "A lot of ministry came out of that meeting." Two of the young girls later married and became wives of pastors; one in England and another in Australia. A young man who was prayed for in that meeting went out to Australia and became a pastor.

Pastor Walker Gorman remembers a meeting in Donaghadee where David started to sing the song, '*Keep me true Lord Jesus, Keep me true...'* Pastor Walker said, "There was such an anointing. The song touched our souls. We sang it for at least 20 minutes. David was playing his accordion. I had never felt an anointing like that before or since. The anointing was on him. It was distinct."

In David and Emily's Christmas letter of 2006, David wrote, "In January 2007 it will be 55 years since I left Bible College in Wales and commenced full-time ministry for my precious Lord. I tell myself and others that we never get old, we only get older. We thank God for His goodness and faithfulness across the years."

Reflection...

Jesus said, *'...unless a grain of wheat falls into the earth and dies, it remains alone; but if it dies, it bears much fruit.'* (John 12:24 NASB). David Greenow believed and lived by Romans 6:8: he had died with Jesus and was raised to live for Jesus. He disciplined himself by John 12:24 and Romans 6:8. I trust that the last few chapters have highlighted the fruit that came from the life of David Greenow. The fruit of people coming to faith in the Lord Jesus Christ and receiving the gift of the Holy Spirit; then those same people, whether in a local or international setting, going on to bear fruit in their own lives to the glory of God. Paul the apostle wrote about following his example. I think we could say, follow the example of David Greenow and live by John 12:24 and Romans 6:8. The secret of fruitfulness: die to your own ways and ambitions and be raised to a life in the Lord Jesus Christ.

CHAPTER FIFTEEN
The Glory People...

I first came across *The Glory People* when I lived in the West Midlands. It was through a friend, Paul Hinks. Paul, his wife Shirley, and his in-laws, would have attended Glory meetings in Newark, Nottinghamshire. Paul told me of his first visit to Newark. He went into the meeting agitated and upset because they were late. The meeting had started and there were people marching around the meeting hall. A lady, who didn't know Paul, broke ranks and came over to Paul and put her arms around him. In Paul's words, *'the heaviness that was on me just lifted off and the love of God flowed into my heart and I went on and enjoyed the meeting.'*

Who are the Glory People?

"The Glory People are a group of Fellowships who have been pioneering the move for Revival in the United Kingdom for 50 years. It all started in 1948 as a result of the Lord anointing a Newark businessman Henri Staples. The ministry that the Lord gave to Henri touched lives in every part of Great Britain and changed many thousands of people. He held meetings throughout the UK and in northern Europe.

The Lord anointed him to minister on the Fruits of the Spirit, and in particular the Joy, which was not obvious in the Church at the time. Ostracised by the established Church he was forced to start an organisation, 'Henri's Evangelical Revival Association'. However, the meetings became known as Glory Meetings because the Glory (Presence) of God was so strong in the meetings. Henri insisted that he had a John the Baptist ministry, that he was the forerunner of a greater move of God. How he would have rejoiced to see the general outpouring of joy that is overtaking the Church in these days. He would have encouraged us all by saying what he often said in his latter years; 'I've had my day, now it is your day to spread the Glory of God - It's in you, Brother, It's in you, Sister. Dare to be strong and do exploits for our God.' Henri went to Glory aged 85 years in 1992 after 40 plus years travelling and evangelising the UK with this Gospel of love."[39]

In the book 'The Glory Way,' Bruce Hyatt writes this in the introduction; "The story of the Glory Way is about a group of people touched by the finger of God. It centres on Newark in Nottinghamshire, the home of a most unusual couple, Henri and Connie Staples. The narrative begins in 1948, although its roots go back very much further. They are Pentecostal. Beyond that they cannot be pigeon-holed. The fact of the matter is, the Glory Way has been a sovereign work of God."[40]

Henri and Connie were laughed at and criticised. Christians were told not to go to their meetings; but people did go, and they met with God. They were not a denomination but ministered in churches as invited and would hold meetings in public halls across the UK. They didn't call themselves the Glory People; others did that. People came to their meetings and said, 'This is the Glory of God.'

There are many testimonies from the Glory meetings which I could include; but I have chosen this one from a visitor to meetings at Portglenone, Northern Ireland; "We thoroughly enjoyed the meetings

39 See www.glory-people.org
40 Hyatt (2001), 'The Glory Way.' New Wine Press, England.

at Portglenone, although we were only able to be there one day. Over twenty years ago God gave me a vision of how His people should praise and worship Him when they meet together. Let me say that I saw that vision fulfilled in Portglenone that afternoon. All the people standing with uplifted hands praising God, also the glory march round the room. There were no hymn books, no long sermons coming from the man at the front, but praise God, we were all in it. This is exactly how I saw it in the vision, so God's way is the Glory Way."[41] David Greenow was one of the ministers at that Convention in Portglenone. There is a picture from the Convention which shows David doing the 'liberty march around the platform.'

Who was Henri Staples?

Again, quoting from the Glory People website... "Henri was born into a family of Methodist lay preachers in 1907 near Newark Nottinghamshire, England.

He was saved in the Methodist Church as a young man. He went to the Jeffreys brothers' meetings in Mansfield in the 1920s, saw many miracles, was greatly blessed, and met Connie, his wife.

He became a manager for Curry's Electrical in the 1930s; business became his god. He started his own shops in 1939; Henri's Radio and six others.

Henri attended the Smith Wigglesworth Meetings in Preston in the 1930s with his family and was filled with the Spirit but not completely set free. After much prayer and fasting by Connie his wife, Henri was playing the piano in a 'dead' Pentecostal prayer meeting in 1948. While Henri was playing the final hymn, God moved on him powerfully.

---

41 The Glory News no 32. Magazine published by The Glory People.

Henri was slain in the Spirit, fell off the piano stool, began holy rolling, speaking in tongues and was filled with joy. He couldn't speak English for a week and was overwhelmed with love.

God called them to pioneer for revival in the church. They started open-air meetings in Mansfield Market Place in the 1950s. Many were saved, healed and set free. He sold all his businesses and started to travel for God: as he said, *'Blazing a trail for revival.'*

God moved spontaneously in the singing, giving many new choruses with a mighty anointing. People began to dance in the meetings in the 1950s and, because the churches had never seen it before, Henri was ostracised for being too free."[42]

Henri and Connie preached, with others who gathered around them, the four-fold Gospel: Jesus Saviour, Healer, Baptiser and Coming King. One of Henri's favourite sayings was, *'This Gospel Works.'* A further dimension to the ministry of Henri and Connie was praise and joy in the Holy Spirit.

On one occasion a friend of Henri Staples pointed out to him that God has a three-legged stool of 'righteousness and peace and joy in the Holy Ghost.' (Romans 14:7) Hyatt writes; "So often the Christian Church has majored on righteousness and peace and has thought that this was enough; but it has lacked a clear expression of joy. The Lord raised up the Glory Way to put the joy leg back."[43]

One man was heard to exclaim after a meeting; 'Well, whatever else you might say, there's no doubt about it, these people really know how to praise the Lord!' Their meetings were full of joy. The songs that were sung had simple tunes and lyrics. Songs like:

---

42 See www.glorypeople.org
43 Hyatt (2001), 'The Glory Way.' New Wine Press, England.

It's setting me free, this Holy Ghost power,
It's setting me free, this very hour,
It's flooding my soul
It's making me whole,
It's setting me free, free, free this Holy Ghost power.

I'm getting ready for the marriage feast,
Yes I am.
I'm getting ready for the marriage feast,
Glory to the Lamb.
We will sing and shout up there,
In that city built four-square,
I'm getting ready for the marriage feast,
Yes I am.

Roy Turner was the *Graham Kendrick* of the Glory Way movement. He wrote many of the songs that were sung and was involved in the worship and praise at the Glory meetings. Many don't realise this; but the song, '*All over the world, God's Spirit is moving,*' was written by Roy Turner, who, as I have said, was used by God musically in the Glory meetings.

CHAPTER SIXTEEN
David's Ministry with The Glory People...

It was at a mission in South Wales that David first met Henri Staples. This is what David wrote about that first meeting and his following experiences with the Glory Way...

"During the mid-fifties we began to hear of times of spiritual refreshing being experienced somewhere in Nottinghamshire. Then we heard further that the services were called 'Glory meetings,' and that the channels being used were brother Henri along with his wife Connie.

There was a lot of difficulty accepting the term '*Henri's Glory meetings.*' The critics were quick to say that they did not want anything to do with '*Henri's Glory.*' Henri would say that it is '*God's Glory*'; Amen. However, the reports of blessing persisted, and we discovered that the blessing location was Newark. People visited Newark and came back with glowing testimonies. Some had difficulty in accepting the reports; all kinds of rumours were flying around.

News of this refreshing continued. In 1958 I was in Wales for meetings at Llwynhendy. We were praying and believing for revival and were busy with our own programme, when a brother who came to our meetings said that he and his wife had been to the Newark Glory meetings, and he gave us accounts of them. He talked so much about these Glory meetings that we were probably rather annoyed by this repeated news of blessing. What did these folks have that we didn't have? I had been tremendously affected by what was called 'the latter rain visitation' in 1951 in Wales. There was a great move of the Spirit that impacted many lives for good.

Then I arrived in Ireland in March 1952 and some of the blessing of the 1951 visitation was moving there. Many fasted and prayed and in 1954 the hand of God moved in a big way, so much so that multitudes found Jesus as Saviour, Healer, Baptiser and Miracle-worker. There was a tremendous sense of the presence and power of God in every gathering. What, then, had these Glory folks that we didn't have?

The day came when Bob Nicholls and some of the Glory team came to South Wales for a holiday. The brother who was always on about the Glory Way asked if they could come where we were for some meetings and fellowship. This was the test, and I can remember discussing with the leading brother as to whether we should receive these Glory folks. We decided that we should and then we would see and be able to judge for ourselves what we thought of it all.

They came and there was much blessing in the first couple of services, and then we heard that Henri himself was on his way down from Newark to join the team. I remember preparing to meet him; after all, we had heard so much concerning him. He arrived and, throwing his arms around me said, '*I do love you, brother.*' I was totally disarmed, and Henri and the team won our hearts completely and great blessing resulted. There seemed to be such a ring of reality about everything they did, and there was such a beautiful flow, nothing forced, in the testimony, ministry and song as they sang 'If ever a time we needed the Lord, we surely need Him now...', and other anointed songs.

Henri said something that first night in 1958 that I have never forgotten and have often quoted since: '*If we love one another, everything else will work out all right.*' I remember thinking, 'How true!' I had experienced much blessing and witnessed God's power in action; but here was an emphasis on, and an experience of, love that I had never encountered before. I remember going to embrace brother Henri after that first meeting and the anointing upon him was of love. I certainly felt it.

The next year was my first visit to the Newark Glory meetings, and what a blessing I received! It was August convention time and there was a glorious atmosphere of love, joy, peace and praise. I had been missioning in the south of Ireland and I felt discouraged and exhausted. Brother Henri called me out in the first meeting and seated me at the front. No one touched me as I sat and wept; and the renewing love of God flowed into me through the brothers and sisters around me. I was revived, Hallelujah! There was a precious flowing together in love, joy and peace. I have never forgotten the end of the final evening when they cleared the floor of the seating and danced and sang: '*Life is wonderful, oh, so wonderful, Life is wonderful now to me. I let Jesus in, He changed everything. Life is wonderful now.*'"

It was my privilege to visit the Newark Glory meetings several times after that. I had the joy of taking part in many of the gatherings in Newark and in different parts of the country where the Glory team ministered. Emily and I along with thousands of others will ever be grateful that we came under the influence of the Glory ministry.

I have since been in a fellowship team with other brothers, preaching and serving the Lord for well over thirty years. We found we could work together in an ongoing relationship. I am convinced that so much of this is due to the bonding of the love of Jesus which we found in the Glory meetings. There was such heart-warming reality about Henri's ministry and the whole church needs this '*baptism of love*' which he spoke of. Certainly, my life and thousands of others were impacted by the Glory move of God; and I have never been the same since. Praise God!

In 1969 the Troubles began in Ireland. By 1972 there was tremendous hate and hurt because of the situation. Henri was in Fleetwood, Lancashire, and I, with friends, made our way over. My heart was hurting with the Northern Ireland problems, but I had an unforgettable time in the meetings as the love of God flowed. In one service, I experienced what I have likened to standing under a waterfall; but this was a *lovefall*, for Jesus' love was pouring down all over me. Hallelujah!

There was so much experienced in those meetings and through the Glory ministry that could never be forgotten by those who were there: the loving welcome and acceptance, the tears of repentance, joy and devotion as people felt the reality of Jesus and His love, the inspiring testimonies and uplifting ministry, relationships being restored or strengthened, hearts overflowing, faces shining, anointed and exuberant singing and dancing unto the Lord.

Henri would say, '*This gospel works. It's the love!*' We had a foretaste of heaven. Family members and friends were changed and blessed by the heart reality that pervaded the atmosphere. Meetings often concluded with the singing of '*Hail Saviour, Prince of Peace,*' or '*God be with you till we meet again.*' Then we left to face whatever the future days might bring, lifted in heart and boosted in our faith, for brother Henri reminded us that, because of Jesus, '*Every day is a good day, but some days may be better than others.*'

Only eternity will reveal how far-reaching the influence of the Glory ministry has been. I for one can gladly testify that my life has been touched and transformed and I am extremely thankful that this love, joy and peace ever reached me, ever came my way. Truly, these were times of refreshing from the presence of the Lord. Thank you, Jesus. Thank God for the Glory."[44]

---

41 Hyatt (2001), 'The Glory Way.' New Wine Press, England.

I have quoted David's contribution in the book, '*The Glory Way*' in full because it does show something of David's heart. When he was in Bible school, he had an experience of the Holy Spirit that made him seek the presence and power of the Holy Spirit constantly in his life thereafter. God was faithful to David by bringing him in touch with the *Glory People*. Also, we see something of David's honesty and humility. He was initially cautious on meeting with Henri Staples and his team but quickly came to realise that the Lord was moving through this group and so he put himself in the place to receive for himself. He was so unlike the disciples of Jesus who wanted to stop others delivering people.

In the Glory News no 16, there is this interesting article; '*Revival at Hereford.*' I am going to quote it in full...

"It was a weekend in August 1959, that David Greenow paid his second visit to Newark and brought along his brother Glyn. Glyn was just at that age when the excitement of life in the world held out its greatest attraction, but the weekend he spent in the Glory Meetings at Newark really settled that; for Glyn was richly blessed in his soul and set on fire for God. His brother David, realising the power and blessing in the Glory Meetings, took back home with him to Hereford a couple of *Glory tapes*. The next thing he did was to listen to these recordings and immediately the move was on. The Spirit fell on several of these young folk as they heard the tape, and before very long there was quite a stir among older Christians too.

It was shortly after this that Henri was visiting Stafford to hold Glory meetings. There we were surprised to see a large coach-load of people from Hereford gathered with us. They were a tonic to our souls and we just praised God more than ever at the evidence of a mighty move of the Holy Spirit. Hallelujah!

The next thing these spiritual commandos did was turn their attention to a small neighbouring town, Kington. There was no real witness in this place and the *Teddy boys and girls* roamed the streets. A disused cinema was hired and the meetings were commenced. It was an uphill fight, but God was pleased to bless the venture. Souls have been saved, the sick healed and many set gloriously free in the wonder working Name of Jesus.

David continues to travel the country taking deliverance meetings wherever there is an open door, but the work in Kington goes on, in the capable hands of Stan Powell and the Glory Band from Hereford." [45]

In another particular Glory News David Greenow is mentioned in an article written by Jean Smith from Halifax. Jean says, "My husband was invited to the Glory meeting at Bradford and the children and myself went along with him. Although my husband seemed to like it, I thought it was silly and longed for the old way. What was the use of singing choruses over and over again? Eventually we all went along to one of Henri's meetings at Leeds, but it had no effect on me. I still did not enjoy it.

Then on Whit Sunday, 1963, dear brother David Greenow came along. I shall never forget that glorious message he gave. He called me out saying, *'I know God has something for this sister.'* He prayed over me and asked God to give me the desire of my heart. At the time I wished the floor would open and I could drop through, as I felt a fool, but I had to obey the voice of the Lord.

On the Monday night it happened. Yes, I got the glory in my soul, so much so, that I had to wake my husband. I was singing, shouting, speaking in tongues and praising the Lord all night. It was a grand Glory meeting; my heart was free and full to overflowing. After all my bondage it was like a river of joy flowing through me. Praise the Lord!" [46]

---

45 The Glory News no 16. Magazine published by The Glory People.
46 The Glory News no 34. Magazine published by The Glory People.

In a further Glory News, there is this testimony from Gwen Sparks. Gwen had been to Glory meetings prior to their starting in Norwich. She writes, "We started our own Glory Meetings in Norwich and they were a real blessing to me, but still I didn't enter into the fullness of the blessings. Then David and Glyn Greenow came to minister; and I was filled with the Holy Ghost. It was the most wonderful experience in my life. I do thank God for a *Glory baptism*. Now I can really enter into the Spirit in the meetings, and I find it is a joy unspeakable and full of Glory."[47]

The following story is of a visit David made to a lady, Cynthia, following a meeting at Evesham. Cynthia had found it strange and unusual but realised that these *Glory people* had something. She said, "On the Wednesday following our visit to Evesham, brother David Greenow came to our home with his tape recorder and played some of Henri's Glory tapes. We had a wonderful time; and when they were finished, David pointed to me, saying that God would baptise me with the Holy Ghost. He laid his hands on me and I felt the power of God go right through me. I fell to the floor under the power of God... I began to speak in other tongues as the Spirit gave me utterance and, when I came to myself, I was full of the power, so much I couldn't stand on my feet. I was two hours glorifying God in the Spirit. Hallelujah!"[48]

David wrote articles for the Glory News. In one magazine his article was headed; "*God's Day of Visitation*", but the sub-heading was, "*A Spontaneous Message recorded in a Glory Meeting by David Greenow.*"[49] The magazine would have been published sometime around 1959/1960. David had already experienced three visitations from God: first, when he was in Bible school in the early 1950s; secondly, the James White revival in Belfast; and, thirdly, the Revival Mission in Portadown in 1955/56. I say this to emphasise this truth: David knew what a move of God looked like.

47 The Glory News no 40. Magazine published by The Glory People.
48 The Glory News no 40. Magazine published by The Glory People.
49 The Glory News no 12. Magazine published by The Glory People.

In this spontaneous message, David said this; "This is a visitation from God. Glory be to God. You can put your old religion on the scrap heap, and let's start living for God."

An important challenge was given by David; "You know: when men hear truth, someone said their attitude towards it determines all their future; and your attitude to what God is doing in these days will determine all your future. Some thought that the Glory Way was crazy, wild and just noise. Some thought that Henri himself was mad." In the article David mentioned the general response to Jesus when He came: 'but many never recognised what God was doing.'

The appeal from David was this; "Oh friends, we need to pray that God will grant spiritual discernment in these days. How we need to pray that the eyes of God's people will be open to that spiritual discernment, that we may see and that we may recognise, that we may perceive the thing that God is doing in these days."

In another Glory News David's article was headed *"Revival Fires are Burning in My Soul."* "Christianity is God living in us" writes David, and he mentions the vision that is pushing him forward, "My whole desire now is to please my blessed Lord, winning souls to the Saviour, healing the sick in His Name and helping to carry the blessing of this great Salvation to all men, everywhere."[50]

A further article that David wrote for The Glory News was titled, *"God's Gifts are Positive,"* and was based on 2 Timothy 1:7; *"For God hath not given us the spirit of fear; but of power, and of love, and of a sound mind."*

On the truth of power, David wrote, "This word 'power' is from the Greek word dunamis, from which we get our English words dynamite, dynamo and dynamic. Glory to God, brother and sister! Every Spirit-filled believer has received this heavenly dynamite and

---

50 The Glory News no 16. Magazine published by The Glory People.

has had placed within them this spiritual dynamo which causes them to become dynamic. Hallelujah."[51]

David Willows, the nephew of Henri Staples, told me this story about David's ministry with the '*Glory People.*' Outreach meetings were being held in Southwell, Nottinghamshire. At one of the meetings David made specific contact with a young woman, Sue Maulson, in the congregation who had glandular fever, rheumatics in her knees and was nearly completely paralysed.

Sue wrote; "For one, at the age of nineteen, who had been in the habit of rushing about in top gear, to be reduced to crawling along at a snail's pace, I did not take kindly to it and I felt very sorry for myself." David came down from the platform and prayed for her. "The power of God swept through her body. She got off her chair and started to dance."[52]

David Willows told me; "It was the last thing she could do; but with someone on either side of her she started to move. Within a short period of time, the young woman was running around the room shouting her praise to God. She had been completely delivered and never suffered again from that illness."

Through attending Glory meetings and conventions, David formed friendships and met fellow evangelists who would eventually form the International Gospel Outreach. David wrote, "The Glory meetings brought a lot of people together from all over the nation: the Camerons from Peterhead and the Pimlots from Norwich met at Newark. It helped to bring us together in the first place, and it certainly helped us to relate and keep us together over the years." David acknowledged the 'melting and bonding' that took place between evangelists who attended the Glory meetings; and some of these evangelists established IGO in 1967. The story of the forming of the International Gospel Outreach (IGO) is told in Chapter 18.

51 The Glory News no 34. Magazine published by The Glory People.
52 The Glory News no 48. Magazine published by The Glory People and Hyatt (2010) 'the Glory Way.'

CHAPTER SEVENTEEN
Barbara Massie...

David's connection with the Massie family started in 1942. David wrote in one of his newsletters... "On May 25th, 1942, I received the Lord Jesus as my personal Saviour, a wonderful and blessed day. I came to know the Saviour under the ministry of a Scottish Pastor, W. Massie in the city of Hereford, England.

"Pastor Massie was a mighty man of God. He was an apostle and church planter and opened many areas in the north of Scotland to Pentecost for the first time. The family moved to Stafford, England in 1947."

David writes, "I entered Bible College in Penygroes, South Wales in January 1950, and found that one of the students was a certain Miss Barbara Massie. It was of interest to me because on May 25th, 1942, I had a very personal encounter with the Lord Jesus in which I passed from spiritual death unto life. The minister in that service was Pastor W.W. Massie, who was Barbara's father."[53]

In May 1951 the College experienced a visitation of the Holy Spirit. I told the story in chapter 4 through the words of Barbara herself. Now we will use David's own words describing what happened in May 1951. "There were two pastors from Wales who had spent some years ministering in the States and Canada, and had been greatly affected by what was then called '*the latter rain anointing.*' These brothers

---

53 "O River of God: A Tribute to the Prophetic Life and Ministry of Barbara Massie." 2008.

came to the Bible College to share their hearts with us, students and staff; and we experienced the Holy Spirit in latter rain visitation in a way never to be forgotten. After they had ministered God's Word, we felt a tremendous and a deep repentance toward God and each other. We came forth from that time with an awareness of the current moving of the Holy Spirit in revival on the earth. Sister Barbara, and any of us who experienced this, were never the same again."[54]

David and Barbara ministered together in the year following, 'in missions and special services, which often knew rich times of anointing and Divine visitation.'[55]

Barbara came to Northern Ireland and spoke at the Plaza meetings in Portadown, but this was after the twenty months of revival meetings that David had led. Following the revival meetings at the Plaza a church was formed and it was with this church that Barbara Massie came to minister. David said that "she brought a ministry that had both clarity and relevance."[56]

In February and March 1960, David and Barbara Massie took over an old cinema in Kington, Herefordshire for six weeks of evangelistic outreach. This was not David's first visit to the town. David, with some glory people from Hereford, came to the town towards the end of 1959.

Barbara writes: "That old cinema was so dirty inside it was impossible to clean! Apart from the Holy Ghost, the only fire we had was a solid fuel stove, which (when it felt like it) belched out more smoke than what went up the chimney."[57] Let me tell you two stories from these revival meetings.

Mary, a seventeen-year-old girl from a mental asylum, was powerfully healed during this evangelistic outreach. Mary was brought by her

---

54, 55, 56, 57 "O River of God: A Tribute to the Prophetic Life and Ministry of Barbara Massie." 2008.

mother to the meetings in the cinema. Barbara Massie recollects; "One night while we were singing, Mary started running up and down the aisle screaming, 'I'm healed. I'm healed. I'm healed.' Her mother, afraid that her daughter was going to become violent and not understanding what Mary her daughter was saying, rushed forward and took her home and put her to bed (without her usual tranquilizers). Mary slept well and woke in the morning bright and alert. She returned to the cinema that night. The change in Mary was miraculous and her healing and deliverance was a great testimony for the Lord in the town."[58]

One night in a service after her miraculous experience, Mary had a vision of Jesus. David was praying. Mary stood up and came running to Barbara Massie. Throwing her arms around Barbara she said, "Oh, Sister Barbara, I've seen Jesus. Jesus is here." Mary was given the microphone and said, "I was sitting by the old stove that smokes, ready to bow my head for prayer, when a shadow fell across me. I thought somebody was standing there and wanted to come in; so, I stood up, but nobody passed. When I looked up, I saw Jesus standing there."

Mary had been in an asylum since she was fifteen and didn't know anything about the Bible. She was asked to describe the person she had seen, and her description was exactly as Jesus is described in Revelation 1:13-16. Mary continued, "I looked at Him and He looked at me, not at anyone else, just at me. Then He smiled, and I saw all of heaven in His smile. Everything I ever needed of joy, peace, forgiveness – everything – was in His smile. And I suddenly felt I had everything in the world I would ever need for all of my life. Then He backed away, came up and stood by me and was gone."[59]

Through Mary's vision of Jesus a number of people were saved that night in the service. They knew that there was no way Mary could have known these things by herself.

Another story from these revival meetings in Kington concerned a

58-59 "O River of God: A Tribute to the Prophetic Life and Ministry of Barbara Massie." 2008.

young man named Wyndom, a coal merchant in the town. Barbara writes: "(I) could feel the burden that was upon his soul. When the service was over, he just sat there staring as if he had been hit with a brick. I walked down to him, took him by the hand and led him to the altar. Kneeling there, he continued to stare straight ahead, and then soon began to confess his sin. Although Wyndom received salvation that night, the conviction of the Holy Spirit remained mightily upon him. Returning the next night, he still seemed to be in a daze. With the life he had led, he couldn't understand or believe that God would forgive him and lift that burden of sin, and for forty-eight hours he walked in that dazed state. Suddenly, on the third night, the joy of the Lord hit him and he began dancing. He danced that night as hard for the Lord as he had danced for the old devil and the whole cinema danced and rocked with him. So great was the change in Wyndom that one woman … came to the cinema to see what had happened to him. She used to be terrified of Wyndom and would leave her house when he and his father came to make a (coal) delivery. One morning she was home when he walked in, his coat and face black with coal dust. She said to him, 'Oh, I'm so glad they had a change of boys. I couldn't put up with that fellow anymore. He was so terrible with all that cursing and swearing. What did they do with him?' Turning to her, he said, 'Oh, missus, I'm him. I went to that old cinema down the road, and God saved me, and I don't swear and curse anymore.' She said, 'Where is it? I'll go there and see. What God can do for you, maybe He can do for my son!'"[60]

When Wyndom was water-baptised, his mother went into the river with him. She was riddled with rheumatism and was afraid of water, especially cold water. She was happy with the change in her son but afraid he would return to his old ways of stealing and drinking but was determined to go into the river with him. Barbara Massie relates, "With his old pals laughing on the bank, Wyndom and his mother both waded into the water. That frail little woman walked in behind her son, ready herself to go under in baptism.

---

60 "O River of God: A Tribute to the Prophetic Life and Ministry of Barbara Massie." 2008.

When they lifted her up out of the waters, her arms shot up straighter than ever. In that cold water, every bit of rheumatism left her body; and she danced her way out of the river: healed!"[61]

Earlier in this chapter I mentioned the visitation that David and Barbara experienced at a Bible school in South Wales. Barbara had been a student at the school and was back for a weekend reunion. During this visitation, the wife of the Principal, Mrs Rowlands, received a dream (see chapter 4). The dream was of the school being a tree of glory and the branches were like sparks going out from the tree and that there were names on the sparks. Mrs Rowlands shared this dream with Barbara as her name was one of the sparks.

I am sure that David Greenow was also one of the named sparks. I believe that the story we are telling in this book gives witness to the dream of Mrs Rowland. Isn't it interesting that one of the groups that David became involved with were called, The Glory People.

What about Barbara Massie? The few stories I have mentioned in this chapter highlights the anointing that she carried. After that experience in May 1951, Barbara went on, under the Lord's guidance, to minister in the UK, USA and Europe. "In the male dominated British Pentecostal environment, sister Barbara was a courageous pioneer, following and fulfilling the call of God to evangelistic and prophetic ministry."[62]

In the USA she shared ministry with many anointed evangelists and saw God use her, especially in the prophetic.

61-62 "O River of God: A Tribute to the Prophetic Life and Ministry of Barbara Massie." 2008.

CHAPTER EIGHTEEN

The International Gospel Outreach...

The International Gospel Outreach (IGO) was founded in 1967 with this motto – '*Recognising the whole church, Reaching out to the whole world.*' David became the first president, a role he occupied for thirty years before handing over to Kingsley Armstrong in 1997.

The IGO grew out of the *Southsea Revival Crusade with* a group of like-minded pastors and evangelists who wanted to work together to fulfil the great commission to go into all the world and preach the gospel. Many of these Christian leaders had first met at Glory meetings and conferences. David wrote, "The Glory meetings brought a lot of people together from all over the nation. The Camerons from Peterhead and the Pimlots from Norwich met at Newark."[63]

One of these men was Bob Searle. He met David for the first time at a convention with the Glory People in 1961 in Newark. Bob writes: "In August 1961 we (Bob and his wife, Ann, and two children, Debby and Cathy) went to a Glory Convention in the Technical College in Newark. It was packed out with people praising God. David Greenow was one of the main preachers there. He dedicated Cathy and prayed for Ann, who had been seeking the Baptism of the Spirit for a long time. I had already been baptised in the Spirit at a Glory meeting in Reading. As we went on to the platform, while Ann was holding Cathy, (a three-month-old baby), she got the baptism of the Holy Spirit. Ann fell backwards and dropped Cathy who was caught by a lady nearby."

63 Armstrong (2007), "IGO International Gospel Outreach: The First 40 Years." Barratt Ministries Publications

After this initial meeting, the relationship between Bob Searle and David Greenow grew. They would meet up at further Glory meetings and when Bob started Glory meetings in Portsmouth, David, with his brother Glyn, were frequent speakers. Other people became involved with Bob Searle; Ron and Margaret White from Southampton and Cecil Stewart from Northern Ireland. Bob and David travelled together overseas holding missions in Belgium, Holland, Denmark and Sweden.

Bob Searle wrote in *IGO International Gospel Outreach: The First 40 Years,* "Soon we were having tent crusades on Southsea common during the summers. Sometimes the meetings would go on well after midnight. They were great rejoicing times. One man, a psychiatrist, used to come and try to fathom us out; as he stood in the doorway one evening, God healed him of deafness."[64]

Also, in this publication, David writes about the role of Bob and Ann in these early days and how relationships that started in the Glory meetings developed: "Bob and Ann organised the conferences and pulled us all closer together. We came to Southsea and had a tent and caused a bit of a stir. In fact, I remember the police arriving as a response to seeing strange things happening. They were confused by what was going on. There were also hundreds, if not thousands, affected by the 'open-airs' in Southsea. I stayed with Bob and Ann in their home and the bond gradually developed."

The *Portsmouth Glory Group* became the *Southsea Revival Crusade* and, in 1967, became The *International Gospel Outreach (IGO).*

In his Christmas pamphlet, December 1967, David gave a report on the last Southsea Revival Crusade held during the month of August 1967. He wrote; "Many souls of both young and old registered decisions for Christ during this period. We held 4 - 5 meetings each day with the purpose of reaching men, women, boys and girls with the Gospel." It was following this Crusade that IGO came into existence.

64 Armstrong (2007), "IGO International Gospel Outreach: The First 40 Years." Barratt Ministries Publications

David remembers the formation of IGO. "In 1967, Bob got us all together and there had been discussions regarding formalising into what was to become IGO. He said to me, 'David will be President.' So, Bob organised that as well. I was never one to push myself and to be landed the presidency was a shock but, looking back, it was good for me and a privilege. I did not think of myself as particularly good at relationships and that forced me into it and that was good for me."[65]

IGO conferences were held twice a year. David writes: "The early conferences were particularly blessed. The presence of God was very real. It was like God was vindicating and bonding us together all the more the IGO conferences became central to all that we did. We arranged our preaching trips around the conference. We made sure that we were present; they became very precious. We got exposed to each other's ministries, and that was good for us. As travelling evangelists, we never got to hear the pastor preaching as we were always doing it; so, the conferences were good for us."

David wrote: "The Glory meetings were terrific but there was a lack of something to belong to. IGO pulled people together and organised us." Glyn wrote about IGO in a similar vein to David: "IGO brought people together with a similar mind and similar experiences. The Glory move was fantastic but did not give any kind of structure. IGO brought ministries together and gave us a movement to belong to. We were together and that brought us stability and strength. It gave us recognition with the ordination. It was the network and the relationships that were produced that proved so valuable."[66]

A network of relationships developed through IGO giving opportunity for members to travel and minister in different churches and house fellowships throughout the UK. At one of the conferences, David remembers Glyn having a mighty touch from God. He was so overcome with Spirit-inspired laughter that he had to be carried out of the meeting.

65-66 Armstrong (2007), "IGO International Gospel Outreach: The First 40 Years." Barratt Ministries Publications

David provided able leadership; his gracious manner and gifting brought people together. He was a father-figure to all involved, giving wise counsel and direction as needed. His wide knowledge of many groups and situations across the country proved to be a unifying force. His focus remained on the individual rather than on the organisation, which he saw as a vehicle for preaching the gospel rather than an end in itself.

But we cannot forget Bob Searle. David wrote; "IGO came into being because we needed Bob to organise things. Bob was an amazing organiser. We were travelling all over, and we needed a Bob to get us sorted."

Reflection...

Before going on, I think it would be good to pause and ask the question: What was the influence of IGO and David Greenow in particular, on the lives of men and women?

David Chaudhary wrote this; "For me, IGO began in the 60s with a man called David Greenow. He played a major part in our lives; he invested into us and encouraged us to go into the ministry in the first place. A lot of people are in ministry today because of IGO."

Andy Paget wrote this: "In 1968 I was ordained as IGO's youngest evangelist. What were some of the key truths that 'rubbed off' then and what have I learned since those early days? I've learned from David Greenow that balance is something beautiful and it should not be confused with compromise. From David and Emily, I've learned to appreciate spiritual parenthood and the true nature of ministry."

Rodney Breckon wrote this; "My first contact with IGO was in 1967, at the Southsea tent convention: the guys were there. These were all living by faith, all pioneering in their own ways... Preaching for me was such an effort and I always wondered if I would ever be able to stand up with the same ease as David, with what appeared to be no preparation, but speaking out of the richness of his experience. They all made such an impression on me making me want to be like them one day. David was always for me, the 'wise old man of IGO.'"

David Willows wrote this: "I got to know about IGO in the late 60s. I heard about IGO through David Greenow and was ordained through IGO about 1971. The thing that attracted me to IGO was the need for recognition of ministers. The glory folk did not offer that and were not for it because Henri had been hurt by organised ministerial things. IGO met a need that nowhere else met. During the glory move we were cut off from anything else. David Greenow was such a good mentor, kind and gracious."

Cecil Stewart wrote this: "I remember a tent in Southsea in 1967. Bob and Ann were there, also David and Glyn Greenow. I remember that it was the beginning of a new fellowship of ministers and we all subscribed to the need for such an organisation. I had known David Greenow since I was a teenager. He was the first one to talk about the Baptism of the Holy Spirit and healing."[67]

IGO provided fellowship and covering for all those involved, bringing together diverse ministries and individuals. In its first 30 years, it never advertised itself; but through relationships and people being invited to the Conferences, IGO grew and it is now a worldwide fellowship of ministries taking the whole Gospel to the whole world.

The presidency of IGO was handed over to Kingsley Armstrong, (son-in-law of Bob Searle) and wife Cathy, the baby who was dropped, in 1997. Kingsley wrote this tribute to David in 2007; "As I have observed IGO over the past few years, I have seen things that are good. God gave us David Greenow and we have all been blessed

---

67 The previous five personal references to David can be found in – Armstrong, K.N. (2007) "IGO International Gospel Outreach: The First 40 Years." England: Barratt Ministries Publications.

through his ministry. When he handed over to me ten years ago, people talked in terms of replacement. Where does this replacement theology come from? God builds on the past; He does not replace it. When I think of David, I think of words like grace, understanding, patience, generous, uncritical and flexible. I am very rarely accused of any of those things! When David walks into a room, people can feel grace. David Greenow carries an amazing authority and Apostleship in his life. It is *who he is* and not *what he does* that has made the difference to people."

CHAPTER NINETEEN
Ministry in England and Scotland...

Southampton, England...

Pastor Ron and Margaret White, friends of David and Emily, are the founding leaders of Victory Gospel Church, Southampton. They very kindly sent me this story of their experience with David.

Pastor Ron writes... "Young man, I say unto thee, Arise." Evangelist David Greenow was announcing his sermon to be preached in the 'Oddfellows Hall' in the great city of Portsmouth. The year was 1959. I was just 19 years old and this was the first time that I had met David and his younger brother Glyn.

David had read from Luke 7:11-17; the account of the raising of the dead, the son of the widow of Nain, with the emphasis on the last sentence of verse 14, 'Young man, I say unto thee arise.' I remember sitting there in the front row intently listening to this man of God, also I became aware that every time he referred back to his text he was looking directly at me, 'young man, I say unto thee arise.' He must have repeated his text at least ten times. Anyhow, that's how it appeared to me; for this was divine confirmation of the Lord calling me into ministry. As the meeting ended, David came and sat next to me and gently but firmly spoke to me concerning the call of God upon my life and that he knew that this message that Saturday afternoon was primarily for me.

A few years later in 1964 Margaret and I were married and were attending a small Pentecostal church in the city of Southampton, when suddenly the pastor left the church and moved away to Reading, leaving many discouraged people who also left, leaving those of us who remained (about a dozen people) wondering what to do? Two weeks passed, then the small group that had remained officially asked my wife and me to take over the role of pastors. As we prayerfully considered the matter, I began to hear those prophetic words from Evangelist David Greenow; 'Young man I say unto you arise.' The rest is history!

The little fellowship began to grow again. David Greenow took it upon his heart to encourage and teach us on his very regular visits to the fellowship and brought sound teaching and instruction regarding the operation of the gifts of the Holy Spirit, laying down a good foundation for the work of the growing church.

On regular visits to the church in Southampton, David noticed a very dedicated man who was always serving others in the fellowship in a very practical way, by the name of David Chaudhary, who with his lovely young wife Sushila, were committed to the work. On one of David's phone calls from Ireland, he mentioned to me that I should encourage David Chaudhary to begin to minister the word in the church - easier said than done!

David Chaudhary firmly insisted that his ministry was the ministry of helps! Setting out the chairs, giving out hymn books etc. The phone calls from Ireland continued, each time enquiring 'have you got that Indian brother ministering yet?' I had to say 'no,' but brother Greenow would only urge me on until eventually I managed to get 'the reluctant preacher' to get up and preach in a Saturday night service. The rest is history!

Hallelujah! Rev. David Chaudhary and Sushila, and indeed all four of their amazing children have made a mighty impact for the kingdom of God here in the UK and across the world."

Perth, Scotland...

David had a strong, enduring link with a fellowship in Scotland called Perth Christian Fellowship. The story is told by Pastor Mervyn and Jane Milne.

Pastor Mervyn writes: "Be kindly affectioned one to another with brotherly love; in honour preferring one another. Romans 12:10; *'Them that honour me I will honour.'* (1 Samuel 2:30)

David Greenow's input into my life and that of my wife Jane, when the Lord Jesus called us into full-time service in the mid-1980s, was incalculable. His encouragements, his inspirations, his words of wisdom were all planned by the Lord in His preparation and maturing of us for His purposes in our lives. I will never forget, and the Holy Spirit never lets me forget, David's first words of wisdom which he gave me personally upon embarking on this ministry calling. He said to me; "Never wander away from the Cross; and remember that the Cross is not a place of negotiation, but a place of surrender." That God-given word of wisdom has been my saving grace through many trials and testings of my faith. I believe the Lord anointed David with the Spirit of wisdom and understanding and caused him to move widely across the body of Christ bringing God's mind into many situations.

David would often remind me that 'God was with me, that God was for me and that God was in me." What often seemed to me to be passing comments in ordinary, natural conversations, in reflection turned out to be God-inspired words of wisdom. When looking for advice about any given situation of difficulty, David always seemed to have the ability (gifting) to give a word in season. He was a man of peace, often a mediator, in steering us through difficult times.

Through my many faults and failings, David could see, by God's grace, the call of God upon my life and sought to encourage and develop that call, despite the obvious shortcomings in me. In those early days he would remind me that *a call* into full-time service for the Lord was one thing; but for that call to mature and be fulfilled in my life it would only happen through '*Cross*' experiences. These words have been proved to be '*oh so true*' over the years.

Now, after over thirty years in full-time ministry, those early words of wisdom still have their impact upon me: '*The Cross is not a place of negotiation, but a place of surrender.*' Sometimes in difficult and challenging times the only thing that makes sense of it all is when you see the Cross of Jesus Christ and you yield to His will.

David would often telephone or drop a note to me enclosing leaflets that he had printed of his teachings, which were of great help to me. Many times, I would use his printed outlines to preach to my congregation. They were so inspired by God.

As a pastor I had no hesitation nor lack of trust in David's ministry amongst the congregation and our full-time team. David was a '*Kingdom*' man rather than denominational. His loyalty was first to Christ; that's why I could trust him amongst the Lord's people, whom He had bought with His own precious blood. David was used greatly by the Holy Spirit to speak God's word into the hearts of many, the fruit of which has manifested.

Being genuinely a humble man, he never sought to promote himself when amongst us. His only desire, it seemed to me, was that Christ be formed in us.

I'm sure David saw through my immaturity and many faults, which at the time I didn't see, and yet he remained a faithful and true friend throughout the years. He would often recommend that I should connect with different people whom he introduced me to. I think David knew that I needed to broaden my view of the wider body of Christ and develop an appreciation and respect of other giftings and ministries within the body of Christ. For that I am deeply indebted to him.

Whenever in the company of David, either on a one-to-one basis or ministering alongside him in our ministry, David always seemed to impart something of the life of Jesus. Jesus said that *"out of our belly shall flow rivers of life"*: this He spoke of the Holy Spirit. I can truly say this was indeed the case with David. Out of him came a Holy Spirit-anointed ministry of the life of Jesus, which impacted Jane and me personally, as well as the congregation and the People with a Mission Ministries (PWAMM) full-time team.

There was another significant occasion when David was used to bring wisdom and understanding to us. Many who know us and Bill and Marion Kettles, will know that God laid on Bill and Marion and on myself and Jane's heart the message of The Everlasting Covenant; the key to a perfect relationship.

Bill would often say; The Everlasting Covenant is God's plan to build God's house, God's way. When David visited, we would often end up in discussion and sharing of scriptures regarding the Everlasting Covenant. At one point, Bill expressed his frustration at the lack of interest amongst Christians to be taught about the covenant, the oath of God.

David's comment was simply to say; many believers are covenant-blessed but not necessarily covenant-based. In other words, they are caught up in the blessings of the covenant without seeking to be anchored or secured by it. Again, his gracious gifting of wisdom and understanding shone through.

There's no doubt in my mind that, without David's God-inspired ministry into my life, things would have turned out so differently over the thirty years of my ministry. Now, of course, the Lord has used others down through the years to encourage and support us, not least Jane's parents, my father and mother-in-law Bill and Marion Kettles, without whom I would never have met David. Yet I can safely say that David was a mainspring of support; especially in the tender years of coming into the practicalities of a call into full-time ministry.

Of all the things of which David was an example to me, the greatest was that of being a 'worshipper' of the Lord Jesus Christ above all other things. His ministry of the Word and operations in the gifts of the Holy Spirit flowed out of that attitude of worship and submission to Christ. He was a worshipper of the Lord Jesus Christ first and foremost, and to me that was obvious. The Lord honoured him greatly, as David honoured the Lord.

Truly, David Greenow was a gift given to the body of Christ. To God be the glory!"

Jane Milne writes –

"When Marcus approached my husband and me to write something to put into his biography about David Greenow regarding our fellowship, we were honoured, but found it a daunting task. It wasn't daunting in wanting to honour David, but we felt we were such a small part of the many ministries and fellowships that David's ministry touched; and we were humbled to be included. We also do not want to promote Perth Christian Centre and the People with a Mission Ministries, but lift up the name of our Lord and Saviour Jesus Christ, as David would have done.

David Greenow was a life-long friend of mine and of my parents Bill and Marion Kettles, Wellwood Christian Fellowship from the 1950s, and from the late 1970s my husband Mervyn Milne, our four children and all at the Perth Christian Fellowship and People with a Mission Ministries (PWAMM).

He would always say I remember you when you were a little baby.... Well, that baby celebrated turning sixty this year; and I can say that each time David and Emily visited (when she was able to), it was a highlight of blessing to me as well as my parents, the Fellowship at Wellwood and then with us in Perth.

David was a wonderful encourager, a worshipper, a faith-builder, always looking for the best in people. He was prophetic; and every time he came, he would build us up in that most holy faith and re-envision us.

His words would always come at the right time, always confirming the word the Lord had laid on our hearts. He was with us from the beginning of the Perth Christian Centre and People with a Mission Ministries, encouraging and speaking prophetically into situations that would arise, even difficult problems over the years. He was a mediator that could be trusted to seek the Lord for the best outcome for both parties. He had a real gentle spirit.

I remember him prophesying at the beginning of the fellowship and ministry that the ministry would be like the sea. There would be wave upon wave where the Lord would move and add to what the ministry was doing or take us deeper as a people, then the wave would calm down for a while and there would be a consolidation of what had been done, and then another wave would rise again and take us forward into what the Lord had for us, and this is exactly how it has been.

He was always at the end of a phone when we needed him; or if we were able to go and visit him and Emily, he would always be gracious and make time for us, again always full of encouragement from the throne room.

I grew up in the Glory days with David and many other lovely people who the Lord brought our way when I was younger. We knew then about the joy of the Lord and the power in praise. It was a special time which we need to get back to in these troubled days.

We also were involved with IGO, the organisation that David set up to be an encouragement to other Christian leaders and ministries. Perth Christian Fellowship and People with a Mission Ministries grew as an offshoot from Wellwood Christian Fellowship first of all as an intercessory house group that met on a Saturday evening to pray for Perth and the nation for revival, then into a fellowship (not our intention) and a ministry.

This prayer meeting came from a call from the Lord to Merv and me to do a work in Perth in 1985. My parents weren't sure about this, and for a little while there was an estrangement. We were young, and they hadn't felt the same call. They had a real burden and heart for the city of Dundee and, of course, for the nation also. David came and was a wonderful mediator in the midst. Shortly after his visit, we joined forces in the ministry God had called us all to. People with a Mission Ministries is the umbrella for the church and ministry. They are made up of a team of about 65 who are either serving voluntarily or being paid part-time.

Many were called out of highly-paid employment and professions to come and follow the Lord and fulfil the mandate He gave us as part of the body of Christ '*to take My power and presence back to the communities of Scotland.* That is what we try to do via various avenues of ministry, relying upon the Holy Spirit to lead and guide us.

Our main focus is evangelism. We have Challenger buses which go into schools all over Scotland under the curriculum for excellence in teaching what Christians believe. Then there are missions and outreach meetings, working with local ministers and leaders in different parts of Scotland. It has been a very rewarding work. David was with us for the opening of the first phase of the ministry in 1986, and that is where he prophesied about the People with a Mission Ministries being like the sea.

Our new building, which is called the *National Christian Outreach Centre*, opened on the 1st February 2008 and houses the Church, the Mustard Seed Coffee shop and bookshop, Footprints Nursery and the office hub from where everything is coordinated.

David spoke at the opening celebration of the National Outreach Centre. Jane kindly sent me a transcript of the message that David shared on the day. (If you would like a copy of the transcript please contact the author).

Reading the transcript my first thought was – this is David. His heart and his passion and his faith shine through everything he said to the congregation that day. We see his thankfulness and gratitude for prayer; we hear encouraging words, compassionate words to the congregation; we encounter the prophetic and apostolic ministry that David carried. The message is Christ-centred and Calvary focused and we can identify the words of knowledge and wisdom that he shared both for individuals and for the life and ministry of Perth Christian Fellowship. As I wrote above, the message shouts David Greenow. It was faith inspiring, Holy Spirit empowering and Christ glorifying. I would have loved to have been in the meeting. I think I would have experienced a real heart transformation as David shared, under the anointing of the Holy Spirit, God's heart and God's purpose for God's people.

David was known, over the years, for giving some Bible truths in short meaningful statements. This sermon at Perth was no exception. Some of the things David said were –

"No one will ever know the infinite cost of Calvary. No one will ever know."

"Be looking for breakthroughs, new breakthroughs in the supernatural."

"We want to do things in such a way there'll be no regrets in eternity."

"The Holy Spirit, the active agent of the Godhead in this age, is now present to make actual what Calvary purchased for us…Trust the Holy Spirit – we need to do that."

"Let me say, the Holy Spirit is faithful to Calvary. He's the executor of the last will and testament of Jesus Christ."

"I want what Jesus purchased for me to be actual and a living reality in my life."

"There are no impossible cases. God can change lives."

In the message David also shared some stories from his ministry on the island of Ireland.

"I had an invitation lately. I was asked to speak at a conference in Northern Ireland on Spiritual Warfare, not one of my favourite subjects but that was the request. I went. A week or two later I got a phone call, 'Please can we meet you. We heard you at the conference.' So, we made an arrangement to meet. Two big men, I tell you I felt 'poor me!' Big men. I'd heard a little concerning them, but I hadn't heard their testimonies. Men with a strong Catholic background – Republican background.

And one of them, an IRA man – strong IRA man – into prison. Got himself into prison; strong Republican IRA background. The biggest of them began to give me his testimony just sitting there as we had a meal together. Into prison; wife and family left him. Someone came along and pointed him to the Lord Jesus – it was prison ministry. God bless those in prison ministry.

Didn't know or have much understanding of truth and so on, but he knew something had happened in his heart. Came out of prison, a nervous mental wreck. Twelve tablets a day he says he was on. Twelve tablets a day to keep him in any way right at all. Someone said to him, 'You need deliverance.' Didn't know what it was but they got him to a place where he was prayed for. Delivered! Got off the twelve tablets, changed completely. The wife and family came back and today he's in business with this other brother that was with him. They're only three years in business, the Lord's blessing them. Blessing them. What changes, changes. And I've been to their fellowship a couple of times now."

The second story concerns a time when he was ministering in Republic of Ireland.

"I remember being in the south of Ireland labouring many years back, and got so ill that I thought I was going to have to lie down on the road before I got home. I felt so ill. I got home and the thing to do of course is to get into bed and yet I felt, no I'm just going to kneel. I'm just going to kneel at my bedside. I got down, I'll never forget it, I'll never forget it. In a moment it seemed like the Holy Spirit showed me God; and all that the devil had planned laying on me, God had already laid on Jesus; and this did not need to be borne twice. It is already laid on my 'sickness' substitute. I stood up, I'm definitely not receiving it. It wasn't immediate, the answer, but I didn't get into bed. Gradually, gradually, gradually it lifted. Now the same provision, as far as I know, I'm sure – I do know – the same provision has been made for every person through Calvary. Hallelujah!

Now I know that you need some wisdom even after an experience like that. I went for fifty years, never was near a doctor after that, but the time came when I found I needed one. And I found that God can heal through the natural; He can heal through the supernatural. Thank God. I came to thank God for the natural and I found – well, it's just wonderful. Jesus is wonderful. I'm probably in better health than I was ten years ago. Thank the Lord."

David finished the message by saying –

"And everybody says, 'Amen.' And shout it 'Amen,' Hallelujah. Come on, let's give the Lord a clap offering. Mervyn, Mervyn, God bless you. Keep going you're on the right path. Keep going. Thanks for listening. God bless you."

As I have already mentioned, David heart and passion for God and for God's people shouts loud through this message. We see his gratitude to God for all the blessings he had experienced in his life. One of David's favourite sayings was, "we must have an attitude of gratitude." His encouragement for all Christians to seek more of God for themselves and not to settle for anything less shines through in the message. As I read the message, I said, "this is David. God's gift to His Church."

***

These are some of the tributes that I received from people who attend Perth Christian Fellowship and had experienced the ministry of David Greenow.

Ruth Holden: "David Greenow - A gift to the body of Christ. As a child I remember him visiting with his wife Emily at Wellwood Christian Fellowship in Longforgan, by Dundee where my uncle Bill Kettles and my aunty Marion pastored. David would play the accordion and sing and share the precious word of God, and prophesy.

I would fellowship with him at occasional glory meetings and also at Perth Christian Fellowship, FGBMFI[68] and as a People With A Mission Ministries member, it was a privilege! He was such a gentle gentleman, with a simple, profound faith in the Lord Jesus Christ. He was a bold evangelist and such an encourager of the Divine. He brought a humble, simple message of faith in song that led you up to higher plains of refreshing. One wee song was 'I marvel at the wisdom of my God, when I see the little lily pushing up the heavy sod. I marvel at the wisdom of my God."

---

68 FGBMFI – Full Gospel Business Men's Fellowship International. Founded in 1953, with roots in Pentecostalism, FGB-MFI is a fellowship of lay businessmen who meet in local groups called chapters. Their main purpose is to bring interest to the Christian gospel. (Wikipedia).

Betty Robertson: (Ruth's mother), "sister of Bill Kettles was also blessed by the ministry of the Lord Jesus Christ through David Greenow's singing, preaching, and prophesying. This was also in the Glory days, at Wellwood Christian Fellowship, FGBMFI and Perth Christian Fellowship."

Douglas (Dougie) Holden: "I first met David in 1979 at an FGBMFI Men's breakfast, then at Wellwood, PCF and PWAMM. David always wanted to encourage you, strengthen you and speak God's word into you, by the power of the Holy Spirit. He had a big heart for people and the body of Christ."

Graeme Moodie: "David gave me a few prophetic words that for me have been valuable over a long period of time. I think of a particular one. It outlined specifically something that the Lord was going to teach me that would become a helpful change of mindset for me. It had to do with learning the importance and value of the 'now' moment, God's oncoming 'now' in my life. All I can say is that this is literally what happened over a number of years.

The prophecy described a period in my life when God made this very concept part of the way that I think, changing my mindset to one of expectancy towards God, expectancy that His blessings were not something only to hope for in the future, but to expect now, as this 'now moment' truly is the only moment that we live in and experience. The prophecy was very exact and clear, and has been (and is still being) fulfilled. To me it has been a very valuable and encouraging word!

David's prophetic words were very specific, very detailed and always bang on the button. Thank you, Lord, for David's direct, exact, but always wonderfully gentle, ministry!"

David Buchannan: "I did not know David Greenow very well, but I knew him to be a man of God. I attended a meeting and during prayer ministry, I received a clear prophetic message through David giving me a word that I should walk through the door that the Lord had opened. That door was to start dating a young lady who is now my wife of 10 years, with many more years to come. Thank God for David Greenow, who heard from the Lord and was able to relay what He was clearly saying."

Jenny Kettles: "I first met David Greenow in 1981, when he was staying at my late father-in-law Bill Kettles' home in Longforgan. Bill was President of the Dundee Chapter of the Full Gospel Businessmen's Fellowship and David was often invited to be the main speaker. David and his wife Emily had been friends with Bill and his wife Marion for many years.

I was still quite a young Christian at the time, and I was very impressed by David's witness for God; how he spoke of his love for the Lord and his fervour for reaching others with the Gospel. He was a very quietly-spoken man, very gentle and kind, but when he preached from the Word of God, he did it with a boldness and earnestness, often with tears, that really spoke to me, and affected me in my walk with the Lord.

David visited Bill and Marion often, and sometimes Emily came with him and it was good to get to know them both. David would speak at the FGBMFI dinner meetings in Dundee and various other meetings. He also came to Perth for the dedication and opening of Perth Christian Fellowship in 1986 and was a regular visitor there over the years.

David Greenow was a genuine human being and a faithful, honest man of God. His gentle ways and holy fervour for preaching God's Word and obeying the call that God placed on his life was a witness for me, my family, and many others, to the Glory of God."

Jackie Cargin: "Whenever David Greenow came to visit and minister at our church, you knew that a man of God and a father in the faith was among us. I remember David as having a lovely gentle spirit, yet he always brought a powerful and relevant Word from the Lord. What stands out most in my memory of him was that he was a man of prayer, so sensitive to the Holy Spirit, and he was gifted with prophecy. He was truly a great gift to the Church of God, and a privilege to have known him."

Catriona Derrick: "David Greenow always had such a glow and sweet presence of the Lord on him. The anointing of the Lord was obvious, and his manner of ministering made you know it was the Lord speaking directly to you. I remember the last time I saw him was at a conference for People with a Mission Ministries at Aviemore. It was a very special time of refreshing.

"I also remember upstairs in the old Centre, not long after the fellowship started, David was invited for the launch of this new ministry and the fellowship which grew out of it. He was the key guest speaker then as well. There was also a prophet's conference, to which David Willows and David Greenow came with Pastor Merv and a couple of others. I still have the tapes somewhere in my house; great meetings, all brand new to us young Christians, but all treasured memories; and so glad David was so much a part of it, in his wonderful sweet way of ministering the Holy Spirit to the body of Christ. Much missed."

Brenda Arnott: "The lasting memory I have of David Greenow is of a man ruled over by and submitted to the Spirit of God: gentleness, meekness and lowliness was what you encountered when you met him. The Adamic flint had been ground down to powder and even as I recall it, it spurs on a desire for that same spirit of grace and gentleness. For me, Brenda, 2 Samuel 22:36 sums up this other David; '*Thy gentleness hath made me great.*'"

Neil Boddy: "Apart from his excellent Bible teaching, one of my most treasured memories is a word of personal prophecy he spoke over me on one of his last trips to Perth. The Holy Spirit said that I would be involved in evangelism with two distinct weapons - a smile and a song! David was totally unaware that I was the People with a Mission Ministries evangelistic coordinator and choir leader commissioned to share the calling throughout Scotland. The word has been fulfilled on many occasions - to God's glory."

John Cameron: "My memories of David are of a man of humility and sincerity in his walk with the Lord; an encourager, full of Godly wisdom. I had not been a Christian long and I still remember his first advice to me: that, as a farmer, I knew the principle that you have to sow to reap. He said I should sow the promise of Christ in my heart to reap a Godly harvest."

CHAPTER TWENTY
Further ministry...

In Republic of Ireland...

David's ministry in Monaghan, which started in the 1950s, continued in the years following.

Remember, it was in Monaghan where David met the Stewart family. Cecil Stewart told me about meetings held in Monaghan in 1965.

This 1965 mission was specifically linked to Henri's Revival Evangelistic Association. The meetings were held in a tent which a young Cecil Stewart had erected. David, with his brother Glyn, ministered during the second and third weeks of the mission. Cecil Stewart gave this report in a Glory News magazine: "We had only planned for one week, but God was moving and we extended the campaign for three weeks, in spite of circulars distributed by other denominations, warning folk not to attend. Many got mad and told us to get back to Northern Ireland, as we had never been invited, but God was moving and 18 souls accepted Christ and over 15 received the Baptism in the Holy Ghost. Several of these testified that they had been warned not to come."[69]

I spent time with Tommie McCracken talking about David and his ministry in Southern Ireland. He told me two stories that are worth repeating.

---

69 The Glory News no 40. Magazine published by The Glory People

The first is about a time when David was with Frank Bray in Cork. Frank was saved at the James White revival meetings in Belfast in 1954. David and Frank were visiting the '*Upper Room*' fellowship to help with open-air meetings. The meeting had started with some singing, and it was time for David to step forward to preach. As he did that, the crowd moved forward with the intention of throwing David and Frank into the harbour waters! A man, some six-foot tall, came forward and stood between the crowd and David and held his hand up. David preached for 20 minutes and the meeting was closed. David, as they were packing their things away, said that they needed to go and thank that man for his intervention, but they couldn't find him!

The second story concerns a time when David and Frank were in Limerick holding open-air meetings. The speakers and microphones were run off a car battery. All was set up, and a crowd gathered to listen to the music; but when the music stopped, the crowd became threatening. David and Frank rushed to put all their equipment away and made a hasty retreat, but they left without the speakers. David and Frank, as they drove off, had forgotten that the speakers were on the top of the car!

When talking to Tommy about David, he mentioned a few personal challenges that he had experienced in his life. Tommy said, "David always appeared when I needed him. He seemed to appear out of the blue."

Tommy really appreciated how David encouraged him and counselled him during those times of personal challenge.

While I was talking with David's wife, Emily, she told me about another incident when he was in Cork. Again, he was with Frank Bray. Frank would have done a lot of outreach work in Cork and David would have covered for Frank when he came back to Northern Ireland on holiday.

There was an occasion, during a meeting, when the police came into the service to question David about the disappearance of some young men from Cork. Families forbade their young people to come to the Gospel meetings that were being held in Cork. The young people did come, but it was in fear and trembling: if they were caught, their fathers would give them a beating.

One night, a young man present was told that his father was coming up the stairs. He escaped by climbing out of a window and clambering down a drainpipe. The incident with the police was because two of the young people had absconded. Their parents went to the police and the police came to David. He didn't know where the two young people had run away to, but the police questioned him, not believing his story. Emily told me that when David finally came back to Northern Ireland, he was in a very stressed state.

He was a frequent traveller in Ireland: this was picked up by the authorities; so much so, that whenever they were in Dublin, they would be followed as they returned to make sure they crossed the border.

In the United Kingdom...

At a mission in Ipswich with Don Double in 1966, Don remembers David sitting on a doorstep with his four-year-old daughter and leading her to give her heart to the Lord. David continued to work with Don Double for many years. Emily told me a story of a prayer meeting in Cornwall where David, Don Double and Harry Greenwood were present. David prayed and laid hands on these two brothers and they were slain in the Spirit.

In late 1966 David was invited to Dennison House, Selwyn Hughes' headquarters, where he preached in several services.

I was told a story of David, with his brother Glyn, and a Pentecostal Mission Hall in Aberkenfig, South Wales, called Beulah. The church was led by Pastor Billy Main. The young people of the church were meeting on a Wednesday and seeking the fulness of the Spirit. In those days, the meetings were called 'tarrying meetings.' They had been seeking the power of the Holy Spirit for a while and, very unexpectedly, the Greenow brothers turned up at the Wednesday night meeting. That night, through the ministry of the laying on of hands, six young people were filled with the Holy Spirit.

In Europe...

In 1963 David and Glynn travelled by car to Sweden, where a revival was taking place. Earlier in the book, mention was made of Glyn and Roy Turner going to Scandinavia. The invitation for Glyn and Roy had come because someone from Sweden had attended a Glory meeting. On the trip with Glyn, an ice breaker had to accompany the ship that brought them into Stockholm; they returned a few months later during a force 9 gale!

In 1966, on another trip, David took Cecil Stewart to Sweden. They used Cecil's car and they came home in a force 10 gale. This trip was a disappointment. The itinerary that was hoped was not arranged. In the end, David and Cecil did minister in different meetings but they were smaller than was anticipated. Their interpreter was Rowland Erickson.

In 1967, David visited Belgium and Holland. He writes; "We enjoyed the presence and blessing of God as we visited Belgium and Holland for ministry at the invitation of brother Marcel Desmit of Belgium, who was our interpreter. We were encouraged in the Lord, and are invited to return to Belgium and Holland next year and expect to do so in the Spring."

In North America...

In 1970, David went to Canada where he travelled extensively, conducting meetings for ten weeks. He later went to Oral Roberts University in America and visited the famous *'Prayer Tower'* where Oral prayed for him. David was thrilled about this. He also attended one of Kathryn Kuhlman's meetings, queuing almost two hours to get in. 5000 people were turned away. 7000 people were in the audience; people were healed from every kind of complaint. Some were even healed as they queued to get into the meeting. A woman got up out of her wheelchair and walked. David said he had never been in such a healing meeting, where the blind regained their sight, the deaf heard and a man with a broken back was totally healed. In a letter to Emily, David said, "It was the real ministry that I have longed to see in Ireland and England."

David visited Canada three times during the years. He had links with men in Canada from his days in the Apostolic Church and from the Revival in Portadown. After Emily's parents died in 1979, she went on one of the trips with David. It was a holiday, but David did minister a number of times.

I found a sealed envelope amongst David's things after his death. On the envelope, written in pencil are these words: "SHARK'S TOOTH FROM FLORIDA. PORCUPINE QUILLS FROM UP NORTH."

Before reading the final chapter, there are some questions I would like to ask you.

Firstly, for those who knew David and sat under his ministry the question is - have you been following through on what David spoke into your life through a prophetic word or through some counselling or through his teaching ministry? It may have been years ago, but God's word still stands. It doesn't wear out or rust. What have you done with the ministry that David brought into your life?

Secondly, for those who never knew David but, through this book, have gained some insight into his life and ministry, what challenges are you now going to run with in your life? David would want you to seek for all that God has for you in Jesus Christ and learn to trust the Holy Spirit to make it all real.

Thirdly, David had an unshakeable conviction that God was going to come again in Revival. David experienced at least three revival seasons in his life. His expectation was that God would visit again with the "latter rains" of revival. Are you carrying the same conviction? Are you willing to be part of this coming move of God? Are you ready and looking for again "seasons of refreshing" from the hand of God?

CHAPTER TWENTY-ONE

The passing of David Greenow...

In the International Gospel Outreach News 2012 there was this headline; 'David Greenow 26th May 1927 – 3rd May 2012.'

The article started with; "David Greenow, IGO Honorary President and Trustee, went to be with the Lord on 3rd May 2012. David had been in hospital following a fall whilst out walking alone, and continued exercising on discharge from hospital. He died whilst on another walk by the river Bann."

I was responsible for going to tell Emily that David had been found dead. With Danny, a family friend, I remember walking up to David's and Emily's home with a heavy heart. It was sudden and, although David had been in hospital two weeks earlier, following a blackout while out walking alone, it was unexpected. The local Christian community were in grief and saddened by his death. He was much loved and respected across all Christian persuasions in Ireland.

Emily, in the immediate and since, bore the death of David with dignity and grace. David's death was a big loss for Emily. But since his death Emily has continued to serve the Lord and be an encouragement to her Christian family. I can think of another lady who lost her husband a few years after David's death. Emily endeavoured to come alongside this lady to encourage and console.

David's funeral was held at Knocknamuckley Parish Church (kindly loaned) on Sunday 6th May 2012. The church can seat several hundred and it was full. The local newspaper wrote; "The sheer numbers in attendance were a reflection of the huge esteem in which he was held from far and near." Those present included people from all corners of the UK. The service was conducted by Pastor Gary Anderson from Lisnadill, Armagh, and there were contributions from David's brother Glyn, his nephew John, and his lifelong colleague and friend, David Chaudhary.

I had the privilege of conducting the service at the graveside at St Saviour's, Dobbin, Portadown. My text was from Psalm 118:24; "This is the day the Lord has made; we will rejoice and be glad in it."

There were three things that I headlined about David. First, he continued the ministry of Jesus in his life. Secondly, David was a gift from God to the Body of Christ and, finally, David experienced fruitfulness in his ministry. I finished my message around the grave with these words: "Is there a challenge for us today? Someone has said, 'We don't honour our fathers by following their ways, but by knowing their God.' David would be the last person to expect us to follow his ways but he would be the first person to encourage us to know HIS GOD. He was so positive and expectant toward God. One of his favourite choruses was, 'Life is wonderful, oh so wonderful...I let Jesus in, He changed everything.' David said this many years ago and he would still say it today, 'Let us open up our hearts to the unlimited power of God.'"

David's nephew, Pastor John Greenow, wrote this tribute: "My uncle David Greenow was more than an uncle. He was a mentor, he was a huge inspiration and example and I always felt privileged just to know him, let alone be his nephew! His qualities are well known: humility, grace, wisdom, Godliness and gentleness.

His apostolic gifting and anointing were carried with seriousness but not religiousness. He always arrived in my life at important times, at the right time, to bring a word in season. He was there at my ordination as a minister and prayed over me. He prayed with me when I was going through the darkest period of my life, and he talked me through the transitions of my life. I especially remember talking to him when I was struggling with the transition to becoming Senior Leader. He articulated what was happening to me and helped massively in my understanding of what I was going through. His prayers, and prophetic and apostolic input, have dramatically impacted my life. When he said he was going to pray for me I knew he was going to pray for me, and I felt the effect.

He was always positive, always interested, self-deprecating... I would talk to him about writing a book about his life and he would seem amazed that he would have anything to say! I will be indebted to Uncle David for his love and friendship, and his massive influence in my life and in the life of my family. I will miss him greatly.

He was a gift to us all and a gift to the church at large, and he is now enjoying his reward. What can we take from his life as an example and inspiration to follow?"

"Love God."

"I knew that Uncle David had a living vibrant relationship with Jesus. His ministry and his life flowed from his walk with God daily. I am challenged to spend time with God and let my life flow from that."

"Love People."

"Uncle David loved people of all ages. He related to people in all walks of life. I never heard him criticise or speak negatively about anyone. I am challenged to love people, believe in people and do what I can to relate to people whoever they are and wherever they are at."

"Love the Church."

"David Greenow loved the Church, whatever group or denomination. He loved people who gathered together to praise God and 'be' the Church; and because of this, he had huge respect across different churches and was able to speak into many situations. I am challenged to love the many aspects and facets of the Church, the bride that Jesus died for."

"One of the meanings of the word 'legacy' is 'gift.' David Greenow was a gift to us all and he left us the gift of his influence and inspiration.

Acts 13:36; *'For David, after he had served his generation by the will of God, fell asleep....'* Let us serve our generation well. That is how we honour David Greenow and our Lord Jesus Christ."

Final comments...

Firstly, I wish to thank John for the great tribute he wrote on his uncle David.

Secondly, it has been a privilege to write this book about the life, the words and the legacy of David Greenow. It has been difficult at times to unearth stories, so I would like to thank everyone for the contributions that have been sent in.

David was not one to publicise himself. He went about his ministry with an authority but also with a gentleness and a quietness. He had no office; he had no staff to organise and promote his ministry. He depended on God, and God opened doors for him. Those doors remained open for him during his years of ministry. David and Emily were always grateful and thankful to God for the people who faithfully supported them in prayer and support.

David wrote this in December 1967: "I want to sincerely thank each one of you who have shown an interest in this ministry by your letters, prayers, hospitality and financial support. It is now over 15 years since I entered full-time faith ministry and it is nothing short of miraculous how God has used His people to meet the needs of my wife and me time and time again. Thanks be unto God."

David was always amazed how God took a young man from a farm near Hereford and used him for His glory. And that is what God did. Think of the people and places mentioned in this book where God used David to be a blessing! And God did that for over 60 years of service in the UK and overseas.

David is no longer with us, but His Lord and Saviour is still with us to save the sinner, heal the sick, deliver the oppressed, and baptise with the Holy Spirit.

Let's go forward and let God write His story in our lives.

PART 3

Special Bonus
David Greenow Teachings

'If any man speak, let him speak as the oracles of God; if any man minister, let him do it as of the ability which God giveth: that God in all things may be glorified through Jesus Christ, to whom be praise and dominion for ever and ever. Amen.'
1 Peter 4:11

INTRODUCTION

David was a prolific writer, yet he only wrote one book. The main focus of his writings was leaflets, bookmarks and pamphlets. David would carry a stock of these around with him on his preaching engagements and hand them out to people as a means of encouragement and instruction. He wrote them himself, and the material is wholly based on the Bible.

A quality that stands out when reading these publications is the thoroughness of the material produced. I think this demonstrates the love David had for God's Word, the Bible, and the heart that he had for God's people.

Paul writes in 2 Timothy 3:16-17; "*All Scripture is God-breathed and is useful for instruction, for conviction, for correction, and for training in righteousness, so that the man of God may be complete, fully equipped for every good work.*" (Berean Study Bible)

David's heart was for people to grow in their knowledge of Christ and grow in their service for Christ. He followed 2 Timothy 3:16-17 for his own life, and he wanted to be a tool in God's hand so that God's people would love the Bible and be fully able to fulfil God's plan in their lives.

David was not only well versed in the Bible but well-read in the field of Christian literature and publications. He was on the mailing list of many Christian organisations and this kept him informed of current thought within the Christian church. Through these magazines, David was also informed of what God was doing worldwide, in His church and in the world.

After David's death, Emily gave me the honour of going into the caravan that David used as a study and taking whatever I wanted. It was an absolute treasure trove of resources. I found books by many different authors. There were Bible dictionaries, concordances and reference books. There were Bible '*Word Study*' books. I remember that there was a book that gave key themes from each book in the Bible. But the material that attracted my attention was the books he had on the Holy Spirit.

I found books by Lindsay, Carter, Stiles, Roberts, Hinn and Linford. Some of these authors are not known today but they show how David was open to learn from a wide spectrum of writers in regard to the work of the Holy Spirit.

David's reading and studying of Christian materials is also demonstrated by the many different quotations that are included in his writings. We have quotes from Wuest, Mueller, Meyer, the Living Bible and other Bible translations, Bishop Ryle, Booth, Kenyon, Wesley, Spurgeon and many others.

In the leaflet entitled '*Giving*', he quotes Jim Elliott, who was martyred for his faith, saying; "*He is no fool who gives what he cannot keep, to gain what he cannot lose.*"

The characteristic that struck me most when looking at the material that David had gathered was his openness to learn and study the things of God. He purchased these materials himself. He didn't have a church expenses account to claim from. He invested in himself financially to learn and study. There was no internet to download material from, but he purchased study books and resources to learn and grow in his knowledge of God's Word and also, to properly apply God's Word to his life and witness.

But with all the books and reference materials that he had, for David the Bible was his main source book. I think of the instruction that Paul gave Timothy: "*Study and do your best to present yourself to God approved, a workman [tested by trial] who has no reason to be ashamed, accurately handling and skilfully teaching the word of truth.*" 2 Timothy 2:15 AMP.

David followed this instruction in his life; and we have known the blessing of that in our lives.

Some of the leaflets David produced had eye-catching titles like...

"Heaven: Latest Travel Information"

"Victory Through Christ: Be A Victor not a Victim"

"Self Invited Burdens or Blessings"

"Reversing the Reverses of Life"

"The Inabilities of the Almighty"

"Satan's Limitations"

All the material that David produced did not advocate a self-help process of change but promoted the Bible. The reader was challenged to base their life on the truth of God's Word. The diagnosis was Bible-based, and the remedy was Bible-based. There were no '*cheap*' motivational statements which we can hear today from church platforms, but statements based on the Word of God that encouraged Christians to believe.

In this section, I am going to highlight some of the Bible topics that David wrote about in bookmarks, leaflets and pamphlets. The range of the material was very wide and some of what was produced was unique. These writings tell us what David believed and what he desired for every Christian and the Body of Christ.

Topic 1
Prayer
Pray without ceasing...

The first topic is prayer. David was a man of prayer and this gave him the authority to teach on it. I remember being told a story about David, when he was one of the guest speakers at a conference in Southern Ireland. The person telling me the story mentioned how, when it was David's turn to speak, this small, thin man walked slowly forward. He didn't seem to have much strength but all that changed as he opened up God's Word on prayer. He lived a life of prayer, and that gave him the authority to teach about it.

Another story that comes to mind is of a colleague who had cancer. David, and a few others, met with the man and the day was spent seeking God for healing. God answered that prayer and the colleague was healed.

I have leaflets about prayer with these headings...

'Prayer Power;'
'Bible Keys That Unlock Prayer Power;'
'Prayer Privileges, Promises & Power;'
'Prayer Power Possibilities;'
'The Ultimate Communication System.'

In the leaflet entitled; '*The Ultimate Communication System,*' these powerful definitions of prayer are given...

➤   A detonator that releases the power of God.
➤   Inviting God and His supplies into the situation.
➤   A meaningful journey to the heart of God.
➤   Not a slavish duty, but a glorious redemptive privilege.

Also included in the leaflet are these statements on prayer...

➤   Calvary is our basis in prayer.
➤   The Bible is our guide in prayer.
➤   The name of Jesus is our authority in prayer.
➤   Faith is our confidence in prayer.
➤   The Holy Spirit is our Helper in prayer.
➤   Our Heavenly Father is our Object in prayer.

David had a large caravan at the bottom of his garden. It was there he would go to learn about prayer and practice this Christian discipline.

In his leaflet '*A Heart-Felt Cry For Revival,*' David gives us an insight into his prayer life. He wrote: "A five-fold prayer that I regularly present at God's throne of grace contains these requests...

➤   A worldwide furtherance of the Gospel.
➤   A daily increase of the Church.
➤   The spiritual growth of each believer in Christ.
➤   The protection, direction and equipping of all in Christian leadership and ministry.
➤   Revival.

What do those requests say to you? There was no personal agenda for David in his prayer life. It was focused on others. Also, those requests are '*BIG*' and David was able to make such intercessions because he had a '*BIG*' God.

I have a book in my library entitled, *'Your God is too Small.'*[70] I think the prayer requests of David say loud and clear, we have a BIG God who is not restricted by geography, history, culture or nationalism. I am reminded of something William Carey said: "*Expect Great Things from God, Attempt Great Things for God.*"

As we read about the specific requests that David prayed, I wonder whether you and I were specifically mentioned in his prayers, or our individual churches were presented before the Lord in prayer. I wonder how many of David's prayers for you and me were answered and are still to be answered.

What about David's request for revival? The leaflet clearly shows what the hopes of David were. He wrote: "*Revival is the Church being restored to normality by the merciful intervention of God.*"

David taught two important truths about revival. Firstly, he believed that revival was for the church and, secondly, it was the Church going back to the days of the Acts of the Apostles. The following verse from a hymn was quoted:

> "*O for the floods on the thirsty land,*
> *O for a mighty revival,*
> *O for a sanctified fearless band,*
> *Ready to hail its arrival. Amen!*"

---

70 Phillips (1952), "Your God is too Small". Epworth Press, London.

Topic 2

The Person and the Work of the Lord Jesus Christ
Jesus, the Greatest One...

The second area of Bible truth I want to mention is around the Person and the Work of the Lord Jesus Christ. David produced a leaflet with the heading, *'Jesus, The Greatest One.'* David believed, taught, lived and preached the four-fold Gospel. This message is built around four particular truths about Jesus: Saviour, Healer, Baptiser in the Holy Spirit and the Coming King.

David wrote this about Jesus; *"His peace calms life's greatest storms; His light dispels the deepest darkness; His truth triumphs over falsehood; His joy brings strength and comfort in life's hurts; His love embraces all men everywhere; His grace can save the vilest; His hand will keep and guide us to the eternal world; His church still stands after centuries of unbelievable difficulty and opposition and continues to emerge in the world as His mighty instrument to reach and bless the nations."*

In the leaflet, *'Jesus, The Greatest One,'* David gave these four outstanding truths about Jesus...

➢   He is the **Only** Person who lived before He was born.
➢   He is the **Only** Person whose life story was pre-written.
➢   He is the **Only** Person who was both God and Man.
➢   He is the **Only** Person whose death has saving power.

There are two further leaflets which I would like to mention.

The first is entitled, 'Calvary's Great Exchange.' The reason I mention this pamphlet is because we see clearly that David believed in the penal substitution of Jesus on the Cross. I believe this truth is being lost to the church today. The truth of substitution is taught; but the truth that Jesus not only died in my place but took all of my punishment on the Cross is not loudly proclaimed across the church.

David wrote, "*We are blessed of God because Jesus was made a curse for us.*" In some sections of the church, this Biblical truth of penal substitution has been compared to *child abuse*. I would make this appeal. Please don't just teach that Jesus' death was a substitutionary death; but teach that He dies carrying our judgement our suffering and God's wrath for our sin. With this truth planted in our hearts, our love for Jesus and our gratitude for the work of the Cross will only deepen, making our praise increase.

In regard to the truth of penal substitution David quoted this verse from a hymn:

> "*The wrath of God which was our due,*
> *Upon the Lamb was laid,*
> *And by the shedding of His blood*
> *The debt for us was paid.*
> *How calm the judgement hour shall pass,*
> *To all who do obey,*
> *The Word of God, and trust the blood,*
> *And make that word their stay.*"

The second leaflet is entitled, 'The Blood of Jesus.' David writes: "*Blood is mentioned about seven hundred times in the Bible, and holds a place of tremendous importance in the purpose of God and the life and redemption of mankind. Christianity has been accused of being a 'blood' religion.*"

Has the truth about the blood of Jesus been lost from the church today? I believe it has. A direct consequence is that we have also lost the important truth that we no longer belong to this world or to satan. Let me quote from David: "*Redeem means 'to buy back,' 'to deliver.' Christ has redeemed us from satan's power that He might possess us for Himself, and we are no longer our own, we are bought with a price. 1 Corinthians 6:19-20."*

Instead of using motivational statements to encourage people to serve and appealing to people with notions of their success, can we not challenge Christians with this biblical truth that *'we are no longer our own?'* You and I have been bought by God for His use and His use alone. The price wasn't in money but the precious shed blood of the Lord Jesus Christ. As someone has said: *'Salvation is free because someone else paid the price.'*

John Stott, in his book, *'The Cross of Christ,'* writes: *"A remembrance that Jesus Christ has bought us with His blood, and that in consequence we belong to Him, should motivate us as individual Christians to holiness, just as it motivates presbyters to faithful ministry and the heavenly host to worship."* [71]

Topic 3
The Promise of Blessing
The gratitude attitude...

Another area that David wrote about was the Biblical truth of blessing. One of David's sayings was: *"Have an attitude of gratitude."* He produced a bookmark on this theme. It was entitled, *"The Gratitude Attitude."* David listed ten reasons why we should have such an attitude of gratitude. This bookmark has been included in part 4 of this book.

I am only going to mention the first three reasons David gives in the bookmark...

---

71 Stott (1989), "The Cross of Christ with study guide." Inter-Varsity Press.

➤   It is a fitting response to God's bountiful giving. (Psalm 106:1; Acts 17:25; Colossians 1:12-14)
➤   It saves us from the sin of ingratitude. (Romans 12:1; 2 Timothy 3:2; Luke 17:17)
➤   It brings us more into accord with Heaven's activities. (Rev. 4:9; 7:9-12; 11:16, 17)

The bookmark ends with this verse of Scripture from Psalm 118:1; *'O give thanks unto the Lord, for He is good.'*

The book that David wrote, which I mentioned earlier, was entitled, *'Bible Blessings.'* It was produced in 1967 by The International Gospel Outreach. I like the title, *'Bible Blessings',* because it says so much about David and follows the great verse in Ephesians that states: *'We are blessed with every spiritual blessing in heavenly places in Christ Jesus.'*

What were the truths that David was promoting as he wrote, taught and preached on the promises and blessings of God?

The first truth that David is highlighting is the fact that the Christian today is in a New Covenant with God: a Covenant that God made with Jesus and, because we are *'in Christ,'* the blessings are ours already. I feel that so much of the teaching we have received over the years has made us think that we are in a Covenant which is a little better than the Mosaic Covenant because we don't have the animal sacrifices and the elaborate systems of that Covenant. We are in completely new arrangements with God because of Jesus; He is the assurance that all the promises of God are ours.

The second truth is this spiritual fact: we are not journeying to some Promised Land here on earth. We are already *'in Jesus'* and everything that we need for a blessed and fruitful life is already ours.

There is a chapter in David's book which mentions an important discipline for Christian living under the New Covenant; '*How to receive from God.*' Jim Cymbala, in his book, '*Fresh Faith,*' writes: "*The greatest Christian is not the one who has achieved the most but rather the one who has received the most.*" [72]

Peter established this discipline at the beginning of Acts. He calls people to repent and then receive; learning and practising to go to the throne of God to receive mercy and grace for every time of need; asking and believing that we have received and then going forward with that confidence: this is the New Covenant arrangement.

The New Covenant is not the Old with all the animal sacrifices set aside. The New Covenant is not even the Old with the family of Levi demoted. The New Covenant is not even the Old expanded to include Gentiles. The New Covenant is the New Covenant. It is a set of arrangements for relationship with our Heavenly Father that have never existed before. These arrangements are absolutely unique. The assurance is not in some stone tablets, but in the One who agreed the Covenant on our behalf, and who sits at the right-hand of God the Father in Heaven.

Topic 4
Faith in God
For we walk by faith, not by sight...

This brings us to another area of Bible truth that David taught about: Faith. In his Christmas letter of December 1967, David wrote; "*Faith is not imagination, but a realisation of things as they really are. Faith is dependence upon God's ability and willingness to fulfil what He promised. Faith is something you have. Romans 12:3. Faith is something*

---

72 Cymbala (1999), "Fresh Faith." Grand Rapids: Zondervan Publishing House.

God expects you to use. Luke 8:25. Your faith will measure to you God's blessing and power. Matthew 9:29. Your faith will always work for your good. Mark 5:34. Your faith has limitless possibilities. Mark 9:23."

Quoting from Jim Cymbala again; *"Never in the four Gospels was Jesus astounded by anybody's righteousness. Never was he impressed with anyone's education. But he was amazed with one thing: people's faith."* [73]

Sad to say, there has been a faith message promoted in the Christian church in the recent past has been perverted into something for self and self alone. Jim Cymbala writes, *"In our time, the whole notion of faith has been derailed in some quarters into an emphasis on saying certain words, giving a 'positive confession' of health, prosperity, or other blessings. You know, a kind of spiritual mantra. A mental formula of 'how the Bible will work for you' is front and centre, while the question of a true heart-faith and communion with the living Christ is rarely emphasised."*[74]

I wonder if this twisted message about faith, has affected our understanding of what Biblical faith is? Have we become afraid to ask and believe? Have we become unsure what we can ask for and believe for? But I also think we may be captured by other thoughts which do not help us live by faith. Questions around what we must do and what we must be before God will ever do anything? We think that there is some invisible standard we must reach before God will ever give or fulfil his promises. The truth is this; we are "IN CHRIST", we are righteous in Him and He is willing to give, give and give.

David wrote and taught faith, but it was faith to believe who God is; what God has given and who God wants you to be.

In the leaflet, *'Have Faith in God,'* David gave these practical helps in building up our faith...

---

73 Cymbala (1999), "Fresh Faith." Grand Rapids: Zondervan Publishing House.
74 Cymbala (1999), "Fresh Faith." Grand Rapids: Zondervan Publishing House.

➤ Have a constant fellowship with the '*Author and Finisher of our faith,*' the Lord Jesus. Hebrews 12:2.

➤ Feed on the '*Word of faith*' day by day. Romans 10:8, 17; Matthew 4:4.

➤ Have a confession of faith. Affirm faith daily. Do not be afraid to let yourself and others hear you declare, "*I believe God.*" Proverbs 18:21. Romans 8:8-10.

➤ Recognise and receive faith ministry. Listen to preaching that builds faith in God and not that which destroys it.

➤ Seek to inspire the faith of others. Sharing faith multiplies it. Never damage the faith of someone else by your unbelieving words and acts.

There are plenty of examples, men and women, in the Bible who lived by faith; but their examples are not the only ones. There have been many in church history that have continued the story of Hebrews 11 and left a faith legacy. I want to suggest that David Greenow, with his wife Emily, have demonstrated Hebrews 11 in their ministry in Ireland and beyond.

When David left the Apostolic church in 1952, he left the safety of a denomination and the security that it brings, to live depending on God for all his needs.

David wrote this paraphrase of Psalm 23; '*I am one of Jehovah's flock, therefore my needs shall always be supplied. Amidst the tender grass He bids me find a tranquil rest, and by the cool and silent living waters I am led by Him. He quickeneth and refresheth my inner life. Following Him I walk the ways that are right; thus no reproach is brought upon His holy name and character. Even if my way should be through the midst of the*

*sunless gulf of death shade, I am not fearful lest any ill should befall me;
Thy presence reassures me. Thou hast Thy club and Thy crook to defend
and guide me, this fact fills me with inward peace. I eat at the banquet that
Thou hast furnished and arranged over against my many adversaries which
linger near, but cannot harm me. The balm of Thine anointing is upon my
head with its enlivening influence, my joy is overflowing. Only that which
is beneficial and that which pertains to the Shepherd's kindness pursues me
in all my daily life; my continual abiding place shall be in the Temple of
Thy dwelling throughout the length of days. Amen. So be it.'*

David went on and broke the Psalm down with different references,
but the whole piece was headed, *'The Testimony of one of the Great
Shepherd's Sheep.'*

David Greenow's story is of someone who knew Psalm 23 but, more
importantly, he knew the Shepherd of the Psalm through his personal
relationship. In 1967 David wrote this; *"It is now over 15 years since I
entered the full-time faith ministry and it is nothing short of miraculous
how God has used His people to meet the needs of my wife and I time and
again. Thanks be unto God!"* David knew the Shepherd of Psalm 23.

David wrote, *"...faith makes it possible for God to fulfil His work and
His promised supplies to reach us; faith not to accumulate the riches of
this world, but faith to see His Kingdom come on earth."*

Topic 5
Divine Healing
God is a Healing God...

This brings us to another area that was close to the heart of David
Greenow. The truth of demonstration, according to 1 Corinthians 2:4-
5: *'And my speech and my preaching were not with persuasive words of*

human wisdom, but in demonstration of the Spirit and of power, that your faith should not be in the wisdom of men but in the power of God.' David believed and practised laying on of hands. God also used David in the gifts of the Spirit, to bring healing and restoration into people's lives.

In a message titled, *'The Purposes of God Today,'* David said; *"All the miracles of Jesus' ministry were a manifestation of the character, authority and abundance of the Kingdom of God. Wherever 'this gospel' is preached today, men and women have an opportunity to surrender to Christ, and enter into the benefits and blessings of His Kingdom. (Matthew 6:33) Jesus said: 'This Gospel of the Kingdom shall be preached in all the world for a witness' or 'with evidence.' (Matthew 24:14) This is the same Gospel that Jesus preached, and it is to be proclaimed throughout all nations with its attendant supernatural evidence, with a view to extending and establishing the Kingdom of God on earth."*

In David's Christmas 1967 letter he writes; *"The work of God goes on, and it is encouraging to realise that the power of God is at work in the Gospel to transform lives and we can point men to Christ with confidence. I am thankful to the Lord for every soul I have been able to help and point to the Saviour this year."*

"There have also been wonderful testimonies of healing. One sister was healed in our Portadown Crusade earlier this year of an internal complaint from which she had suffered for 11 years. Another sister tells me that after prayer she has been certified clear of the dreaded disease of multiple sclerosis which had threatened to destroy her life. Yet another sister tells how she was instantly healed of a serious spinal complaint when I called her out for prayer. Her child was also wonderfully delivered after prayer. Hallelujah! It thrills me to know that the God of miracles lives today. He is still answering prayer."

David had a very thorough Biblical basis for his belief in Divine healing. In an article headed, *'Why I Believe in Divine Healing,'* David gave five reasons.

First, because of the healing nature of God. Quoting scriptures like Exodus 15:26 and Malachi 3:6, David wrote very firmly, '*God is a healing God.*'

Secondly, because of the healing ministry of Christ. David wrote, "*He healed them ALL. Matthew 12:15. There was none of those who came to Him that He could not or would not heal. Christ is the same today and continues His ministry through believers. Hebrews 13:8, John 14:12.*" I can hear David saying to us, "*Believe this, Believe this.*" I remember one of the songs that David sang and played on his accordion, "*He has healing hands. The hands of Jesus are healing hands.*" It is an accepted truth that Jesus was the '*Word made flesh.*' Jesus did not only come to be the sacrifice for sin, but he came to reveal the heart and character of the LORD God.

There was a space of four hundred years between the end of Malachi and the beginning of the Gospels. Israel had heard nothing from God during that time; but Jesus came and revealed who the LORD God is: He is the God who heals, Jehovah-Rophi.

Think of the times Jesus said, during his ministry on earth, "*your sins are forgiven,*" and also remember He healed the sick. The question is this: why would Jesus want to stop healing the sick on His return to Heaven? He is still forgiving people their sins, so why would He stop healing the sick? (Mark 16:18). Healing displays the care and the compassion that the LORD God has for people. Healing displays the heart of the LORD God.

The three other reasons David gave in the leaflet, '*Why I Believe in Divine Healing,*' were...

➢   **Because** of the atoning work of Christ. Matthew 8:17 (Isaiah 53:4), John 19:30.

➢   **Because** of the healing power of God's Word. Numbers 23:19, Psalm 107:20, Psalm 119:89, Jeremiah 1:12, Matthew 8:8, 1 Peter 1:24-25.

➢   **Because** of the quickening presence of the Holy Spirit. Luke 6:19, Acts 1:8, Romans 8:11.

The *'dunamis'* that flowed out of Jesus in Luke 6:19 is the same *'dunamis'* that we receive through the fullness of the Holy Spirit. David wrote: "*The presence and power of the Spirit brings healing and health.*"

There is a truth that does need to be mentioned at this point. David believed in Divine Healing, not because of some book he had read or some healing evangelist that he had heard, but because the truth in the Bible had been revealed to him. Further, David believed that the miraculous not only confirmed the message, but brought the reality of the Lord into the midst of men and women.

David wrote this in September 2002: "*Compared with other continents, Europe is the one in which Church growth is least evident. Surely this is a cause for deep concern for Christians. I believe that one of the reasons for this is the sad lack of the manifestation of the supernatural power of God giving evidence of His reality. It is time to repent, if it can in any way be said of us, 'He (Christ) could there do no mighty work... and he marvelled because of their unbelief. (Mark 6:5-6).' May we determine in our hearts that in this needy day we are going to be believing Believers.*"[75]

---

75 Christian Lifestyle magazine: Magazine published by The Apostolic Church.

Topic 6
The Person and the Work of the Holy Spirit
Just like Jesus....

I have heard it said in recent times that the Holy Spirit is the most misunderstood person in the Trinity. I remember reading a story about a house group who were studying Acts chapter 2. The group leader said, "Let's not talk about the Holy Spirit. It's too controversial."[76] Reading the material that David produced on the character and the work of the Holy Spirit, that charge could not be laid against David. He knew the Holy Spirit for himself, and also knew how central the Holy Spirit is in everything that Jesus, as Head of the Church, seeks to build in His Church today.

When David started to minister freelance in Northern Ireland, the prominent belief in the local Christian community in regard to the Holy Spirit would have been Cessationism. (the Holy Spirit was given for a former time, not now). The three mainline UK Pentecostal movements were present in Northern Ireland, and God had really used these movements to build His Church; however, the prominent teaching in the country was the evangelical, reformed faith of Presbyterianism.

It must be mentioned that the three mainline Pentecostal denominations in Northern Ireland did suffer ridicule from certain quarters of the evangelical church in Northern Ireland. I know of one evangelical minister who would publicly mock the Pentecostal experience from his pulpit. It must also be remembered that it was in the 1950s that the Free Presbyterians under the leadership of the Rev. Ian Paisley came into prominence in Northern Ireland. They took Northern Ireland by storm, but they were Cessationist in belief and practice.

---

76 Warner (1997), "Alive in the Spirit." Hodder and Stoughton.

But God was stirring the nest.

For David, this was God restoring to His church the latter rains that were promised in Joel, Isaiah and Hosea. A movement sprang up in Canada in the late 1940s called the '*Latter Rain Movement.*' Their influence spread across the whole Body of Christ in North America and subsequently the UK, Europe and Africa. This movement was not a denomination but drew together ministers who were looking for a recovery of the days of the Acts of the Apostles.

As I have already mentioned, David came under the influence of this move of God while he was at the Apostolic church Bible school in Penygroes. Ministers from the Apostolic church in Canada and the USA who had experienced this fresh move of the Spirit in North America came to the Bible School in 1951. David and the other students had a powerful encounter with the Holy Spirit. This experience never left David and he would often have talked about the tears and the breaking that took place in his heart at that meeting in the Bible school.

There was also the growing influence in the Christian church of the Charismatic Renewal, which started in the 1950s and championed the things of the Spirit. David du Plessis, Dennis and Rita Bennett and in the UK, Michael Harper and the Fountain Trust, were some of the influences behind the Charismatic Renewal in the UK and Ireland, however for Protestants in Northern Ireland, there was something else about this movement that didn't sit well with them: that was the involvement of the Catholic Church in this renewal.

Finally, there was the increasing influence in Northern Ireland of the healing revival evangelists from America. The revivalist that David took over from in Portadown in 1955 modelled himself on these evangelists. There was also the visit of James White to Belfast in the 1950s, which so impacted David and thousands of others in the

Province. There was a Christian bookshop, Mall View, in Armagh, that stocked magazines and books about these healing evangelists and revivalists. Their shop stamp is on many of the books and magazines that were in David's library.

Below is an extract from a magazine called the Voice of Healing: (the Mall View bookshop advertised in this magazine) *"After the lean spiritual years of World War II, two major national movements revitalized the American church. One was the evangelical movement spearheaded by Billy Graham and other was the healing revival represented by William Branham and Oral Roberts and a host of other lesser-known ministries like A. A. Allen and Jack Coe. It declared itself as 'a signs-gifts-healing, salvation-deliverance, Holy Ghost miracle revival.' Between 1947 and 1958 scores of healing evangelists traversed America and went into the entire world praying for the sick."* [77]

Billy Graham came to the UK and these healing evangelists came to the UK and to Northern Ireland. As already mentioned, one such evangelist was James White, with whom David shared a platform in Belfast. David would have spoken at length about these meetings and the vast crowds that attended.

In the June 1959 copy of the Voice of Healing the headline was, *'Revival Strikes Ireland with David Nunn Party.'* (David Nunn had a team of associates with him.) While David is not mentioned specifically in the article, someone who David did work with is mentioned, Frank Bray. One of the outcomes of the Nunn visit was that Bray was commissioned to start a revival centre in Cork. David worked with Frank Bray in Cork in the years following.

This was the situation in which David started his itinerant ministry; Northern Ireland was a stronghold of Cessationism, but there were stirrings in regard to the Holy Spirit.

---

77 Voice of Healing: magazine published by the Last-Day Sign Gift Ministries.

I shall take a step back and deal more with the teaching of Cessationism.

R.T. Kendall writes in *'Holy Fire;'* *"Cessationism is a hypothesis. It is not a teaching grounded in Holy Scripture – like the virgin birth, the deity of Christ, the resurrection of Jesus, and salvation by the blood of God's Son. Cessationists have chosen to believe that God does not reveal Himself directly and immediately today... Cessationists do believe in the supernatural in Scripture of course, but have no expectation that God will intervene supernaturally today except, perhaps, through providence...the notion of the gifts of the Spirit being in operation today, as in 1 Corinthians 12:10-12, is out of the question... The Holy Spirit can therefore be quenched by a doctrine that does not allow for Him to show up."*[78]

Personally, and David would have agreed with me, Cessationism is not supported by the Bible or Church History.

A key Bible passage for Cessationists is 1 Corinthians 13:8-10. Quoting again from R.T.Kendall; *"...Cessationists take the view that Paul actually forecast Cessationism when he said prophecies would pass away, tongues would cease, and that the 'perfect' would come. Some take the 'perfect' to be the Bible, i.e. when the church finally agreed upon the exact canon of Scripture; whereas I too agree that the Bible is perfect, that is not what Paul means in 1 Corinthians 13."* What then is *'the perfect?'*[79]

Kendall believes it refers to *'perfect love.'* Others see it in regard to Jesus coming back and some refer to the time when we get to heaven. Martin Lloyd-Jones used to say; *"The Bible was not given to replace the miraculous but to correct abuses."*

What about Church History? It depends very much on which books you read. Some writers seem to blank the Holy Spirit out completely from their writings. David Carnduff in his book, *'Ireland's Lost Heritage'*, mentions that during the Ulster

78 Kendall (2014), "Holy Fire." Florida: Charisma House.
79 Kendall (2014), "Holy Fire." Florida: Charisma House.

Awakening of 1859, there was evidence of speaking in new languages and the manifestation of the gifts of the Holy Spirit.[80]

Just think about the Welsh Revival 1904. I have already mentioned the testimony of Frank Hodges: "*I was really desperate for the baptism of the Spirit. I thought I would go down to Wales for the blessing... I went to a little house close to the home of Evan Roberts. (renowned leader of the Welsh Revival) There I saw for the first time a person baptised in the Spirit.*" Frank received his baptism in that meeting. In later years, he would become David's pastor in Hereford. For a previous book I wrote, I did some research on the 1904 Welsh Revival and I believe that, in some meetings, Evan Roberts moved in the gifts of wisdom and knowledge.

David Pawson, '*Word and Spirit Together,*' David Allen, '*There is a River,*'and Eddie Hyatt '*2000 Years of Charismatic Christianity,*' all give examples of how the Holy Spirit and the gifts of the Holy Spirit never ceased to be experienced in the Church of Jesus Christ in the years after the Acts of the Apostles. In my book, '*The God of our Fathers,*' I wrote; "*It is evident from Church history that the key truths of 1st Century Apostolic Christianity were not totally lost, but became increasingly sidelined and clouded with superstition by the established church over the centuries.*"[81]

What about now?

The fastest growing Church stream today is the Pentecostal stream. William Kay writes: "*The Pentecostal and Charismatic Movement is one of the wonders of the twentieth century.*"[82] A further point to note is this: the belief in and an experience of the Holy Spirit is now sought, desired and promoted in many historical denominations where the things of the Holy Spirit had previously been avoided and spoken against. I remember meeting a minister in Zimbabwe who described himself as a *Baptocostal!*

80 Carduff (2003), "Ireland's Lost Heritage." Northern Ireland: IPBC Publications.
81 Thomas (2016), "The God of our Fathers."
82 Kay, W.K. (2009). "Pentecostalism." London: SCM Press.

David believed and taught that there was a distinct and separate experience of the Holy Spirit for Christians. Also, there were gifts of the Holy Spirit to seek and experience in ministry. But before we look further into what David taught about the Holy Spirit, I trust that I have established two key truths.

First, David had a Biblical mandate to teach these things. The things of the Spirit, according to Acts 2 and 1 Corinthians 12, had not come to the end with the completion of the canon of scriptures.

Secondly, there was a long history of the Spirit continuing to work in the lives of men and women post the Acts of the Apostles. In particular, the 20th century was the time when God restored back to His Church and spread across the Body of Christ, the experience that first came on the Day of Pentecost.

David Greenow, in character and calling, was the right man to break down all of the opposition to the Holy Spirit in Northern Ireland and foster a coming together of Protestants and Catholics around the Holy Spirit.

I know of individuals who were part of the Anglican community whom David led into an experience of the Holy Spirit; and they are still living in that experience today. A weekly interdenominational house group met near David and Emily's home. Methodists and Presbyterians attended this group and David was often the speaker. He would have taught about the Holy Spirit and encouraged people to seek for themselves.

David wrote in the leaflet, '*Be Filled with the Spirit: Eph 5:18;*' "*The Baptism and Fullness of the Holy Spirit is a definite God-given spiritual experience, promised in the Scriptures, ministered by Christ subsequent to the new birth, for the empowering of all New Testament Believers. It is vitally important to our Christian obedience, service and character that we seek and receive the gift and fullness of the Holy Spirit.*"

David prepared a study entitled, '*Lessons from the Book of Acts.*' In regard to Acts 1:8, he wrote: "*The word 'power' used here is from the Greek word 'Dunamis,' which has the meaning of ability power. It is rendered ability, efficiency, might in the Amplified Bible. It suggests inherent power capable of reproducing itself like a dynamo. God's own ability is given to Christ's disciples through the Holy Spirit to proclaim the Gospel. Acts 4:33, 10:38.*"

The Great Commission gives the church a huge task to fulfil. The church in Acts saw its fulfilment for their day because the leaders and the people had an ongoing experience of the Holy Spirit. Why do some think that, in our day, the Great Commission can be fulfilled in other ways with different tools and strategies? God desires to make His Presence felt and experienced. It has always been the case. God has always wanted people to know that He is not some distant landlord but that He is present on the earth. For us, this is now experienced by the Holy Spirit.

The big question that people seem to have in regard to the fullness of the Holy Spirit is the issue of speaking in tongues or speaking in other languages.

Firstly, let us understand that there was a bigger dimension to the Day of Pentecost than just people speaking in languages that were not native to them or that they had learned. David, in his study on Acts, details the other evidence of Pentecost that the early church experienced and demonstrated. Joy, unity, liberality, godly fear, favour, increase, were some of the other ongoing evidences of the presence of the Holy Spirit from the Day of Pentecost. Another point to mention is this: Jesus became the focus. In the Gospels the questions were whether Jesus was Elijah or Moses or Jeremiah or some other prophet. The Day of Pentecost established that Jesus is Lord and Head over the Church. The experience of the Holy Spirit that the disciples had on the Day of Pentecost was sent by Jesus. The focus for Israel and the world was now the Lord Jesus Christ.

Secondly, what about speaking in new languages? In a Bible study that David prepared entitled, *'Being Filled With The Holy Spirit,'* he gave four answers to this introductory statement: "The purpose of speaking in a new language by the prompting and guidance of the Spirit;"

➤ A new prayer and praise communication with God; 1Cor 14:2, 14-15.

➤ An upbuilding of the believer's personal life; 1 Cor 14:4.

➤ Serves at times as a sign to unbelievers; Isaiah 28:11, 1Cor 14:21-22, Acts 2:5-11.

➤ For the edification of the whole church when, as a ministry gift of the Spirit, it is interpreted; 1Cor 14:13.

David had a very thorough and all-encompassing understanding of the Person and the Work of the Holy Spirit in the Church today. This is reflected in a study sheet David produced, entitled, *'Four Main Ways The Holy Spirit Works In The Believer.'*

When Jesus was teaching the disciples about the Holy Spirit, as recorded in John chapters 14-16, He said this about the work of the One who was coming; *"He will glorify me."* (John 16:14 NIV). David writes this in regard to the Spirit –

➤ **The Fruit of the Spirit** – *"These fruits of the Holy Spirit are expressions of the life, nature and character of Jesus produced in us by the Spirit."*

➤ **The Gifts of the Spirit** – *"These gifts are for power and ministry: as the fruit are for life and character, these gifts reveal the supernatural Ministry of Jesus."*

➤ **Prayer in the Spirit** – *"The Holy Spirit seeks to develop the prayer life of Jesus in us."*

Before mentioning the fourth way, notice how clear David is in his beliefs and understanding of how the Spirit works in unity with Jesus, who is Head of the Church, to produce His image in the church and to fill the Body of Christ with the life and fulness of Jesus.

The fourth way of the Holy Spirit is, **Worship in the Spirit**. Again taking the words of Jesus in John 4:23-24 and remembering what Jesus said in Matthew 22:37; *"Love the Lord your God with all your heart and with all your soul and with all your mind."* (NIV). This further establishes that the Holy Spirit is not working to His agenda, but to Jesus' plan for the church.

At the end of the leaflet '*Be Filled with the Spirit:* Ephesians 5:18,' David wrote: *"May God bless you richly in the Spirit-filled life."* For David, in his personal and ministry life, the Spirit-filled life was the Biblical norm. He desired this for every born-again Christian, and thank God, he was used, along with Emily, to lead many people into this kind of life.

Topic 7
The Ministry of Encouragement
Encourage one another and build each other up...

In writing this book, I have met and spoken to many people. One quality of David's that is mentioned without hesitation is that he was an encourager. Nicky Gumbel writes; *"Encouragement is not flattery or empty praise; it is verbal sunshine. It costs nothing and warms other people's hearts and inspires them with hope and confidence."* [83] David was such a person himself, and he wrote to encourage people to believe and receive from the Lord everything that they had been given in Christ.

---

83 Gumbel, N. Bible In One Year Day 269.

All of David's writings were about encouragement. Titles like, '*Trust in the Lord*,' '*Strength for Your Day*,' '*Bible Blessings for Your Life*,' and '*Victory Through Christ*.' They were encouraging Christians to seek more, receive more and share more. At the bottom of the leaflet entitled, '*Seven Steps to a Miracle*,' David wrote; "*The God of miracles lives today. Fear not to put your trust in Him. There is nothing too hard for the Lord.*"

David did write one pamphlet specifically on '*Christian Encouragement*.' He wrote: "*Encouragement has the meaning of: to urge forward, to give new courage to, to hearten, reassure and persuade. Each one of us has the ability to be an 'encourager' if we will, and the choice is very definitely ours... Encouragement helps to bring out the best in people, and we should determine to urge folk to take new heart and look to God in His Word which is the greatest source of uplift and certainty.*"

David wrote lecture notes on Christian service and let me mention one statement - "*The Christian worker should be like a good watch: open-faced, busy hands, pure gold, well-regulated and full of good works.*"

The notes are very comprehensive and Biblically based. What I found interesting, and perhaps no surprise, is the one person he featured in the notes, a person that we can model our service on: Barnabas, 'son of encouragement.' (NASB Acts 4:36). We, no doubt, could think of many others from Scriptures to present as models; but for David it was Barnabas. David gave eight characteristics of Barnabas that we could seek to live out for ourselves but for me, I see that the eight characteristics were exemplified in David himself. I wondered whether Barnabas was David's example and model. Let me give the characteristics –

➢   He had a cooperative spirit.
➢   He recognised the doings of God.
➢   He rejoiced in the blessing and success of others.

➢   He exhorted believers to make steadfast dedication to the Lord.
➢   He lived in a constant fullness experience of the Holy Spirit and Faith.
➢   He had an attractive Christian experience.
➢   He sought to include and encourage the ministry of others.
➢   He was trustworthy.

Was David a Barnabas to many people? Was David a *'son of encouragement'* in the Body of Christ? I believe he was. He wrote about encouragement; he encouraged many to live in their inheritance but also, he was, in his person, an encouragement.

Topic 8
A Personal Walk with the LORD
Never give up...

One key area of the Christian life that David encouraged people in was their personal walk with the Lord and his focus was the building of Christian character.

An article that David wrote in 2002 was headed, *'Never Give Up.'* David was encouraging steadfastness. The article was Bible-based with six illustrations from the scriptures regarding the steadfast life.

He wrote; *"We live in a world that is being increasingly shaken, and lives that are not built on the spiritual foundation rock of Christ Jesus will be caught up in the world's instability and uncertainty."* He gave this challenge at the end of the article; *"Let us present our lives in covenant commitment that from now to eternity, come what may, we will be devoted lovers of God, dedicated followers of Christ and determined workers in His Church and in the great harvest field of the world."*

A chorus from Henri's Glory was quoted;

> *"I'm going on, I'm going on,*
> *I'm going on towards the mark,*
> *Toward my home.*
> *Too many lives depend on what I do,*
> *Give me the strength, Dear Lord, I'm going on with you."*

The article included this prayer, *"May God grant you out of the rich treasury of his glory to be strengthened and reinforced in the inner man by the Holy Spirit. Amen."* (Ephesians 3:16)[84]

Another leaflet on this theme was called, *'Faint Not.'* Again, the Bible was the base to everything David wrote. He stated: *"God has a message for us in His Word no matter what may be our experience, and He says to us time and again, 'FAINT NOT!' Don't become a quitter and fold up inside. God is with you. Isaiah 41:10. "Fear thou not, for I am with thee."*

The leaflet closed with a verse from a hymn;

> *"Faint not, nor fear, His arms are near,*
> *He changeth not, and thou art dear;*
> *Only believe, and thou shalt see,*
> *That Christ is all in all to Thee."*

David wrote a great deal about the power and promises of God but he also wrote to challenge Christians about their personal walk. When reading the titles that headed many of David's leaflets, we would be mistaken to think that he was just advocating some populist mantra to confess and declare but he knew that there were attitudes and qualities that a Christian was required *'to put on.'*

He wrote about steadfastness. The material David wrote on prayer was encouraging people in their devotional life with the Lord. In the

---

84 The Christian Lifestyle magazine May 2002. Magazine published by The Apostolic Church.

leaflet, 'Releasing the Power of God,' he wrote; "The early Christian made an impact on their generation by dedicated Christian living and co-operating with God for the display of His power."

David was not a 'holiness preacher' but did preach a message of ongoing sanctification before God and by the Holy Spirit. He did preach a positive message, because there were many promises from God to be experienced. For those who sought a growing walk with God and to grow in the things of God, these promises would be realised in abundance.

There are four particular pamphlets of David that I would like to refer to in regard to our personal walk with God. David didn't want Christians to just exist on confessing some spiritual mantra, but he wanted Christians to allow the Holy Spirit to develop their hearts to be like Jesus.

In the leaflet, 'This is your Health,' the challenge is to be humble, having no pride or presumption when coming to Jesus. Another truth emphasised is to acknowledge the Lordship and Authority of Jesus in our lives.

The second pamphlet is headed, 'Christian Attitudes and Actions.' David lists all the 'one another' commands that are in the New Testament and writes; "There is a tremendous need of obedience to these commands and exhortations among God's people today, that the Church may demonstrate Christ-likeness in character and ministry to a waiting and watching world. God grant that we shall see selfishness losing hold of the Church and largeness of heart and vision taking its place as true Christians everywhere recognise and compassionately consider one another."

The third leaflet is called, 'Self Invited Burdens or Blessing.' Based on the book of Proverbs, David writes about unconfessed sin, the undisciplined life, the unstable character, and the unrestrained tongue. We find challenges about having hearts that are hard, stubborn, rebellious, selfish, and uncontrolled. What answer does David give for such a heart? David writes: *"The remedy is surrender to the Lordship of Christ and obedience to His word which will bring a new strength and order into life."*

The final leaflet is, '*Reversing the Reverses of Life.*' In the introduction, David recognises that Christians will face difficulties and problems in their lives; *"As far as I know, no one is exempt, and Bible characters, including Jesus, all had their particular tests and trials to face. Perhaps it should be some encouragement to us to know that we are not alone as we face the problematic situations of life."*

In the last sentence of the introduction, David adds this thought: *"Jesus will help us with our real problems but sometimes it seems that we make things difficult for ourselves; and it might be helpful to ask some relevant questions. Hebrews 2:18."*

The questions that David asks are –
➤   Are your problems real or imaginary?
➤   Are your problems being exaggerated?
➤   Are your difficulties receiving too much attention?
➤   Are your problems self-created?
➤   Do you really believe that God can help you overcome your problems?

David always exuded a positive attitude regarding what God can do in the lives of people. David always wanted the best for people in their Christian lives, but he was not afraid to ask some hard questions. I think that the questions that David lays out in the leaflet are relevant and meaningful to ask. David wanted people to live above their circumstances but was honest in his counsel. Sometimes, people don't like to face questions that challenge their selfishness.

Let me repeat what David wrote – *"Jesus will help us with our real problems but sometimes it seems that we make things difficult for ourselves and it might be helpful to ask some relevant questions."*

Topic 9
Revival
Visit us again in power ...

The first topic that we looked at in regard to David's writings was prayer. I mentioned the leaflet, *'A Heart-Felt Cry For Revival.'* This leaflet gave us an insight into his prayer life. He wrote; *"A five-fold prayer that I regularly present at God's throne of grace contains these requests..."*

➤   A worldwide furtherance of the Gospel.
➤   Daily increase of the church.
➤   The spiritual growth of each believer in Christ.
➤   The protection, direction and equipping of all in Christian leadership and ministry.
➤   Revival.

I want to now look specifically at David's writings about Revival. It is good to mention in passing that David was linked to Selwyn Hughes and the revival and evangelistic work that Hughes birthed in London.

The initial meetings in Portadown that David became part of in February 1955 were headed, *'Portadown Healing Revival.'* The meetings continued, under David's ministry, with this banner headline, *'Revival Continues in The Plaza.'*

As I mentioned in the section on David's life, he was involved with Henri's Glory. In their meetings in Monaghan in 1965 the headline was, *'Henri's Revival Evangelistic Association.'* The invitation was, *"Come, see and feel Revival in operation NOW."* David, along with Cecil Stewart and Roy Turner, was a member of the *'Revival Party.'*

There has been a long-running debate in Christian circles regarding the source of revival. There are two main schools of belief. There is the Jonathan Edwards school which believes that Revival is a sovereign act of God; we cannot predict or organise Revival. The other school of belief is the Charles Finney school, which says that a revival can happen anywhere and at any time provided certain activities took place, for example, prevailing prayer.

Pastor Jim Cymbala in his book, *'Fresh Wind, Fresh Fire,'* gives us some insight into how Charles Finney would organise his revival meetings. Cymbala writes; *"Father Nash, as some called him, would quietly slip into a town three or four weeks before Finney's arrival, rent a room, find two or three like-minded Christians to join him, and start pleading with God."* Finney's revivalism was birthed in prayer. What is interesting is this; four months after Father Nash died, Finney left his itinerant ministry to become the pastor of a church in New York. Cymbala writes; *"His partner in cracking the gates of hell was gone."*[85]

David, I think, stood with the Charles Finney school. He quotes from Finney in the leaflet, *'A Heart-Felt Cry for Revival;'* Charles Finney said; *"Revival is nothing else than a new beginning of obedience to God."* As Father Nash would lead people to pray for revival, David took up the same stance. He prayed for revival personally and he encouraged others to follow. David wrote: *"I am aware that it can be a delusion to be always waiting for God to move in revival while we do nothing."* David, instead of doing nothing and just waiting, prayed and encouraged others to pray. Revival was one of his daily prayers.

David was very clear about three things in regard to revival.

85 Cymbala (1997), "Fresh Wind, Fresh Fire." Zondervan Publishing House.

First, revival was for the Church, not the world. David made seven statements about revival in the leaflet. The focus of each statement was on God's People. I just want to mention two; *"Revival is a cold Church being set ablaze with holy fire"*, and *"Revival is a powerless church coming back into the ability of God's Holy Spirit."*

Secondly, revival was the Church going back to the Acts of the Apostles. David wrote: *"Pentecost is God's great specimen day for revival."* David's friend and colleague in ministry Selwyn Hughes wrote this: *"Every revival contains some feature of the Day of Pentecost, for Pentecost is God's pattern of blessing for His Church."*[86]

The sad thing is this. Many of the books written on revivals have been written by people who do not believe that the work of the Holy Spirit, as revealed in the Book of Acts, is for today. They are called cessationists and I have written about this particular stance in topic 6 of this section. There have been books written on the Welsh Revival that contain nothing about the Pentecostal elements which were revealed during this mighty outpouring of the Holy Spirit. In my research of this Revival for another book I wrote, I found that the people who were baptised in the Holy Spirit and spoke in 'other tongues' during this Revival in Wales. I mentioned, earlier in the book, the story of Frank Hodges who was filled with the Holy Spirit and spoke a new language in a house not many doors away from Evan Robert's house.

The gifts of the Holy Spirit were also revealed during the Welsh Revival. Noel Gibbard in his book, *'Fire on the Altar,'* writes about Sarah Jones. She lived in a village in South Wales, and exercised many of the spiritual gifts, including prophesying, healing and speaking in tongues. Evan Roberts visited Sarah on at least one occasion.[87]

Thirdly, David wrote, *"Revival is the Church being restored to normality."*

---

86 Hughes (2004), "Revival: Times of Refreshing." CWR.
87 Gibbard (2002), "On the Wings of a Dove." Bryntirion Press.

For what purpose, you may ask? Again, quoting David; "*Revival and Harvest are inseparably linked and if revival is God working in His Church by the Spirit's power then Harvest is the Church working in the world by the Spirit's power.*"

For David, revival was key to the harvesting in these last days. He looked at the Book of Acts and saw a church that was the specimen for today. He would have encouraged us today to seek the Lord, not follow some American model, but the model of Church as seen in the Book of Acts.

I have a pamphlet where David, with a prophetic edge, speaks into Ulster, the great verse of 2 Chronicles 7:14: "*If my people, which are called by my name, will humble themselves and pray and seek my face and turn from their wicked ways then will I hear from heaven and will forgive their sin and will heal their land.*" This scripture has often been used by preachers to challenge God's people to come back to their God: a verse that carries the call to seek God for revival. David wrote; "*In this verse of scripture, God gave Israel and to us four definite steps to three tremendous blessings which the church and nation are in great need of at the present time.*"

The specific challenge that David gave to the church in Ulster was this: "*Ulster has been a highly favoured part of God's earth, founded upon Christian principles, and a stronghold of evangelical Christianity and missionary outreach. Nevertheless, those whom God gives a lot to, He expects a lot of, and He will not allow us forever to take the privileges His grace has given for granted or to live indefinitely upon the accumulated spiritual capital of bygone generations, thinking that we are God's special pets as we self-righteously look down our noses at those we consider beneath our standing.*

"*God has abundantly blessed us, but the hour of reckoning is upon us in church and nation, and the truth which we have possessed will become the very measure of our accountability. This is an hour for absolute honesty before God on the part of His people for an inevitable showdown is coming for all unreality, hypocrisy and religious sham. ONLY REALITY COUNTS NOW. Too much is at stake and too many souls are facing eternity without Christ even for our nation for the Church to continue in its attitudes of lukewarmness, religious pride and indifference."*

The final line of the pamphlet was; *"CHRISTIANS OF ULSTER, AWAKE."* This quotation puts into perspective what David believed about revival. It would take revival to bring the Church back into its true position with the Lord. Revival, for David, was not just about having a happy time on earth where everything would be good, but revival was key to the Church rising and bringing in the harvest before the return of Jesus Christ.

Topic 10
Jesus, the Coming King
Behold, He Cometh...

David gave this call to Christians in one of his pamphlets; "IT IS LATER THAN WE THINK! IT IS ONE HALF MINUTE TO MIDNIGHT! JESUS IS COMING SOON!"

This brings me to another area of Bible teaching that David wrote about; the return of Jesus Christ, the fourth truth of the Full Gospel: Jesus - Saviour, Healer, Baptiser in the Holy Spirit and Coming King.

As I mentioned in an earlier section, David went to a Pentecostal Bible school in South Wales for two years. This denomination, The Apostolic Church, taught and preached these truths about Jesus; they believed in the virgin birth, sinless life, atoning death, triumphant resurrection, ascension and abiding intercession of our Lord Jesus Christ; and His second coming and millennial reign upon earth. The denomination, which still exists today, were pre-tribulationist in belief. They believed the rapture of the Church would take place before the tribulation and after the seven years of Jacob's trouble upon the earth, Jesus would return to earth and establish His millennial Kingdom.

David writing in the leaflet, 'Behold He Cometh,' confirms his acceptance of the truths that were taught to him in Bible school; *"The Second Advent of Christ is to take place in two distinct stages. First, He will come to the air **for His saints...** Secondly; Christ shall come **with His saints** to the earth to reign."* David had this expectation *"The greatest Divine Intervention into human affairs in 2000 years, is about to take place in our time."*

David wrote this poem in regard to the hope that he had:

> *Beyond the curtain of time there's a land that's sublime,*
> *And our loved ones are there in its glory so fair,*
> *And some day it will be that our Saviour we'll see*
> *When we pass beyond the curtain of time.*
>
> *Beyond the curtain of time there's no death bell to chime,*
> *And no tears ever flow as they do here below,*
> *All redeemed ones will sing ever unto their king,*
> *When we pass beyond the curtain of time.*
>
> *Beyond the curtain of time in eternity's clime,*
> *There's no sin will e'er blight in that Heavenly light,*
> *We shall never more roam from our blood purchased home,*
> *When we pass beyond the curtain of time.*

In a leaflet titled, "Anticipating Eternity," David wrote; "A few years ago, I asked the Lord how I could be a wiser man. I share with you His answer: 'Live in an increasing awareness of Deity, Calvary and Eternity'." He asked himself a question in the leaflet: "What I Anticipate In The Heavenly Eternity". He gave eight things that he was anticipating in the Heavenly Eternity.

One thing was very personal for David. He wrote, "There will be the greatest time of reunion ever known. In our locality two sisters who became separated during childhood were reunited after 70 years. Imagine the joyous celebration; what is that compared with the rejoicing in Heaven as loved ones meet again to part no more. I will meet a mother who I had for only the first month of my life. Don't tell me that won't be exciting."

One further thing was: **To appear at the Judgement Seat of Christ.** David writes; "This is where rewards for service will be determined… We do not work for reward but because we love our Saviour and Master, yet He insists that we shall all appear before Him and have our life's work tested with searching Divine fire." This is not a judgement about whether we will go to Heaven, because those who appear at this judgement are already saved; those who 'died in Jesus' and are already in Heaven; and there will be those Christians who are transported to Heaven when Jesus comes to the sky. (1 Thessalonians 4:16-17)

This appearance at a judgement seat is about our service for Jesus after coming to faith. We are not saved by works but we are saved to work. Have we been light? Have we been salt? Have we carried forth those works which Paul writes about in Ephesians, "created in Christ Jesus"?

David writes this about this judgement; "This will separate what is superficial from that which is genuine and of lasting worth. The Scripture tells us there are crowns of reward and if it should be that after the test there is a rewarding crown for me I would love to take it and, with the Elders of Revelation 4:10, lay it down at Jesus' feet and say Thank you Lord!"

How often is this Bible truth about Christians appearing before the Judgement Seat of Christ preached and taught about in churches today?

The return of Jesus Christ has implications for the Church, the World, Israel and satan. For Christians, we must be ready and looking for His appearing. David writes; "Immediately after the rapture of the Church, and for approximately seven years there will be a terrible time of persecution, judgement and tribulation. All this will be climaxed in the battle of Armageddon. Revelations 16:13-16. Then Christ shall come with His saints and destroy the Antichrist and his allied evil forces that at that time will be converging on Israel with the purpose of utterly destroying the Jewish nation. 2 Thessalonians 2:1-10; Revelations 10:11-21; 14:14-20; Isaiah 34:1-8."

What is the trigger for these events in the world and in Israel? The return of Jesus to the sky to take His saints away will start a series of events which will bring devastation to the world. With the rapture, Christians will face the Judgement Seat of Christ but we will also be included in the Marriage Supper of the Lamb. But for the world there will be increasing years of war, death, famine across the face of the earth until Jesus comes back and stands on the earth once again.

This then is the truth that must be emphasised. We don't know when the rapture of the Church will take place. In another leaflet, "Christ is coming! No man knows the hour. LIVE READY!" David wrote; "We must be in Christ to be preserved from coming judgement and tribulation, as Noah was in the Ark and was kept by the power of God from the destruction that came upon the rest of the world."

From what is preached in many circles today you can understand why many Christians have the idea that life is just going to go on and on, like that famous battery. For David, Eternity, Heaven, the appearance again of Jesus Christ, the rapture of the Church, were all part of the Gospel story. For David the Gospel story didn't finish at the Cross or with an empty tomb, or even with the Day of Pentecost. The final chapter is Jesus meeting with His Bride, the Church, and establishing His Kingdom on earth.

In the leaflet, 'God's 5-Fold Goal Through The Gospel,' David identifies the fifth goal: **To inspire Gospel believers to look for the Lord Jesus and be in readiness for His second coming.**

David wrote: "The early Christians seem to have had far more enthusiasm regarding Christ's coming than the present day Church. Their watchword was 'Maranatha' – The Lord is coming!" I found this little poem amongst David's handwritten papers and notes:

No need to worry o'er the future,
It is all in the Master's hand.
No need to fear about tomorrow,
It will be as He has planned.
Whether the sky be stormy,
Whether the day be fair,
No need to worry,
No need to hurry,
God will be right there.

Topic 11

Demonology

We have an enemy who has an army ......

This is a subject that is not talked about much in the church today. I found a study that David had prepared on this Bible topic. There are two things to remember as we look into what David wrote on this subject.

Firstly, Mark 16:15-18 says; "And then he told them; 'You are to go into all the world and preach the Good News to everyone, everywhere. Those who believe and are baptised will be saved. But those who refuse to believe will be condemned. And those who believe shall use my authority to cast out demons, and they shall speak new languages. They will be able even to handle snakes with safety, and if they drink anything poisonous, it won't hurt them; and they will be able to place their hands on the sick and heal them." (Living Bible)

Secondly, all the demons that Jesus dealt with in his ministry are still around. I have never come across or heard of a cemetery where the demons that revealed themselves in Jesus' day are buried. The demons that were dealt with in the life of the Gadarene man are still around. Think of the other incidents in the ministry of Jesus where individuals were delivered from the demonic. For example, consider the young boy who would be thrown into a fire; and the Syrophoenician's daughter. I want to mention Luke 9:49; John is saying to Jesus; *"Master we saw someone casting out demons in Your name."* The demons of the Gospels are still around, and they are still causing heartache and distress for individuals and their families.

David wrote *"These spirit forces of satan are constant in their attack against the things of God. They are in eternal opposition to all that is of God and seek to hinder His purpose; bind His people, and mar and destroy His creation through all kinds of evil."*

Again, with the exactness of a surgeon, David breaks down this topic and lays a Biblical foundation for the identification of demon activities, the defeating of such forces, and the building up of the person set free.

He gives this practical advice at the end of the leaflet: *"Avoid an unhealthy over-emphasis on Demonology. Let your life be Christ-centred, and everything else will be held in right perspective and become part of your overall Christian knowledge and experience."*

Topic 12
The Church
Serving together...

David was an itinerant evangelist and Bible teacher. He never had an office, a personal assistant or a ministry title. The leaflets, pamphlets and bookmarks simply had this note: *'by Evangelist D.J. Greenow'* or *'by Evangelist DAVID GREENOW, Bleary Road, Portadown, Craigavon, N. Ireland, BT63 5NE.'* He didn't attempt to establish a church where he could have been the Senior Pastor or establish a para-church ministry with their own conferences, books and holidays.

David, with others, was instrumental in establishing the ministry, International Gospel Outreach (IGO). From my experience of IGO, one thing that stood out for me was they were to support local churches in their mission locally and globally. David's heart was for the Body of Christ and every local expression of that. No local church leader should have felt threatened by David. He would have only encouraged every Christian to be involved in their local fellowship and seek to serve within that sphere.

David prepared some very comprehensive material on Christian Service. In the material he highlighted five things that were required in our service for Christ:

➤   Calvary motivated. 2 Cor 5:14; 1 Cor 2:1-5.
➤   Christ centred. Col 1:18.

➤   Holy Spirit Anointing. Zech. 4:6.
➤   Bible based. 2 Tim 4:2; Isa 8:20.
➤   Church orientated. Matt 16:18

Christ is committed to building His church. Are we?

David, in his early Christian life and through his attendance at a Bible school, would have been taught about the vision and purpose that Christ had for the Church. This never left him. One of David's regular prayer requests was for '*a daily increase of the church.*' His writings on Revival and the call to pray for Revival had this focus: "*Revival is a powerless church coming into the ability of God's Holy Spirit.*" David's encouragement and teaching on Revival was centred on the Church of today coming back to the Day of Pentecost.

David wrote a paper on '*The New Testament Church.*' As with everything that David wrote, this paper was Bible-based and extensive in the pulling together of verses and truths from the Bible. David was a skilled craftsman in linking Scripture to Scripture in whatever theme he was writing on. I am not going to quote extensively from this paper. David is very clear in regard to what the Church is not: it is not a building made by man; it is not any one particular sect or denomination; it is not a mere social or religious organisation.

Regarding what the Church is, David wrote: "*They are a Body of people called out by God, through the Gospel, from the world, sin and satan's kingdom, to gather unto Christ. These born-again Christians belong to this one Mystical Universal Church of Jesus Christ, which finds visible expression through a vast number of 'local churches' scattered throughout the world.*"

David wrote this regarding the purpose of the Church: "*It is the business of the Church to make clear by word and deed the facts that Jesus is alive today. God's Word is utterly reliable, and His power has not changed."* He believed in the Church of the Lord Jesus Christ, and lived to support and encourage every local expression of the Church.

Topic 13
The Prophetic
Seeing with the eyes of the Lord...

There are a number of aspects regarding the prophetic ministry that David carried and displayed in his life.

Firstly, David had a gift of prophecy in accord with 1 Corinthians 12. He used this gift to encourage, build up and comfort the Body of Christ.

Secondly, he wrote about the prophetic agenda and the future return of the Lord Jesus Christ. I have already mentioned what David believed and taught about the Coming of the Lord Jesus Christ.

Thirdly, his prophetic insight and spiritual concern for Ulster. He was a prophet. David lived and ministered in Ulster and the Island of Ireland throughout the Troubles. I have a leaflet entitled, '*The Ulster Crisis.*' When I read the leaflet I thought immediately, how courageous David was to put pen to paper to write about the crisis. He '*pulls no punches*' as we say. Also, his analysis of the situation was historically sound and culturally relevant. He was not writing from any political bias or prejudice. Writing from a spiritual persuasion, he said; "*If ever Ireland needed prayer it is now, and will you please accept the burden of intercession for this nation... As I have written this, the atmosphere in Ulster is tense and in the last few minutes news has come through of another explosion in Belfast with several dead and many injured. I trust every child of God will share the prayer burden for a people caught up in the tragic events of this present hour that a new day of spiritual awakening may dawn for Irish people. Amen. Prayer changes things and people."*

In this leaflet, David quoted the well-known verses from 2 Chronicles 7:14: *"If My people..."* David produced a leaflet on this verse entitled, '*A Message from God for Crisis Days.*' He made this comment; *"We who live in Northern Ireland are facing a tremendous challenge against the very life and existence of the nation as we have known it, and liberties and privileges, so long taken for granted, are in danger of being taken from us."*

David was a prophetic voice into Northern Ireland. He wrote further; *"These are the days in which we are tempted to pass the blame to someone else, and so the government is ridiculed, or one section of the community continually accuses the rest of society. Many people are confused and frustrated regarding the situation in which there appears to be far too much religion and precious little true Christianity."*

Remember, David wasn't somewhere on the mainland writing these challenging comments. He wasn't some international Bible teacher who would just fly in for conferences in Northern Ireland and speak into the situation and then fly out. During my time ministering in Northern Ireland, I saw that many times. They would fly in and speak into the nation and then fly out.

David had lived in Ulster since 1952 and the place and the people were in his heart. He was living near Portadown and Lurgan; two hotbeds of the troubles in Northern Ireland. He travelled to South Armagh. An area that was known as "bandit country." He had walked through the horrendous situation when the Mountain Lodge church was attacked by terrorists. Lurgan was known as the most divided town in Northern Ireland. Portadown had its flash points also. When Emily's parents died in 1979, Emily asked David if he wanted to move to England. His answer was "no." David lived the situation and God used him to be a prophet to the people of Northern Ireland and Ireland. He didn't run away like a Jonah; he didn't hide like Elijah did on one occasion but he continued to serve and speak for His Master during years of conflict and troubles that touched many families in the province; Christian as well as non- Christian. I think David demonstrated not a little boldness and courage to let God use him to speak into the situation in Ulster. What was the key to this? David knew he had a calling from God and he also knew the placing of God in The Kingdom.

Topic 14
Our Response
The Challenging Now...

In the late 1980s David produced a leaflet titled, 'The Challenging Now.' In this pamphlet, David wrote "It is almost 47 years since I accepted Jesus Christ as my personal Saviour and almost 37 since I ventured into full-time ministry for my Lord. It has been a great joy and privilege to give of my time effort to the greatest purpose in the world, that of being in Divine service. During the years that are now past I have travelled many thousands of miles in different countries and constantly acquired new experiences as I have to tell men of their need of Christ and to build up the Christian believer in the most holy faith. As a result of God's dealings with my life, a whole range of scriptural and present-day facts have made impact upon me and as I share some of these with you I pray that God will speak into your hearts." The seven facts were as follows...

➢   **THE LATENESS OF THE HOUR** – "Bible signs of the end of this age are abundantly manifest on every hand."

➢   **THE DEMAND FOR REALITY** – "With every passing day the Church is being crowded into the position where only reality counts."

➢   **THE DOWNWARD COURSE OF THE WORLD** – "Never have I been as conscious that this world is on the wrong road."

➢   **THE INFLUENCE OF YOUTH** – "We are told that half the population of the earth is under 25 years of age… The Church must have a positive message for youth as well as for the whole family."

➢   **THE MARCH OF CHANGE** – "God is calling for change in His Church as His end-time purposes increasingly come into view."

➢   **THE CHURCH'S GREATEST ENEMY** – "The Church has many enemies such as modernism… Nevertheless, there is no enemy as deadly as that which can exist in the hearts of those who profess to follow Christ, and that is the attitude of indifference resulting from the loss of first love for Jesus."

➢   **ENCOURAGING END-TIME EVENTS** – "Tremendous changes for the good are taking place in our day as dedicated believing children of God explore the possibilities of new breakthroughs into further dimensions of spiritual reality." There were three particular events that David highlighted.

Firstly, the multitudes that were finding Christ through the preaching of the Gospel. David wrote this pamphlet in 1989 and quotes "an average of 90,000 persons are born again into the kingdom of God daily, and about 1000 new local Churches are opened weekly. The Cross of Christ still saves. Romans 1:16." I know that those figures, that David quoted, have increased and continue to increase as we go into the third decade of the 21st century.

Secondly, David wrote: "the power of God is producing the greatest number of healing testimonies since Bible days and this is arousing tremendous interest in many circles. Jesus is alive and Bible days are here. Heb. 13:8." It is so sad that over many, many years there has been a belief promoted in the Church that healing has been with drawn and so there has been the emphasis of preaching the Word. The commission of Mark 16 is not time or generation bound. God still heals today. In the last couple of weeks in my own life, I have proved the healing power of God. In the church I presently attend, we saw someone healed through a Zoom prayer meeting a few weeks ago. Healing demonstrates the power of God and, as in Jesus's day, it gets people's attention for the preaching of the Gospel.

Thirdly, David highlighted the "unparalleled outpourings of the Holy Spirit are being experienced by Christians of various denominations as God fulfils His promises to send the latter rain of His Spirit in the end time. Thirsty hearts are being filled and moved to compassionate action, clearer vision, deeper dedication and richer relationships, as Christ moves to fulfil His declared purpose in the earth: that of building His people into an overcoming Church that is destined to have increasing impact on the world." David saw this as a continuing fulfilment of Acts 3:19, "times of refreshing" being sent "from the presence of the Lord" for the Church and, as a result, an empowering for mission into the world.

I honestly think that these facts are still relevant for us, if not more relevant since David wrote the leaflet, 'The Challenging Now.' David finished the leaflet with this challenge: "From now until the dawn of eternity may we, each one, determine to live in the light of Calvary and in the now of God's purposes." What better response can we give, in honour of David Greenow, but more importantly, in honour of Almighty God to serve this generation with Calvary and the Day of Pentecost being living realities in our lives.

I trust you have enjoyed, been encouraged but also been challenged regarding what you believe and what you live for as we have looked at some of the writings of David Greenow.

I remember a time in November 2017 when I was faced with some serious questions and decisions about ministry. I keep a journal, and Lamentations 3:21-26 had been an encouragement at the start of the month. My wife and I were confused and disappointed regarding the situation that we found ourselves in. I was working on this book at the time, and a bookmark that David had produced just popped out. It was headed, 'God Meant It For Good. Gen 50:20. Our **ALL** wise, **ALL** loving, **Al**mighty Heavenly Father will **Al**ways work for our highest good, in **ALL** He permits in **ALL** of our lives.' (Romans 8:28 was also quoted) This small orange bookmark was a great encouragement to me. I have it pinned to my journal entries around that time in November 2017.

As I have already mentioned, I trust that these writings of David's have been a blessing and also a challenge to you. I have certainly enjoyed studying and reading them. In a few days of finishing this section I started some studies with a group of Christians on the Person and Work of the Holy Spirit. I used some of David's leaflets on the Holy Spirit to hand out to those attending the studies.

David's writings are still relevant today because they are Bible-based, Christ glorifying and, with a heart to seek and know, the Holy Spirit will use them to challenge our hearts.

David was also famous for his sayings. When I had the privilege of burying David. I quoted this saying; "Let us open up our hearts to the unlimited power of God."

Again, quoting from another article that David wrote for the Christian Lifestyle magazine, which was titled, 'Releasing the Power of God,' David gave these pithy and meaningful comments -

"There may be many mighties but only one Almighty."

"He is not dependent on the majority because He has the monopoly."

"God's power is not limited by any problem."

"Some tell us that the 'age of miracles is past' but there is no age of miracles, only a God of miracles."[88]

As I draw this section to a close, I was wondering what David would want for us to experience and know from his writings. I think he would want us to know –

His Loving Heavenly Father who has given us untold promises in Jesus Christ.

The person of the Lord Jesus Christ: Saviour, Healer, Baptiser in the Holy Spirit and Coming King.

The Person and power of the Holy Spirit to continue the works of the Lord Jesus Christ.

---

88 Christian Lifestyle magazine. Published by The Apostolic Church.

A Christian life that is overcoming and abundant.

The Christian's discipline of prayer and Bible meditation with ongoing fillings of the Holy Spirit.

To be part of the Body of Christ that grows and is gifted by the Holy Spirit.

You may be saying, 'that is a lot of things.' Yes, but David had a **BIG** God, who is, and who can do more than we can imagine or think.

PART 4

A SELECTION OF
BOOKMARKS THAT
DAVID WROTE

Pray to God the Father. John 15:16, 16:23. Matthew 7:11

Rely on God's promises. Numbers 23:19. Jeremiah 1:12. Hebrews 10:23.

Ask in the Name of Jesus. John 14:13-14, 16:23-24. Acts 4:29-30.

Yearn earnestly for the answers. Mark 11:24. Proverbs 10:24. Psalm 34:17.

Enter His presence with Praise and Thanksgiving. Psalm 100:4. Philippians 4:6. 1 Thessalonians 5:18.

Reject all doubt and unbelief. Hebrews 3:19, 4:2, 11:6.

Persist when tempted to be discouraged. Luke 11:5-10, 18:1-8.

Open your heart in forgiveness to others. Mark 11:25. 1 Peter 3:7. Matthew 18:23-35.

Wait patiently when answer is delayed. Psalm 40:1-3. Acts 1:4. Hebrews 6:12.

Ever seek to glorify God. John 14:13. 1 Corinthians 10:31. Isaiah 42:8.

Reckon on God's love, power and the enablement of His Holy Spirit. 1 John 4:8-10. Jeremiah 32:27. Romans 8:26-27.

STRENGTH FOR YOUR DAY
....

SOURCE
Isaiah 26:4 "In the Lord Jehovah is everlasting strength."
Genesis 17:1; 1 Chronicles 29:12.

PROMISE
Deuteronomy 33:25 "As thy days so shall thy strength be."
Isaiah 41:10; Psalm 29:11.

CONDITIONS
Isaiah 40:31 "They that wait (expectantly) upon the Lord shall renew their strength."
Daniel 11:32 Know God.
Hebrews 11:33 & 34 Trust Him.

PRAYER
Psalm 119:28 "Strengthen Thou me according to Thy Word."
Nehemiah 6:9; Psalm 22:19.

AFFIRMATION
Isaiah 49:5 "My God shall be My strength."
Psalm 71:16 Philippians 4:13

EXAMPLES
Ezra 7:28 "I was strengthened as the Hand of the Lord my God was upon me."
2 Timothy 4:17 2 Samuel 22:33,40.

INVITATION
Isaiah 27:5 "Take hold of My strength."
Isaiah 41:1 Ephesians 6:10

Psalm 46:1
"God is our refuge and strength, a very present help in trouble."

JESUS – THE SAME – TO-DAY
Heb. 13:8

1. IN HIS TENDER COMPASSION. When He saw the multitudes He was moved with compassion on them. Mt. 9:36.
2. IN HIS WILLINGNESS TO FORGIVE. Be of good cheer! Thy sins be forgiven thee. Mt 9:2. Neither do I condemn thee, go and sin no more. John 8:11.
3. IN HIS FAITHFULNESS TO HIS PROMISES. He who promised is reliable and faithful to His Word. Heb. 10:23 (A.B.)
4. IN HIS UNLIMITED POWER. He is able to save to the uttermost. Heb. 7:25. He healed them all. Mt 12:15. He is able to keep you from falling. Jude 24.
5. IN HIS PURPOSE FOR MANKIND. I am come that they might have Life More Abundantly. Jn. 10:10.
   "Still He loves to save the sinful, Heal the sick and lame,
   Cheer the mourner, still the tempest. Glory to His Name."

GOD'S
BIBLE ULTIMATES

NO GREATER

Person ever lived – Lord Jesus Christ. Colossians 1:14-20. Phil 2:5-11. Hebrews 1:1-12. Revelation 1:5-8, 18.

Event in human history - Christ's Calvary sacrifice for sinners. John 19. Isaiah 53. 1 Peter 2:24; 3:18.

Message ever told - Good news of Christ's full Salvation Blessings. Romans 1:16; 10:15; 15:29. 1 Corinthians 15:1-3.

Gift ever offered - Eternal and abundant life in Christ the Saviour. John 3:16. Romans 6:32. 2 Corinthians 9:15. Romans 8:32.

Life –change to be experienced - Passing from spiritual death to life through a new birth. John 1:12; 3:3-8; 5.24. Acts 26:15-18. 2 Corinthians 5:17.

Assets can be acquired - Incalculable riches in Christ Jesus. Ephesians 1:3,7,8,11; 3:8. 1 Corinthians 3:21,22. 2 Corinthians 8:9.

Assignment ever delivered - To go to the world and tell every person the good news of a Saviour. Mark 16:15. Luke 2:10,11; 24:26,27. John 20:21. 1 Thessalonians 2:4.

Guide to life and living – God's Word, the scriptures of truth. Psalm 119:9,105. 2 Timothy 3:16. Deuteronomy 4:10. Romans 15:4.

Communication system available – Talking to our Almighty Father in prayer. Jeremiah 33:3. Matthew 7:7-11. Mark11:24, 25. Hebrews 4:16.

Security possible – kept by the Power of God. 1 Peter 1:5. Psalm 91; 121; 125:2. Colossians 3:3.

Requirement ever made – to love God and people. Matthew 22:35-39. Jude 21. Ephesians 3:17-19; 5:2. 1 Thessalonians 3:12.

Lifestyle to adopt – Christlikeness in life and ministry. 1 Peter 2:21. John 12:26; 5:8. Ephesians 4:11-13. 1 John 2:6.

Success level achievable – Total obedience to the will of God. Joshua 1:8. John 14:23; 15:10. Matthew 7:21. Psalm 40:8.

Adventure known – Walking in fellowship with God. Genesis 5:24. Malachi 2:6. 1 Corinthians 1:9. 1 John 1:3.

Investment returns – Eternal rewards. Matthew 16:24-27; 19:29. 1 Timothy 4:6-8. John 12:24-26. Revelation 22:12.

Assured destination – God's Home, Heaven. John 14:2,3. 2 Corinthians 5:1. Luke 10:20. Revelation 7:9. Hebrews 11:13-16.

J JIREH – THE LORD WILL PROVIDE
Gen. 22:14. Phil. 4:19. Rom. 8:32.
E ROPHI – THE LORD OUR PHYSICIAN
Exod. 15:26. Mat. 8:17. Mark 6:56.
H SHALOM – THE LORD OUR PEACE
Judges 6:24. Isa 53:5. Eph 2:14.
O NISSI – THE LORD OUR CAPTAIN
Exod. 17:15. Heb. 2:10. 2 Cor. 2:14.
V RAAH – THE LORD OUR SHEPHERD
Psa. 23:1. John 10:7-16.
A TSIDKENU – THE LORD OUR RIGHTEOUSNESS
Jer. 23:6. 33:16. 2 Cor 5:21.
H SHAMMAH – THE LORD IS PRESENT
Ezek. 48:35. Mat. 28:20. Heb. 13:5.

THE HEAVENLY FATHER AND HIS FAMILY

I will be a Father to you and you shall be my sons and daughters says the Lord Almighty.
2 Corinthians 6:18

He imparts His life and nature to them.

2 Peter 1:4
John 1:12
1 John 3:2
Galatians 3:26; 4:4-7
Ephesians 2:19
Romans 8:15

He shares His love and fellowship with all His children.

John 14:21,23; 16:27
Psalm 103:13
1 John 1:3, 7
2 Corinthians 13:14
1 Peter 5:7

He gives attention to their prayer desires and requests.

Matthew 7:7-11
John 15:16; 16:23, 24
Luke 11:1-13
Philippians 4:6 & 7
1 John 3:22; 5:14 & 15

He guards and protects them all times.

1 Peter 1:5
John 10:27-29
Jude 24
Psalm 91:4, 11, 12;
Psalm 121:5-8
Psalm 125:1 & 2

He lovingly corrects, instructs and disciplines them.

Proverbs 3:11 & 12
Hebrews 12:5-10
Deuteronomy 8:5
Job 5:17; 23:10
Psalm 94:12
Psalm 32:8

He accepts responsibility to supply all their needs.

Romans 8:32
Philippians 4:19
Matthew 6:8-13; 25:32
Psalms 34:10; 23:5

He provides a spiritual and eternal home for them.

Himself – Psalms 91:1; 90:1
Local Church – Hebrews 10:25
                        Acts 2:42;
Heaven Itself – John 14:2 & 3
Hebrews 11:16

He gives His all wise Holy Spirit to constantly indwell, instruct and enable them.
Luke 11:13; 24:49
John 14:16, 17, 26; 16:13 & 14
Acts 1:5 & 8; 2:33, 38 & 39

He plans only the highest good for all their future.

Romans 8:28
Ephesians 1:3; 2:4-7
1 Peter 1:3-5
Luke 12:32
1 Corinthians 2:9

He gives them His Word for encouragement and help in daily living.

Matthew 4:4
Acts 20:32
2 Peter 1:4
Ephesians 6:17
Romans 15:4
Psalm 119

SATAN'S LIMITATIONS

HE CANNOT

Annul God's Covenant Word
John 10:35; Psalm 89:34; 119:37;
Ezekiel 12:25; Mark 13:31; 1 Peter 1:25.

Reverse the work of Christ's Cross
John 19:30; Ecclesiastes 3:14;
Hebrews 2:14; 9:12; Romans 5:8;
1 Peter 3:18; Colossians 2:14,15.

Dethrone the God Exalted Christ
Ephesians 1:20-22; Phil 2:9;
1 Peter 3:21,22; Psalm 110:1-7;
1 Corinthians 15:25; Matt 28:18.

Overpower the Almighty
Genesis 17:1; Jeremiah 32:27;
Isaiah 14:12-15; Luke 10:17-19;
Mark 5:1-20.

Demolish the Christ built Church
Matt 16:18; Ephesians 2:6-7; 3:21;
1 Peter 1:3-5; Revelation 7:9-12.

Outwit the Wisdom of God.
Rom 11:33-34; Dan 2:20-22, 28;
Ephesians 3:10; 1 Corinthians 2:6-8.

Withstand the dedicated God indwelt
Gospel believer. James 4:7; 2 Peter
5:8,9; 1 John 4:4; 5:4; Revelation 12:11.

Undo the events and results of
Pentecost. Acts 2:1-4, 38, 39, 42-47;
Titus 3:5,6; 1 Corinthians 12:1-11;
Galatians 5:22,23; Romans 15:18-20;

Hold in captivity the person who knows,
believes and acts upon Gospel Truth.
Isaiah 60:1; John 8:32; Acts 26:16-18;
Romans 8:12; Galatians 5:1.

Escape His divinely appointed destiny.
Isaiah 14:12-14; Rev 12:10; 20:10;
Matthew 25:41.

10 COMMANDMENTS FOR YOUR FAITH

Be strong in the Lord and the
power of His might.
Ephesians 6:10 Be strong
1 Corinthians 16:13.
2 Timothy 2:1.

Be anxious for nothing.
Phil 4:6 Pray!
John 14:1. Ephesians 6:18.

Be of good cheer.
John 16:33. Phil 4:4.
Psalm 32:11. Cheer up!

Be not dismayed, discouraged.
Isaiah 41:10.
I am thy God Isaiah 43:1,2.
1 Samuel 30:6. David
encouraged himself in the Lord.
Hebrews 10:35.

Be thankful in all things.
Colossians 3:15 Be ye thankful
Psalm 100:4. 1 Thess 5:18

Be transformed by the renewing of
your mind. Romans 12:3 Changed
thinking-changed living.
Phil 4:8. Joshua 1:8

Let the peace of God rule in your
hearts. Colossians 3:15.
Let it! John 14:27. Job 22:21

Cast thy burden upon the Lord.
Psalm 55:22. He will sustain you
1 Peter 5:7. Matthew 6:32

Be not overcome of evil but
overcome evil with good.
Rom 12:21. be an overcomer!
1 John 2:13; 4:4; 5:5

Keep yourselves in the love of
God. Jude 21 Trust it.
1 John 4:16 Respond to it.
1 John 4:19 Share it.
1 John 4:7. 1 Thess 3:12
1 Corinthians 13.

JESUS– OUR – PEACE Eph. 2:14

ANNOUNCED AT HIS BIRTH. On earth PEACE, goodwill toward men (Luke 2:14). His Name shall be called...The Prince of PEACE (Isaiah 9:6).

DEMONSTRATED IN HIS LIFE. PEACE, be still (Mark 4:39). Thy faith hath saved thee; go in PEACE (Luke 7:50).

BEQUEATHED AT HIS DEATH. PEACE I leave with you, My PEACE I give unto you...Let not your heart be troubled, neither let it be afraid (John 14:1,27).

PURCHASED THROUGH HIS SACRIFICE. Having made PEACE through the blood of His cross (Col. 1:20). The chastisement of our PEACE was upon Him (Isaiah 53:5).

IMPARTED THROUGH HIS WORD. These things Have I spoken unto you that in Me ye might have PEACE (John 16:33). Jesus says, PEACE BE UNTO YOU (John 20:19).

THE LORD OF PEACE HIMSELF GIVE YOU PEACE ALWAYS BY ALL MEANS (2 Thes. 3:16).

Christ's throne will never pass away; Above the storms of life He reigns,
The life He gives can ne'er decay, Throughout the years His Peace remains.

TRUST IN THE LORD
Prov. 3:5

TRUSTING IS THE SECRET OF –

1. PEACE
   Thou wilt keep Him in perfect peace, whose mind is stayed on Thee; because He trusteth in Thee. Isa. 26:3. Rom. 15:13.
2. HAPPINESS
   Whoso trusteth in this Lord, Happy is he. Prov. 16:20. Psa. 33:21.
3. STABILITY
   They that trust in this Lord shall be as Mount Zion, which cannot be removed, but abideth for ever. Psa.125:1. 112:7.
4. PROTECTION
   His is a shield unto them that put their Trust in Him. Prov. 30:5. 29:25.
5. DIVINE FAVOUR
   He that Trusteth in The Lord, mercy shall compass him about. Psa. 32:10. 31:19

I WILL TRUST AND NOT BE AFRAID: FOR THE LORD JEHOVAH IS MY STRENGTH AND SONG. Isa 12:2

MY GREAT PHYSICIAN

The Lord is my Physician.
I shall not fail to trust His care for me.
He maketh me to know that He "Himself took our infirmities and bore our sicknesses and with His stripes we are healed".
He leadeth me by the still waters of "The Fountain of Life".
He restoreth my body to health.
Though I walk through the valley of the shadow of doubt I shall not fear to take God at His Word, for He saith, - "I am the Lord that healeth thee".
Thy rich promises comfort and strengthen me.
Thou preparest a life of victory for me in the presence of discouraging symptoms.
Thou anointest me with the oil of the Holy Spirit for healing.
My cup runneth over continually with Praise to my God.
Salvation, Healing and Holy Living will be mine all the days of my life; and I shall **keep trusting Jesus as my great Physician forever.**

Antom Darms

THE GRATITUDE ATTITUDE

1. Is a fitting response to God's bountiful giving. Psalm 106:1; Acts 17:25; Colossians 1:12-14.
2. It saves us from the sin of ingratitude. Romans 1:21; 2 Timothy 3:2; Luke 17:17.
3. Brings us more into accord with Heaven's activities. Rev. 4:9; 7:9-12; 11:16,17.
4. Brings pleasure to the heart of God. Psalm 69:30,31; 107:22; 116:17.
5. Aligns us with the thanksgiving commands and exhortations of the Bible, God's Word. Colossians 3:15; 1 Thessalonians 5:18; Psalm 105:1; 107:1,22; Leviticus 22:29.
6. Shows we are following the example of Christ and others gone before us.
   Christ – Matthew 11:25; Luke 22:19; John 11:41.
   David – 1 Chron. 29:13; Ps 116:17;
   Judah – 2 Chron. 29:31; 33:16
   Paul – Acts 28:15; 1 Tim. 1;12;
   Colossians 1:3.
7. Fills our mouths with something beneficial. Ephesians 5:4,19,20. Prepare our hearts for further blessings. Luke 17:15-19. The thankful heart receives more to be thankful for. Ruth 2:10-17.
8. Is a companion of prayer and praise. Philippians 4:6; Colossians 4:2; Hebrews 13:15.
9. Prepares the way for God's victory in our lives. 2 Chron. 20:22; Acts 16:25,26; Jonah chp 2; 2 Corinthians 2:14.
10. Essential in our approach to the presence of God with its blessings. Psalm 92:2; 100:4; 2 Chronicles 5:13,14.

**O give thanks unto the Lord for He is good.
Psalm 118:1.**

BIBLE KEYS THAT UNLOCK PRAYER POWER

1. GOD'S HEALING NATURE
   Exod. 15:26 I am the Lord (Jehovah Rophi) that health thee.
   1 John 4:7, 16. God is Love. Love heals.
2. GOD'S HEALING WORD
   Psa. 107:20. He sent His Word and healed them.
   Mat. 8:8. Speak the Word only and my servant shall be healed.
   Prov. 4:20-22. My Words...they are...health to all their flesh.
3. GOD'S HEALING SON
   His Ministry. Mat. 8:16. He healed all that were sick. Luke 4:18,19.
   His Name. Acts 3:16. Faith in His Name hath made this man strong. 4:10.
   His Atonement. Mat 8:17. Himself took our infirmities and bare our sicknesses. Typified. Num 21:1-9; Prophesied. Isa. 1-5. Exemplified. 1 Pet. 2:24.
   His Risen life. 2 Cor. 4:10,11. Life of Jesus manifest in our body. Rom. 5:10.
4. GOD'S HEALING SPIRIT
   Rom. 8:11. He shall also quicken (enliven) your mortal bodies by His Spirit that dwelleth in you.
   1 Cor. 12:9. Gifts of healing by the same Spirit. Acts 10:38.

   GOD'S SUPPLY IS GREATER THAN OUR NEED – TRUST HIM TODAY.

CONTACT THE AUTHOR
Email: desmondmarcusthomas@gmail.com

INSPIRED TO WRITE A BOOK?

Contact
Maurice Wylie Media
Your Inspirational Christian Publisher

Based in Northern Ireland, distributing across the world.

www.MauriceWylieMedia.com